M000206765

NEWSROOM LAW

NEWSROOM
LAW

A LEGAL GUIDE FOR COMMONWEALTH
CARIBBEAN JOURNALISTS

KATHY ANN WATERMAN LATCHOO

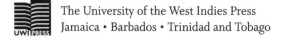
The University of the West Indies Press
Jamaica • Barbados • Trinidad and Tobago

The University of the West Indies Press
7A Gibraltar Hall Road, Mona
Kingston 7, Jamaica
www.uwipress.com

© 2020 by Kathy Ann Waterman Latchoo

All rights reserved. Published 2020

A catalogue record of this book is available from the
National Library of Jamaica.

ISBN: 978-976-640-753-7 (paper)
      978-976-640-754-5 (Kindle)
      978-976-640-755-1 (ePub)

Cover photograph of the Trinidad and Tobago Hall of Justice in Port of Spain
© Andrea de Silva Viarruel.

Cover design by Robert Harris

The University of the West Indies Press has no responsibility for the persistence or
accuracy of URLs for external or third-party Internet websites referred to in this
publication and does not guarantee that any content on such websites is, or will
remain, accurate or appropriate.

Printed in the United States of America

For journalists who love what they do

you and I
between us
words

—Susan Shim

CONTENTS

TABLE OF CASES

FOREWORD

"The tort of defamation is an ancient construct of the common law. It has accumulated, over the centuries, a number of formal rules with no analogue in other branches of the law of tort. Most of them originated well before freedom of expression acquired the prominent place in our jurisprudence that it enjoys today. Its coherence has not been improved by attempts at statutory reform."

—Lord Sumption in *Lachaux v. Independent Print Ltd and Anor.*[1]

"It is a feature of the common law of defamation that neat conceptual solutions do not always provide satisfactory answers to the endlessly varied fact-sets with which judges and (in some jurisdictions) juries have to wrestle, for the purposes of achieving an outcome which properly accords with justice and common sense."

—Lord Briggs in *Simon and Ors v. Lyder and Anor.*[2]

This is a valuable work written by Kathy Ann Waterman Latchoo, a sitting judge and a former prosecutor and journalist. *Newsroom Law* is a welcome and necessary addition to busy journalists' arsenal of informed professional judgment as they go about their vital task in a world of instant deadlines and "fake news".

This work will also aid those media lawyers who might otherwise miss the wood for the trees and will prove to be a readable account for media and law students alike. That Madam Justice Waterman Latchoo has found the time and energy to complete this task is impressive enough. More impressively, she has brought years of experience of both journalism and law. No serious media person will want to do without this work at the ready.

The quotations from Lord Sumption and Lord Briggs shine a spotlight on the law of libel and slander. Lest I give the impression this work is limited to the law of libel and slander – perish the thought. Although the author provides a readable account of that area, she goes further and intentionally provides a broader and deeper practical and legal context. The author tackles the challenge of stating succinctly the law that governs media professionals and newsrooms.

If, as the two quotations suggests, the law of defamation is a jumble, then what any astute reader requires is a good guide to the complete media legal landscape. The media legal landscape includes the constitution with its twin freedoms of expression and the press; the law of libel and slander (which many would be surprised to discover can impose civil and criminal liabilities); the law of contempt; the statutory law governing freedom of information and data protection as well as the special restrictions on publishing information about children and court cases. The author has filled a yawning gap with her comprehensive and thoughtful survey of this vast array of law that exists in the Caribbean countries that the author has covered.

The publication of the written word has come a long way since Gutenberg. Journalists now work across traditional media and the Internet. The most dramatic changes in the last two decades involve technology, the Internet and the media. The first Blackberry hit the market in 1999, and the first iPhone in 2007; Facebook was founded in 2003; Twitter in 2006, and WhatsApp in 2009. It is obvious that technology enables us to communicate, and its impact is far and wide and still only incompletely understood.

In 2016, the election of Donald Trump as the president of the United States led to an inquiry as to whether Russia had sought to influence the election outcome. In 2017, the United Kingdom voted to leave the European Union. The role of the media in both those events is still unfolding.

Alongside these technological and cross-border challenges are the long-term decline of print media and the emergence of differing media models. Nowadays, several respected global media voices attract the support of foundations; others have global digital footprints that dwarf traditional reach.

In other words, the world and the world of media have undergone dramatic change. The law must change in response to those transformations. Hardly anyone under the age of twenty-five reads an actual newspaper; they get their news digitally. Everyone of that age is entitled to vote and participate in the civic and democratic life of their community in myriad ways. The quality of that participation will, in part, depend on the integrity of the information the media provides to them. The law of media has had to play catch-up, and this work catalogues those legal trends and developments and explains them to readers.

I heartily commend this work and congratulate the author as I look forward to another edition updating this valuable work.

Ian L. Benjamin, SC[3]

ACKNOWLEDGEMENTS

This idea for this book was first sown in the 1990s by Lennox Grant when he was editor in chief of the *Express,* in Trinidad and Tobago, and the writer was a journalist on his team and a newly minted attorney.

Tajmool Hosein, Queen's Counsel (QC), now deceased, approved that first copy, which was intended as an in-house guide, and recommended a separate chapter on investigative journalism. The in-house guide remained unpublished because, at the time, it seemed that the Libel and Defamation Act was going to be reviewed and amended.

Many years later, the perspicacious writer and editor Judy Raymond revived the idea and kindly edited the first drafts of some chapters and lent helpful advice. By then, I had decided that the work should be expanded to help journalists in the Commonwealth Caribbean, instead of limiting it to Trinidad and Tobago. Finally, my husband Maximus Latchoo announced, "It's time. Get it done", and he contributed not only funds but also his tireless support and faith that it would be done.

Attorney-at-law Ian Benjamin encouraged, prodded and never let me forget what needed to be accomplished. He introduced me to attorney Sadnha Lutchman, who conducted valuable research and fact-checking. Journalists Camini Marajh and Wesley Gibbings; vice president of the Trinidad and Tobago Publishers and Broadcasters Association Kiran Maharaj; attorneys-at-law Andrew Mitchell, QC, Ravi Rajcoomar and Faarees Hosein; Professor Eddy Ventose; Justice Brian Cottle of St Vincent and the Grenadines; and Chancellor Yonette Cummings-Edwards of Guyana also read chapters and offered their comments and advice.

Susan Shim, whom I have known since we were both eleven years old, blessed this work with the beautiful haiku for the dedication page. My endless thanks also go to the editorial support team at the University of the West Indies Press, the Media Association of Trinidad and Tobago, the Press Association of Jamaica, the Association of Caribbean Media Workers, Justice Kimberly Cenac-Phulgence, Justice Shiraz Aziz, Justice Colin Williams,

Tishara Armstrong, Dwaymian Brissette, Zahra Burton, Parnell Campbell, QC, Jo Elliott, Francesca Hawkins, Nikola Lashley, Dr Sharon Le Gall, Linda Straker and all those, too many to mention, who offered their advice, encouragement and support.

INTRODUCTION

Journalists are busy people.

With the clock tick-tocking, they must navigate the law of libel, contempt, privilege, copyright, breach of confidence and official secrecy.

This book is meant to guide, comfort and support journalists. Although they may chafe against the many legal restrictions, they should know that they can do and say a lot within the law.

With a better understanding of their legal rights, journalists can go about their business with greater confidence, knowing when to yield and when to stand firm.

This book is no substitute for the services of a competent and experienced lawyer, but with this guide, journalists and their editors or producers should be able to hold their own in war rooms. Media lawyers can be scarier than editors.

The Commonwealth Caribbean countries whose law has been primarily described are Antigua and Barbuda; the Bahamas; Barbados; Dominica; Grenada; Guyana; Jamaica; St Kitts and Nevis; St Lucia; St Vincent and the Grenadines; and Trinidad and Tobago. Reference is made to relevant law in Belize, Bermuda, British Virgin Islands and Cayman Islands.

Some difficulty was encountered in obtaining up-to-date information on particular aspects of the law in the various jurisdictions, and any shortcomings in this regard are mine alone. The book focuses on the existing law in the region rather than policy and reform and the actual how-to of journalism, although some recommendations are made.

The book begins by placing journalism in a constitutional context and ends with an overview on damages for defamation and a glossary of legal terms. It describes our legal systems and the hierarchy of courts, which every journalist should strive to understand, whether or not assigned to the court beat. In particular, *Newsroom Law* seeks to demystify libel law, including the *Reynolds* public interest defence that has put fresh emphasis on what constitutes "responsible journalism". Other chapters alert journalists to the legal pitfalls in covering Parliament, elections and court cases. The chapter on investigative journalism seeks to answer common questions such as whether photographers may use telephoto lenses to capture people in private areas like their bedrooms, and whether it is ever okay to break the law (such as bribing a public official) to expose a greater wrong (such as corruption).

Newsroom Law does not attempt to cover every nook and cranny of media law but rather concentrates on the most relevant and bothersome areas that generate discussion and, at times, befuddlement in the newsrooms.

It is not a study of ethics, but journalism is nothing without ethics, and where the law leaves off, ethics must step in. In acknowledgement of this relationship, the book includes as an appendix the revised code of ethics of the Association of Caribbean MediaWorkers.

Although this book is aimed primarily at journalists, it is hoped that lawyers and law students, too, will find a space on their shelves for it.

CHAPTER 1

FREEDOM OF EXPRESSION

Without effective freedom of expression, materialized in all its terms, democracy vanishes, pluralism and tolerance start to break down, the mechanisms of citizen oversight and complaint start to become inoperable, and, in short, fertile ground is created for authoritarian systems to take root in society.

—*Herrera Ulloa v. Costa Rica*[1]

Freedom of expression is the best expression of freedom.

It is a barometer of a healthy democracy; a safety valve for social dissent; a checkpoint for independence; and a brake on government power, interference and abuse.

It guarantees the realization of all human rights. An excellent modern statement on the importance, function and scope of this freedom comes from the Supreme Court of Uruguay, which had this to say:[2] "In fact, without freedom of expression, full democracy does not exist, and without democracy, the sad history of the hemisphere has demonstrated that everything from the right to life to the right to private property is seriously endangered."[3]

Freedom of expression is one of the fundamental rights and freedoms enshrined in the Bill of Rights in the regional constitutions, as inviolable as the right to life, the right to personal liberty and equality under the law.

Freedom of expression belongs to everyone, whether journalist, evangelist, politician or the man or woman at home in the recliner armchair. It has a dual dimension – encompassing not only the individual right of all people to express their own thoughts, ideas and information but also the collective right of society at large to seek and receive any information, to learn about the thoughts, ideas and information held by others and to be well informed.[4]

Without such freedom, you would not be able to read a newspaper or a book; listen to a broadcast; or breathe a thought, unless Big Brother said so.

And as stated by the European Court of Human Rights, that freedom extends not only to inoffensive or indifferent ideas or words but also to those that offend, shock or disturb.[5]

In the famous words of Justice Stephen Smedley in England in a case against a roadside preacher: "Free speech includes not only the inoffensive but the irritating, the contentious, the eccentric, the heretical, the unwelcome and the provocative provided it does not tend to provoke violence. Freedom only to speak inoffensively is not worth having."[6]

Freedom of expression includes freedom of the press, which is the right to publish factual information and opinion in a variety of forms, including newspapers, television, radio and social media. The Trinidad and Tobago Constitution, exceptionally, speaks of freedom of the press and freedom of expression separately, which acknowledges the critical role played by the press in that democracy.

The relevant sections in the constitutions of the independent Commonwealth Caribbean nations draw their origins from Article 10 of the European Convention on Human Rights,[7] which states: "Everyone has the right to freedom of expression. The right shall include freedom to hold opinions and to receive and impart information and ideas without interference by public authority and regardless of frontiers."

But no freedom is absolute. So the article continues in this way:

> The exercise of those freedoms, since it carries with it duties and responsibilities, may be subject to such formalities, conditions, restrictions or penalties as are prescribed by law and are necessary in a democratic society, in the interest of national security, territorial integrity or public safety, for the prevention of disorder or crime, for the protection of health or morals, for the protection of the reputation or rights of others, for preventing the disclosure of information received in confidence, or for maintaining the authority and impartiality of the judiciary.

The article is recognized in the respective sections of the various Commonwealth Caribbean constitutions,[8] which typically begin: "Except with his own consent, a person shall not be hindered in the enjoyment of his freedom of expression."

Restrictions are placed on such freedom to protect reputations, maintain order, protect public health and national security, and so on. For example, Section 20 (2) of the Barbados Constitution states:

Nothing contained in or done under the authority of any law shall be held to be inconsistent with or in contravention of this section to the extent that the law in question makes provision:

a.   that is reasonably required in the interests of defence, public safety, public order, public morality or public health; or received in confidence, maintaining the authority and independence of the courts or regulating the administration or technical operation of telephony, telegraphy,

b.   that is reasonably required for the purpose of protecting the reputations, rights and freedoms of other persons or the private lives of persons concerned in legal proceedings, preventing the disclosure of information received in confidence, maintaining the authority and independence of the courts or regulating the administration or technical operation of telephony, telegraphy, posts, wireless broadcasting, television or other means of communication or regulating public exhibitions or public entertainments; or that imposes restrictions upon public officers or members of a disciplined force.

Journalists, therefore, are limited in what they can publish and when they can publish it. Although freedom of the press is guaranteed, journalists are not entitled to unfairly damage people's reputations, interfere with the administration of justice or disrupt the fairness of general elections.

Freedom of expression is valued for its own sake but it is also instrumentally important. *R v. Secretary of State for the Home Department ex p Simms*[9] Lord Steyn stated that

> freedom of speech is the lifeblood of democracy. The free flow of information and ideas informs political debate. It is a safety valve: people are more ready to accept decisions that go against them if they can in principle seek to influence them. It acts as a brake on the abuse of power by public officials. It facilitates the exposure of errors in the governance and administration of justice of the country.

Freedom of expression also means that journalists should be free from government interference. If government officials feel aggrieved by what is published about them, they have to seek redress through the courts like everybody else.

And journalists who believe the state is arbitrarily violating their free speech right can file constitutional motions in the High Court.

Constitutional clashes between the state and the media have arisen over such matters as withholding or cancellation of broadcast licences; restrictions on importation of necessary commodities such as newsprint; and laws that criminalize statements critical of public figures and bodies.

Several landmark Bill of Rights cases illustrate how the courts have sought to resolve such conflicts. The burden is always on the would-be censor to show that the restriction is reasonably required.

These cases underscore the importance of freedom of expression to the proper functioning of a democratic society and the need for our watchdogs and sentinels to remain vigilant.

NO PRINT FIT FOR NEWS

In Guyana, in 1971, President Forbes Burnham issued several trade orders prohibiting the importation of newsprint and printing equipment except by licence issued by the competent authority.[10] The New Guyana Company, which published the *Evening Mirror* and *Sunday Mirror,* challenged the validity of the orders on the basis that the orders had the effect of hindering their freedom of expression without interference in accordance with Article 12 of the constitution.

The judge at first struck down the trade orders, but the Court of Appeal overturned his ruling, holding (myopically) that there was no fundamental right to import newsprint or printing equipment. In the opinion of the Court of Appeal, the government had the right to conserve scarce foreign exchange and there was no direct impact on the newspaper or intentional trespass on the constitution.

Similarly, in an Antiguan case, the Privy Council adopted the "no direct impact" reasoning when a biweekly newspaper challenged the constitutionality of the Registration of Newspapers (Amendment) Act.[11]

The 1971 act forbade the printing or publishing of a newspaper unless there was a deposit of $10,000 with the accountant general, to satisfy any judgment of the court for libel. The relevant government minister could waive the deposit if he were provided with a bank guarantee or insurance policy.

The *Antigua Times* contended that the requirement was repugnant to Section 12 of the constitution. The court ruled in favour of the newspaper, holding that such a provision impeded freedom of expression. But the Privy Council saw it otherwise – the objective of the provision was to raise revenue, which was reasonably required and not excessive. The requirement of the fee was not devised to impede the press, even though such expenditure might reduce the resources of the newspaper otherwise available to improve its circulation, and so was not contrary to the constitution.

It was another decade and a half before the Privy Council abandoned this strangulating approach and sanctified the importance of the right of freedom of expression in a democracy, observing that such a right would be a "fragile thing if it could be overridden by general political or economic policy". The Privy Council also underscored the need for the courts to adhere to a "firm performance of their proper constitutional role" in assessing limits on fundamental rights.[12]

The fresh approach was marked in 1990 by another Antiguan case involving Tim Hector, and the infamous Public Order Act, discussed later in this chapter.

In contrast, Trinidad and Tobago newspapers were successful in having restrictions on the importation of newsprint deemed unconstitutional. In 1989, pursuant to the Exchange Control Act, the Central Bank restricted newspapers' ability to purchase newsprint. The High Court found such action infringed on the constitution.[13] Lucky J distinguished the Guyana case because Section 4 (k) of Trinidad and Tobago's constitution sets out freedom of the press as a separate and fundamental freedom. Therefore, it must be given a broad and purposive meaning. In Guyana and other Commonwealth Caribbean countries, freedom of press is encapsulated by freedom of expression.[14]

Lucky J declared that newspapers could not be placed in the same category as any other importer of goods who could not claim a fundamental right and freedom enshrined in the Bill of Rights. He rejected the argument that freedom of the press did not include the right to import newsprint; without the commodity in which they communicated, newspapers would be forced to close.

He expounded on the vital role of the press in a democracy and why courts must jealously guard freedom of the press: "Freedom of the press is not the right of the media only, it is a fundamental right of the individuals or people of this country, it is the right of society. Therefore, any infringement of that right against any person, be it a newspaper or the electronic media, is an infringement against society."

ON THE AIR

In Belize, a member of the opposition party sought permission of the television station to broadcast a programme on matters of public policy – the state of the economy. Regulation 10 of the Broadcast and Television Regulations of 1984 called for the permission of the authority before "any political speech or activity" could be aired. The secretary wrote to the applicant formally refusing permission, characterizing the proposed broadcast as a "party political broadcast". The Court of Appeal agreed with the applicant, ruling that the basis on which permission was refused was arbitrary because the broadcast authority had not seen the script of the proposed broadcast.[15]

In Trinidad and Tobago, Surujrattan Rambachan, an academic and opposition politician, alleged a breach of his right of thought and expression when the Trinidad and Tobago Television Ltd, a public authority, had denied him the right to reasonable airtime.[16] The court ruled in his favour:

> In this modern age, a free press is indispensable to the right to express political views and to freedom of thought and expression. If the free press goes, by any form of government action or censorship, then inevitably the other two related freedoms are affected and will ultimately perish. More and more, these three fundamental freedoms become the three sides of a triangle; they really form one whole and upon them hinge the liberty of the individual and the freedom of the nation.

LICENCE FOR THEIR MOUTH

In Antigua, the government, terminated a call-in radio programme, *Talk Your Mind*, on government-owned Radio Anguilla after it attacked government plans to introduce a national lottery.[17]

The presenter was John Benjamin, chairman of the Anguilla Democratic Party, one of the two parties in the coalition government. Benjamin's idea was that the programme would fulfil a promise of open government made by the Anguilla Democratic Party and would allow people to express their views on matters of concern to the community.

The Privy Council held the cancellation to be a breach of the freedom of expression guarantee because the minister clearly intended to impede free speech by cancelling the programme as a reprisal for its criticism. This was the relevant motive and there was no excuse of falling ratings or jaded audiences. Its cancellation was capricious and arbitrary, and the presenter was entitled to damages.

Lord Slynn of Hadley remarked that as long as people were not criticizing the government on sensitive issues, the government seemed content to let the programme continue. But the government-controlled media must, like the government, comply with the constitution as must any other citizen.[18]

The court in *Benjamin* applied the historic decision of *Olivier v. Buttigieg*,[19] in which a weekly newspaper, the *Voice of Malta*, had offended the

Catholic Church and was condemned by the archbishop. The chief government medical officer then decreed that the entry into hospitals and branches of his department of newspapers condemned by the church authorities was strictly forbidden. The Privy Council used Malta's free speech clause to strike down the ban.

In *Observer Publications v. Matthew and Attorney General of Antigua*,[20] the Privy Council made it clear that everyone has the presumptive constitutional right to a broadcast licence and its bestowal is not an executive privilege. A newspaper that had been critical of the government applied in 1995 for a licence to operate an FM station. The grant of such licences was in the discretion of Cabinet. Seventeen months after the application, the applicant had received only a euphemistic reply that the matter was under consideration.

The only licensed radio stations, other than the government-controlled radio and television station, were a commercial radio and cable television station all owned and controlled by members of the prime minister's immediate family. The Privy Council held that although no one had an absolute right to a licence, its denial could only be on constitutionally justifiable grounds. In this case, no reason had been advanced or could be inferred. Violation of the applicant's rights was therefore plain.

PUBLIC ORDER

In Antigua, Section 33B of the Public Order Act was declared unconstitutional after Tim Hector, editor of the *Outlet* newspaper and a fierce critic of the government, published an article in which he made statements critical of the government and the commissioner of police.

It was alleged that the statements were false and likely to undermine public confidence in the conduct of public affairs. The Privy Council found that the provisions offended against the constitutional provisions in relation to freedom of expression and were accordingly of no effect.

Lord Bridge said such a provision that criminalizes statements likely to undermine public confidence in the conduct of public affairs ought to be viewed with the utmost suspicion: "In a free democratic society it is almost too obvious to need stating that those who hold office in government and who are responsible for public administration must always be open to criticism. Any attempt to fetter or stifle such criticism amounts to political censorship of the most insidious and objectionable kind."[21]

CHILL FACTOR

Freedom of the press can also be suppressed by government officials in less overt ways, which do not usually give rise to constitutional motions but can have a "chilling effect" in newsrooms. Such measures include advertising boycotts;[22] blacklisting particular journalists and media organizations from official state functions and news conferences; and gruff phone calls to editors and producers.

Journalists also practise varying degrees of self-censorship to avoid reprisals. The broadcast media continue to express concern over the discouraging effect of broadcasting codes and conditions attached to their licences, such as governments' entitlement to free airtime. (See chapter 11, "The Broadcast Journalist".)

Perhaps the best antifreeze is constant persistence and publicity. The Declaration of Chapultepec[23] sounds the call: "The struggle for freedom of expression and of the press is not a one-day task; it is an ongoing commitment. It is fundamental to the survival of democracy and civilization in our hemisphere."

CHAPTER 2

HOW THE COURTS WORK

Do not pervert justice. Do not show partiality to the poor or favouritism to the great, but judge your neighbour fairly.

—Leviticus 19:15

SOURCES OF LAW

In the Commonwealth Caribbean, sources of law are the constitution; statute or legislation; common law; custom; international law; and equity.

The constitution lays down fundamental principles by which the state is governed. It is the most important legal source because it is the parent law by which all other laws are measured; it is the supreme law of the land.

Statutes are created by an act of Parliament. An act begins life as a bill, is passed by the House of Representatives (or House of Assembly or National Assembly) which is the lower house and the Senate or upper house; is assented to by the president or governor general, and a date is set for it to come into force. Some countries such as the British Virgin Islands, Dominica, Guyana, St Kitts and Nevis, and St Vincent and the Grenadines have one legislative chamber or a unicameral parliament.

Common law or case law develops on a case-by-case basis in the courts. Sometimes it is called judge-made law. It is based on the doctrine of judicial precedent.[1] Where there is no statute on a particular point or issue, the judge must look at case law, that is, how other courts have dealt with the issue. The decisions of superior courts are binding on all subordinate courts within the jurisdiction. Where the decision is from a court of equal or lower jurisdiction, or from another state with similar law, it is persuasive. So the decisions of the Court of Appeal of Guyana, for example, will be of persuasive authority on the Court of Appeal of Jamaica. Similarly, decisions of superior courts in the United Kingdom, Canada, South Africa, Australia and other countries with a common law tradition can be highly persuasive in jurisdictions in the Caribbean.

When Caribbean countries achieved independence, much of the English common law was expressly adopted, or codified by statute. With the exception of Guyana and St Lucia, the legal system of the English-speaking Caribbean countries is based on the common law system, derived from England. The legal systems of Guyana and St Lucia may be described as "hybrid", because Guyana has the influence of the Roman-Dutch tradition, while St Lucia has a strong influence of the French civil law.[2]

Equity developed in English law to soften or correct the sometimes too-rigid rules of the common law, which could result in injustice. A court can exercise its discretion to grant relief where there is an injustice, but the common law provides no remedy. An example of equitable relief is the granting of compensation for breach of confidence (discussed in chapter 13). Equity embraces principles of fairness that were developed and applied in the civil arena.

Custom is a rare source of law in the region. Custom is usually not written down but has existed from time immemorial. It is restricted to a particular locality and is an exception to the common law. An example of how customary law influenced legal reform is in the area of family law; legislation has abolished the concept of "illegitimate" children, reflecting long-held West Indian custom.

Parliaments in the region often incorporate rules of international law into national legislation. International judicial precedents bear much significance, particularly in the area of human rights and constitutional law. The European Court of Human Rights and the United Nations Human Rights Committee are the two main international human rights bodies.

HIERARCHY

The courts are divided into two main areas: civil and criminal. In both arenas, there are four levels of courts, starting with the lowest: the magistrates' court (parish courts in Jamaica[3]), High Courts, appeal courts and the Judicial Committee of the Privy Council. The Privy Council, which hears appeals from Commonwealth jurisdictions, is the final court of appeal in many Caribbean jurisdictions, but is being replaced by the Caribbean Court of Justice. The Caribbean Court of Justice was established in 2001 and is based in Port of

Spain, Trinidad and Tobago. Guyana,[4] Barbados, Belize and Dominica have acceded to the Caribbean Court of Justice as their apex court or court of last resort.

The hierarchy of courts depends on the system of binding precedent, or *stare decisis*. That means that the decisions of each court are binding on those lower in authority. The decisions of courts of equal jurisdiction are not binding on one another, but magistrates and judges will examine such decisions and see whether they ought to be followed or distinguished.

Sometimes magistrates and judges make mistakes and their decisions can be appealed and corrected. Decisions of the magistrates' court are reviewed by judges of the appellate division; the composition of the court varies among the various jurisdictions, and may require one or two judges instead of the usual three as is the case for appeals from the High Court. In Guyana, three judges of the High Court usually hear magisterial appeals unless the appeal concerns an indictable matter that was tried summarily; then the appeal will lie to the Court of Appeal. In the Bahamas, the High Court hears some magisterial appeals.[5]

High Court rulings are heard by three judges of the Appeal Court; occasionally, where there is a complex or novel point of law, five judges will sit.[6] Rulings of the Appeal Court are reviewed by the Privy Council or Caribbean Court of Justice. The parties are known as the appellant (the person appealing the decision) and the respondent (the party replying to the submissions of the appellant). In criminal trials at the High Court, a jury's verdict is final, however.

Nine states[7] that belong to the Organisation of Eastern Caribbean States share a unified Supreme Court – the Eastern Caribbean Supreme Court, which includes a High Court and Appeal Court. The Eastern Caribbean Supreme Court is headquartered in St Lucia and headed by a chief justice. Resident judges preside in the High Courts, but there is a single Court of Appeal. Three judges sit at the appellate level, and they visit the various territories to hear appeals from all subordinate courts.

CIVIL ACTION

Civil actions deal with private controversies and involve one person or company suing another. The objective is not punishment, but to restore the parties so far as possible to previous positions. The title of the action will be written like this: *Jones v. Brown*. The claimant's or plaintiff's name appears first and then the name of the respondent or defendant. Do not pronounce the "v" when naming the case; instead say "and". Most civil actions arise out of a dispute over a contract or tort. A contract is an agreement between two or more parties, giving each certain rights. A contract does not have to be written to be enforceable. A tort is a wrong and includes nuisance, negligence and defamation.

Minor claims are heard in magistrates' courts, the more serious in the High Court. In a civil action, the claimant draws up a document called a claim form (the old-fashioned term is "writ") and delivers it to the defendant. Copies are also filed in the registry of the High Court. The claimant must set out his cause of action in a statement of case and serve it with the claim form. For example, in a running-down action, he may claim that the defendant violated the traffic regulations by breaching a major road and failing to keep a proper lookout.

The defendant then serves a defence, responding to the claim. Discovery[8] (an information-gathering process) takes place and eventually the matter will be set down for trial. When the matter is settled, we do not describe the respondent or defendant as guilty. We say he has been found liable and, usually, ordered to pay compensation or damages.

In defamatory actions, before claim forms are served, the claimant will send a pre-action protocol letter with details of the words complained of and the defendant will reply, usually within fourteen days. This is because many such matters can be resolved out of court to avoid wasting judicial time.

Civil trials are usually before a judge alone, although jury trials are still available in some territories. Guyana, St Lucia, and Trinidad and Tobago do not hold jury trials in civil matters. Jamaica does. Where statute does not stipulate any definite mode of trial, it is within the discretion of the judge to grant a jury trial if good cause can be shown. Grenada, for example, has abolished civil jury trials except in "exceptional circumstances".[9]

CRIMINAL ACTION

Criminal courts deal with people accused of crime, decide whether they are guilty, and, if so, determine the consequences they shall suffer. Prosecution is held on behalf of the public. Therefore, the title of the matter will be written as "*The State v. John Doe*" or "*The Crown v. John Doe*".

Criminal law is the representation of underlying principles of political morality in a liberal society. The function of criminal courts is controlling misbehaviours and enforcing ethical conduct. They deal with people accused of crimes, and if defendants deny committing the acts with which they are charged, the court must choose between their version of the facts and that of the prosecution. Sometimes those arrested and charged with crime plead guilty. There is then no need to determine guilt. The remaining question is whether a defendant should go to jail, pay a fine or be subjected to other corrective treatments.

Most criminal actions begin with the police arresting someone. However, anyone may bring a criminal charge in his own name, against a defendant, and this is called a "private prosecution".[10] This rarely happens, and people do so when the police do not charge, perhaps because they find the matter trifling. Even in private prosecutions, the director of public prosecutions has the power to discontinue any criminal proceedings.

Police may arrest with or without a warrant. A warrant is not necessary where the police have reasonable grounds to believe that an arrestable offence (one for which the penalty is more than five years in prison)[11] has been committed, is being committed or is about to be committed. So to chase after a thief fleeing with a pedestrian's wallet and arrest him requires no warrant.

A defendant may also be brought to court by way of summons, if the offence is not a serious one. The summons is a document the court issues for a defendant to attend on a specific date, and informs him of the charge and the date and time of the alleged offence. The summons will be served by the police on the defendant himself, or may be left at his usual address with an adult.

The suspect appears before a magistrate; the mode of trial depends on the nature of the offence. Summary matters are minor offences, such as assault, possession of a few marijuana cigarettes, or using obscene language. These are dealt with by the magistrate, who may discharge the defendant or find him guilty.

More serious matters are called indictable offences,[12] such as murder, rape, robbery or kidnapping. For indictable offences, magistrates hold preliminary inquiries to determine whether there is sufficient evidence to send the matter for trial at the High Court. The prosecution is expected to lead all the evidence it relies upon to prove the charge and its witnesses are subject to cross-examination. At preliminary inquiries, the accused (alternatively referred to as the defendant) often invokes his right to silence, and reserves witnesses for the High Court trial.

The magistrate will then either commit the accused to stand trial before judge and jury, or discharge him. Bear in mind that the discharge is not the same as an acquittal, because the inquiry is not a trial, and the accused is not even called upon to plead.

Even after a discharge, the prosecution can still bring the accused to trial by relaying the charge; by holding a further inquiry, if further evidence is brought to the fore; or by the director of public prosecutions seeking permission from a High Court judge to prefer (bring) an indictment (a formal statement of the charge) without going through an inquiry.

Antigua, Barbados, Jamaica and St Lucia[13] have abolished old-style preliminary inquiries that require witnesses giving oral evidence. Instead, the magistrate or judge decides whether to commit the accused based on written statements and exhibits. In some other jurisdictions where old-style inquiries are held, there are provisions for "paper committals";[14] the magistrate may decide on the basis of written statements and exhibits and, importantly, "without consideration of the evidence", which means the defence has no right to cross-examine prosecution witnesses.

Some matters are called "triable either way". This means the accused has a choice whether to have the matter heard summarily before the magistrate or before a judge and jury.

At the High Court, a trial is before judge and jury.[15] Some exceptions are Belize, the Cayman Islands, Trinidad and Tobago, the Turks and Caicos Islands, and Jamaica's Gun Court. Generally, a jury of twelve sits on capital matters and nine in noncapital matters. In the Bahamas, Guyana, St Kitts and Nevis, and Antigua, an array of twelve sits for all types of offences. In Barbados, Grenada, St Lucia, St Vincent and the Grenadines, and Trinidad and Tobago, a jury of twelve is required for capital offences and nine for noncapital cases.

Alternates may also be selected, in case one of the members of the jury panel should fall ill or is unable for some other reason to complete his or her service. This is the position in Trinidad and Tobago, Antigua, Grenada and St Lucia. In Trinidad and Tobago, alternate jurors first sat in the murder trial of Dole Chadee,[16] a reputed gang leader and drug dealer. The full slate of six alternates was selected, in a headliner trial involving nine accused who were all convicted and hanged.

In capital trials, all twelve jurors must agree before a guilty verdict can be returned or accepted. In other matters, a majority verdict may be accepted. Where a jury cannot come to a decision, the judge has the discretion to order a retrial.

In magistrates' court, it is common for police officers to prosecute criminal charges, although trained lawyers from the Office of the Director of Public Prosecutions handle more complex cases and those of high public interest.

In the High Court, however, only trained attorneys have rights of audience, which means they are permitted to argue cases and address the judge.[17]

STANDARD OF PROOF

Whether civil or criminal, at the trial, parties may call witnesses and present evidence according to rules of procedure. The standard of proof in civil cases is called the balance of probabilities. This means that one party will have to prove to the judge that his version of events is more probable than not. This is lower than the criminal standard of "proof beyond reasonable doubt". It is therefore possible for a person to be acquitted of a criminal charge and yet be held liable in the civil courts on the same facts. For example, a driver may be acquitted of causing death by dangerous driving in the criminal arena, but if the family of the deceased bring a civil action against the driver, the judge may be convinced on a balance of probabilities that the defendant is liable for wrongfully causing the death of the deceased. American football star O.J. Simpson was held liable in the civil court in 1997 for the 1994 deaths of his ex-wife Nicole Brown and her friend Ronald Goldman, although he had been found not guilty of the murders in a criminal trial.

In Trinidad and Tobago, a special reserve policeman Nicholas Leith shot and killed seventeen-year-old Anisha Neptune outside a police station in 2001. He was tried for manslaughter and freed when the judge upheld a no case submission by the defence. However, Mary Neptune, mother of the deceased, pursued a "wrongful death" claim in the civil court and in 2011, a judge found Leith had acted recklessly. He was ordered to pay damages to the mother of the deceased.[18]

SPECIAL COURTS

Several other types of courts have the powers of a High Court: they deal with such matters as tax appeals, industrial disputes, and offences committed by military personnel. Unlike the criminal and civil courts, judges in these courts need not be attorneys.

For example, in Trinidad and Tobago, Jamaica and Barbados, a court martial tries people subject to military law (and is not nearly as dramatic as the movie *A Few Good Men,* starring Jack Nicholson and Tom Cruise). An ordinary court martial is presided over by a president and no fewer than two officers who do not necessarily have any legal training. The offences they hear may include aiding the enemy, desertion, cowardly behaviour and disgraceful conduct.[19]

Court martials sit in open court, and so the news media are allowed to attend and report on the proceedings, subject to the court's power to hear matters *in camera* (in private) on the ground that it is necessary or expedient in the interest of justice or national security to do so.

The Environmental Commission of Trinidad and Tobago, established in 2002, is the only environmental court in the Caribbean. It has six commissioners, but only three sit on an adjudicating panel, which includes either the chairman or deputy, who must be attorneys with more than ten years' standing. The other four are people of different expertise, and have included a marine scientist and petroleum engineer.

Trinidad and Tobago also has an industrial court, which is a superior court of record that settles disputes between trade unions and employers under the Industrial Relations Act.[20] It has all the rights, powers and privileges of a High Court concerning the attendance of witnesses, production of documents and the enforcement of its orders. Its composition includes members who need not be attorneys-at-law, but people experienced and qualified in industrial relations, economics and accountancy. Trinidad and Tobago is the only CARICOM country with such a court: the industrial court in Antigua is not a superior court of record. Some other states have industrial tribunals.

In Trinidad and Tobago, the Tax Appeal Board, established in 1966, is also a superior court of record, established to hear appeals against assessments of a number of taxes and duties, such as income tax, value-added tax, corporation tax, customs duty and anti-dumping and countervailing duties. This means it has the same status as a High Court. The court is composed of a chairman, the presiding officer and two members. All appeals are heard before the full panel, although provision exists for the chairman and one member to hear matters where the parties consent. The consent of the parties is also required for people who do not have an interest in an appeal to be present in court at the hearing of an appeal, in accordance with Section 8 of the Tax Appeal Board Act.[21]

Similarly, the Revenue Court in Jamaica hears and determines appeals from taxpayers, but it is staffed by a High Court judge with specialization in accounting and taxation. The relevant legislation is Section 4 (1) Judicature (Revenue Court) Act.

In Belize, the indigenous Maya community uses alcalde courts, which fall under the executive and not the judiciary. The alcalde courts hear minor criminal and civil matters, and their jurisdiction is summary in nature, in accordance with the Inferior Courts Act.[22]

CHAPTER 3

DEFAMATION

My initial response was to sue her for defamation of character, but then I realized that I had no character.

—controversial American basketballer Charles Barkley, in 1994, on hearing Tonya Harding proclaim herself "the Charles Barkley of figure skating"[1]

DEFINITION

It has always been a bad thing to bad-mouth others. Think of the thunderous biblical command in Leviticus 19:16: "Thou shalt not go up and down as a tale bearer among thy people." And the treacherous Iago's exhortation to Othello: "But he that filches from me my good name / Robs me of that which not enriches him / And makes me poor indeed."[2] In tenth-century England, King Alfred used to have the tongues of slanderers cut out.

People usually value their reputations above all else, and the law of defamation protects people from having their good names stolen.

Various definitions of defamation have been crafted, some giving rise to much confusion. The test has been variously described as "lowering the plaintiff in the estimation of right-thinking people generally"; "injuring the plaintiff's reputation by exposing him to hatred, contempt or ridicule"; and "tending to make the plaintiff shunned and avoided".

A helpful description is found in a 1970 British Columbia Court of Appeal decision *Murphy v. LaMarsh:*[3]

> (Defamation is where) a shameful action is attributed to a man (he stole my purse), a shameful character (he is dishonest), a shameful course of action (he lives on the avails of prostitution), or a shameful condition (smallpox). Such words are

Sure, everybody is repeating it,
but it doesn't mean it's true...

CartoonStock.com

considered defamatory because they tend to bring the man named into hatred, contempt or ridicule. The more modern definition of defamation is words tending to lower the plaintiff in the estimation of right-thinking members of society generally.

The key points of defamation law[4] in the Commonwealth Caribbean are:

- It does not matter if the defamation was intentional or the result of negligence.
- The remarks must be harmful.
- The words must refer to the claimant.
- The remarks must be conveyed to a third person.

LIBEL OR SLANDER

Defamation comes in two forms: libel and slander. Libel is defamation in permanent form, such as writing or drawing. Slander is defamation in transitory form, for example, words spoken. Film, video, television and radio broadcasts may be considered libel because the words spoken are stored in permanent form. Sometimes, it is difficult to differentiate between slander and libel. A television documentary (as opposed to a spontaneous live broadcast), in which copies were distributed to the public and the interviewee, was considered libel and not slander.[5] But a television broadcast of words read from a prepared script was deemed slander.[6] In *Ready v. Gabriel and others*[7] the issue arose recently, in Trinidad and Tobago, and the trial judge decided that a television broadcast was slander.[8] But a competing decision from the same jurisdiction followed, in *Jwala Rambarran v. Dr Lester Henry*.[9] Justice Devindra Rampersad stated:

> The time has long passed for the categorization of the transient nature of slander in the modern era to be revised. To my mind, especially in circumstances where radio stations are no longer limited by the strength of their broadcasting signal but now extend over the Internet to an international audience via a multitude of online live streaming software, apps and other technology, all with the capability of recording such programmes, along with the requirements of the law and or lawful procedure for the maintenance of recordings of radio programmes, the court would be hard-pressed to accept that radio broadcasts are the sole domain of the category of slander. The transience of the spoken word in the golden age of radio has been replaced by the relative permanence in the current era of global information and technology.

Guyana in Section 3 of its Defamation Act,[10] treats words in radio and television broadcast as being in permanent form. Barbados and Jamaica have abolished the distinction between slander and libel, referring only to defamation.[11]

The claimant who brings a libel action does not have to prove he suffered any loss or injury as a result of the defamation. Slander, on the other hand, at common law, requires proof of actual loss, such as loss of a job or profits – except in cases where the words are calculated to disparage a person in any office, profession, calling, trade or business held or carried on by him at the time of the publication; the words impute a crime for which the claimant can be made to suffer physically by way of punishment; or the words impute the claimant has a contagious or infectious disease.

British politician and author A.P. Herbert, who enjoyed exposing the absurdities of English law, summed up the difference like this: "in practice it is safer to insult a man at a public meeting than to insult him on a postcard, and that which is written in the corner of a letter is in law more deadly than that which is shouted from the house-tops".[12]

Publication

For defamation to be actionable, the words must be conveyed to someone other than the claimant. So, if someone insults you, undermining your standing and reputation to your face but no one else is around to hear, you would have injured pride but no cause of action. If, however, he puts such insults into a letter and faxes it to your office and your co-workers read it, then you could file a writ. Anonymous callers on radio and television talk shows sometimes make defamatory remarks and that can cause the radio or television station to be slapped with a suit.[13] It is no defence for a host, broadcaster, managing director, editor or producer to say one has no control over the callers, and a disclaimer is of no assistance. Broadcasters who take the risk of live broadcast without a time delay have to face the consequences if the material turns out to be defamatory.

Publication can come in any form – effigy, cartoon, chalk marks on a wall, signs, pictures, placards. Jennifer Howlett, a former mayor of Castle Point, Essex, England, won a libel suit in 2003, against a millionaire who used to trail banners from his private aeroplane, calling her a thief.[14]

It is usually not difficult for a claimant to prove publication. If slander is broadcast over a public address system or libel is contained in a national newspaper, it would be accepted that it was heard and read.[15] If published on a website, the claimant will be unable to rely on the presumption of law that there has been a substantial publication; however, reasonable inferences can be drawn.[16]

Every time the libel is repeated or further published, a fresh cause of action arises. This is known as the "multiple publication" common law rule,[17] dating back to the nineteenth century. In 1830, the *Weekly Dispatch* defamed the Duke of Brunswick, an eccentric and corpulent ousted despot who liked to paint his face and eat an abundance of sweets. Seventeen years later, the duke, then living in Paris, sent his manservant to buy a back issue of the paper; another copy was obtained from the British Museum. The newspaper contended the action was time-barred, but the court held that delivery of the paper to the duke or his agent constituted a fresh publication in respect of which suit could be brought action.

If you are publishing a correction, be careful not to repeat the libel. Say "Yesterday's article headlined '3 held for bank robbery' incorrectly stated the name of the accused. His correct name is X."

WORDS MUST BE DEFAMATORY

Whether the words complained of are capable of bearing a defamatory meaning depends on the context and content of the whole article, and the impression they would convey to an ordinary reader. The meaning of words is not determined in isolation, but the whole of the article and all circumstances of the publication. "Words, like people, are judged by the company they keep."[18]

The classic statement of the principle that the whole of the publication or the "bane and the antidote" must be taken into account lies in a passage from the judgment in the nineteenth-century English case of *Chalmers v. Payne*: "In one part of the publication, something disreputable to the plaintiff is stated, but that is removed by the conclusion; the bane and the antidote must be taken together."[19]

Some statements are clearly defamatory. Calling someone a thief, a liar, a murderer, a terrorist or a drug addict is clearly capable of bringing someone into hatred, contempt or ridicule. Standards of "right-thinking people" change over time. It was once considered defamatory to call someone a German during World War II, for example. To allege incompetence at playing the steel pan would not lower someone in the estimation of right-thinking members of the society, unless the person happens to be a professional pannist.

In *Byrne v. Deane*,[20] a member of a golf club alleged that a fellow golfer had defamed him by putting up notices to the effect that he had reported to the police that illegal gaming machines were kept at the club. It was held that such publication was not defamatory, although it might get the claimant kicked out of the golf club for being a snitch.

In the United Kingdom, Elton John successfully sued the *Sunday Mirror* for alleging that he was suffering from bulimia. The initial award of £350,000 was slashed to £75,000 by the Court of Appeal. Liberace, the flamboyant pianist, sued the *Daily Mirror* in 1956, after its celebrated and cantankerous columnist Cassandra (William Conner) described him as the "summit of sex – Masculine, Feminine and Neuter. Everything that He, She and It can ever want" and a "deadly, winking, sniggering, snuggling, chromium-plated, scent-impregnated, luminous, quivering, giggling, fruit-flavoured, mincing, ice-covered heap of mother love". Liberace, who wore an understated suit without a single sequin to the trial, claimed that the words labelled him as a homosexual. He was awarded £8,000, one of the largest settlements in English legal history, and later joked that he cried all the way to the bank. (Despite changing perspectives on sexual orientation in the twenty-first century, it is still defamatory to call someone a homosexual.)

Clive Lloyd, the former West Indian cricket captain collected US$100,000 from the *Age* in 1984 after a stringer wrote a column under the headline "C'mon Dollar C'mon", suggesting the World Series Cricket games were fixed.[21] Ken Gordon, former chairman of Caribbean Communications Network, in Trinidad and Tobago, was also awarded damages after Prime Minister Basdeo Panday called him a "pseudo-racist" at an Indian Arrival Day celebration in 1997. Panday appealed, declaring, "Thank God for the Privy Council", but the Law Lords upheld the decision.[22]

Gordon, by then, knew his way around defamation trials, having been a favourite target of Patrick Chookolingo, *Bomb* editor. In 1988, the Privy Council held that Gordon had been libelled when the *Bomb* called him a hypocrite, alleging he had taken part in a prayer session led by the eccentric prime minister of Grenada, Eric Gairy.[23]

The lessons to be learned from the Panday/Gordon matter were ignored by a credit union executive who defamed a well-known attorney on radio in 2008.[24] Robin Montano was the attorney representing depositors of the Hindu Credit Union in Trinidad and Tobago who were denied access to their money. He sent a letter on behalf of one of his clients, seeking recovery of TT$2,167, 201.94, which was pursuant to a judgment in default obtained against the credit union. Harry Harnarine, president of the credit union, was a guest speaker on Radio Shakthi, when he described the letter Montano wrote as a "racist nasty letter" and accused him of "playing Indians' friend". So Montano was defamed as not only a racist but a hypocrite too. The court awarded him general damages in the sum of TT$250,000 plus costs.

An even worse example of danger unheeded occurred when a Sunday *TnT Mirror* columnist viciously attacked a religious and cultural activist, who was also an *Express* columnist, by calling her a racist. [25] The libel was contained in four articles written over an eight-month period, and five later articles referred to her in the most despicable manner. The malicious intent of the defendant was underscored by his descriptions of the claimant as "facially grotesque" and "hideous" – which were the least of the attacks. The claimant was awarded TT$700,000 plus costs to compensate her for the "serious distress, hurt and humiliation suffered, for the injury to her reputation, and as a vindication of reputation".

Charmaine Forde, a Trinidadian singer, was also successful against the *TnT Mirror*, which alleged she had died of AIDS and her body had been shipped home under an assumed name. After her lawyer sent a letter to the newspaper, pointing out that she was alive and well, the paper scornfully published the letter and repeated the libel. Forde was awarded TT$90,000.[26]

In 1987, the two daily newspapers in Jamaica, the *Daily Gleaner* and the *Star*, which were both owned by the same company, published libellous articles about Anthony Abrahams, who had been minister of tourism for Jamaica between 1980 and 1984. The libel stemmed from an Associated Press report that alleged that Abrahams had been suspected of accepting bribes from an American advertising firm in return for the island's advertising and public relations contract. The Associated Press report had been released in error before the writer had completed her inquiries and obtained a reply from Abrahams. The *Star*, an afternoon tabloid, first published the article without amendment and without any thought to verifying the information. Abrahams delivered to the newspaper a rebuttal statement that was not published. Rather, the *Gleaner* reprinted the article the following day.

In 2003, the Court of Appeal reduced the damages from J$80.3 million to J$35 million, which was the equivalent of £533,000. The court pointed out the sum included punitive and deterrent elements, and reflected the baselessness of the charges. The Privy Council dismissed the defendants' appeal on the basis of excessive damages.[27]

Although it may sound archaic, slanderous words that impute unchastity or adultery (usually of a woman) are also actionable, and without proof of special damage. Trinidad and Tobago's Libel and Defamation Act, Section 6,[28] specifically protects women from such slurs, but Guyana's Defamation Act, Section 6,[29] is gender neutral and refers to "any person". In a Trinidadian case, *Ramkhelawan v. Motilal*,[30] the defendant called a married woman a "nasty whore and prostitute" and said she brought men to her house. The court had little difficulty finding that such vituperation was calculated to expose the claimant to contempt, hatred and ridicule, and judgment was in favour of the claimant.

RED FLAGS

Certain words and phrases should send up red flags to journalists and editors. Say someone gave a bad performance, not that he or she is bad actor. It takes more than one foul-up for someone to deserve a derogatory label. A liar means a habitual liar or someone who has told a monster lie, not a fibber. A doctor who made an isolated mistake is not a butcher. If you call someone a thief and it turns out he has one conviction as a juvenile for shoplifting a packet of chewing gum, you may find yourself in deep waters.

Be wary of referring to events and persons as the only, the first, the last. For example, to describe a doctor as the only one who is qualified to perform a particular type of surgery is capable of giving rise to a libel action, if a second doctor is also qualified. Examples of defamatory statements are those that impute dishonesty, criminal activity, immorality, financial difficulties or unfitness for office or profession.

Seemingly innocuous statements can turn ugly when certain facts emerge. Example: A newspaper publishes a "police blotter" report that Mr. Driver was robbed at gunpoint while sitting in his car on the Lady Young lookout with his girlfriend. It is one of several brief items of crime news, which the reporter collected from his usual source at the police station. After the article appears, Mr. Driver, who is married and serves as a counsellor in his church's marriage preparation programme, states that the woman is not his girlfriend but rather a family friend he was consoling on the recent death of her father. Mr. Driver would have a cause of action against the paper because the report paints him as an adulterous hypocrite.

In *Tolley v. Fry and Sons*,[31] the claimant was an amateur golfer who was depicted in an advertisement for the defendant's chocolate. He successfully contended that people familiar with the golfing world would think that he had been paid for the advertisement, thereby violating his amateur status.

The test is aptly described in *Hough v. London Express Newspaper*:[32]

The only question is, might reasonable people understand them in a defamatory sense? So when circumstances are proved which will clothe words otherwise innocent with a defamatory meaning the question must equally be: might reasonable people who know the special circumstances understand them in a defamatory sense? If words are used which impute discreditable conduct to my friend, he has been defamed to me, although I do not believe the imputation, and may even know that it is untrue. So if it be said of A that he is a forger, no witnesses are necessary or can indeed be called to say that they believed the charge: if, then, he being a married man, it is said of him "yesterday he married Miss X" it defames him to those people who know that he already has a wife even if they did not believe he had actually committed bigamy.

The UK *Sunday Times* in 2009 reported inaccurately that Elena Baturina, wife of the mayor of Moscow and known as "Russia's richest woman", had bought a mansion in London for millions of pounds. Although there is nothing defamatory in saying someone has bought a property that she has not, things got complicated when it was revealed that Mrs. Baturina had been required under Russian law to declare her assets, which she did and the house was not listed. The innuendo was that she was hiding assets. After a two-year libel battle, the paper apologized and agreed to pay costs and damages.[33]

On the other hand, there is no telling the things that will offend people who have a lot of time (and money) on their hands. A Saudi Arabian prince launched a libel suit in 2013 against *Forbes* magazine,[34] saying it defamed him by underestimating his wealth at US$9.6 billion less than his own arithmetic had determined. Among other insults, the magazine had stated that the value the prince placed on his holdings at times felt "like alternate reality". The prince complained that the magazine had portrayed him as engaging in price share manipulation, and systematically exaggerating his wealth. *Forbes* replied that the motive of the claimant was vanity and insecurity as the prince for twenty-five years had been "lobbying, cajoling and threatening" the magazine in relation to his ranking on the billionaires' list. The dispute was eventually settled out of court in 2015.

PHOTOGRAPHS, HEADLINES, CAPTIONS

Photo editors and writers of headlines and captions have to be alert to lurking libel. A single word, a careless adjective, even in a tiny caption, can provoke a libel action. In one English case, a reporter described business tycoon, Owen Oyston, as "disgraced" in a caption. At the time, the tycoon had not been officially disgraced. There were merely rumours about him being investigated by the police. He sued and the paper settled out of court. Six months later, Oyston (in 1996), was sentenced to six years for raping a fifteen-year-old girl at his country house in Lancashire. But too bad for the paper. It cannot get a refund. It's the person's reputation at the time of the publication that matters. Of course, if the newspaper was able to establish that the reputation of the claimant was indeed as it had suggested, they would be able to appeal out of time, and the onetime victorious claimant put at risk of conviction for perverting the course of justice or perjury, as happened with the famous author and politician Jeffrey Archer.[35]

Similarly, headlines themselves can be defamatory. However, the court will consider the article as a whole, because newspapers are not published for people who look only at the headlines and move on. In the United Kingdom, two actors sued the *News of the World*, which published a doctored photograph of their faces on naked bodies engaged in a sexual act.[36]

The headline screamed, "Strewth! What's Our Harold Up to with Our Madge?" Beneath the photograph, the article went on to describe a new computer game in which the faces of soap stars were superimposed on the bodies of others. The plaintiffs contended that some readers would look only at the photograph and the headline without reading the fine print below. The House of Lords held that it was not possible to divide the readership of a publication into different groups for the purposes of deciding what is defamatory; the article must be read as a whole. The actors lost their case.

Be careful about using generic pictures to illustrate a story. In *Triangle Publications, Inc. v. Chumley*,[37] an American newspaper and a magazine published a photograph of a teenage girl embracing a man and an excerpt from a diary saying she was pregnant. The illustration was an advertisement for a television documentary series on teenage pregnancy. The court held the photographs were defamatory.

Television stations must also be careful when selecting film footage that may convey defamatory remarks of a person. Example: Journalists representing newspapers and television stations cover a protest outside a bottling factory. The demonstrators carry placards bearing caricatures of the directors of the factory with the words "Thief from thief does make God laugh." If the papers and television stations publish photographs or footage of the placards, they, as well as the demonstrators, could be sued for defamation by the directors.

Sometimes, the juxtaposition of headline and photograph causes a problem. Remember, libel laws do not forgive carelessness, and your honest intentions do not count. No judge will say, "Oh, well, the sub-editor clearly made a mistake. He didn't intend to give offence." Through mix-ups with photographs and captions, innocent men and women have been horribly defamed, such as having one's name printed under the photograph of a convicted child molester.

ADVERTISEMENTS

Sometimes, members of the public who have axes to grind choose to place ads in the paper to get back at an enemy or rival. Both the person placing the ad and the newspaper publishing it would be liable. For example, an advertisement announcing that X is interested in learning the whereabouts of Y because Y owes her large sums of money should be declined with all possible speed. A woman, competing for the affection of a married man, once tried to place a birthday greeting in the *Daily Express* newspaper in Trinidad to the man with her name and picture, in which she presented herself as his darling wife. If her plot had not been foiled, the man could have sued on the ground that he had been made out to be a bigamist or an adulterer.

It is an old trick, apparently. In the 1902 case of *Morrison v. Ritchie and Co.*,[38] an unknown person placed a notice in the *Scotsman* to the effect that twins had been born to the claimants. This was considered defamatory (at that time) because the couple had been married for only one month. It was held that the action against the newspaper was relevant, notwithstanding that the newspaper had no knowledge of the pursuers or intent to injure them.

A mistake in the printing of a telephone number could also be disastrous. One man's phone number was printed in an advertisement that offered sexy massages. He, his wife and daughter were harassed all weekend by phone calls from potential clients until the advertisement could be removed. He did not pursue his legal options, maybe because he was exhausted from answering the phone.

CALYPSOS

Everyone is grist for the calypsonian's mill. Sinner or saint, politician or priest – none shall escape unscathed. But calypsos have no special privilege and neither do the news organizations that publish defamatory lyrics. In Barbados, in 1989, a former employee of a chicken farm reported to the Ministry of Health that he saw diseased and already dead chickens being processed and sold to the public. A public health inspector visited the farm, and the *Nation* newspaper published photographs of unhealthy chickens. This led to a national uproar, known as the chicken controversy, and calypsonians responded with characteristic wit:

> You sell me chicken wid de flu, E.I.E.I.O.
> You trick me once, you trick me twice
> And now my belly paying the price
> Cause every day, you laugh and hide and sell me fowls who commit suicide.[39]

The Barbados Rediffusion Service broadcast several calypsos: "The Madd Chicken Song", "Pluck It" and "Tit for Tat" that were calypsos composed and sung by a group called Madd, and two other calypsonians, "Red Plastic Bag" and "Classic". The calypsos contained defamatory words about the chicken farm. The chief justice ruled that no privilege attached to the publication of calypsos. Similarly, in *Dr. Edmond Mansoor v. Eugene Silcott*,[40] calypsonian Kaseba was ordered to pay compensation to the claimant for defamatory remarks contained in a composition called "The Golden Review", which he performed in a tent in front of hundreds of spectators. The trial judge Michel J pointed out that calypsonians do not have immunity from suit.

Then he offered the following guidance:

> The way in which a calypsonian avoids being sued for statements which he makes in song is by heeding the advice of the Mighty Chalkdust, the grand master of political commentary in calypso. Chalkdust has, for over four decades, delivered biting political commentaries criticising every Prime Minister of Trinidad and Tobago, from Eric Williams to Kamla Persad-Bissessar, but none has sued him, because – according to him in his calypso entitled "the Art of Spin Bowling" – when you want to sing that type of calypso, you don't bowl straight, but you have to learn to spin slow. He sang too in that song that you have to spin the ball from the back of your hand so that you don't say what you really want to say but the audience knows what you say. Kaseba – in his calypso entitled "Divine Intervention" – did not spin the ball, but bowled straight by singing that "Mansoor bribing Ministers, imagine how much he got for computers". You can only say that about someone whether in an article, a speech or a calypso – if you can establish the truth of the statement. The Defendant could not do so and ought never to have written, said or sang it.

INNUENDO

Journalists are like boxers. Sometimes, they go for the knockout punch. But on other occasions, they prefer to bob and weave. Libellous remarks are not only direct punches to the jaw ("She's a liar") but may also be glancing blows ("Like Pinocchio, her nose must be growing"). Both are extremely damaging. Reasonable people will know exactly what you mean, even when you try to be coy. So notwithstanding the advice of Chalkdust and Justice Michel with regard to the art of double entendre, innuendo is not a prophylactic. But at least in Trinidad and Tobago, recipients of calypso barbs, however hurtful and damaging, have a tradition of taking it all on the chin. Not because calypso or humour in any form are protected, but because to take legal action is likely to make the subjects look like even bigger jokes – who cannot take one.

HUMOUR

A joke that destroys the image of someone at whom it was aimed remains defamatory, even if it is funny to everyone apart from the victim. Humour, satire or parody do not belong to any enclave of protected expression.

The deputy headmaster in a large South African public school successfully sued three schoolboys for defamation after they created a computer-generated caricature of the headmaster and deputy headmaster by superimposing their heads on the bodies of two naked men sitting next to each other in a suggestive pose. The image was posted on the school notice board and remained there for about half an hour. The majority of judges at the appellate review held that although the intent was humorous, the caricature was defamatory.[41]

However, where the satire or humour are outrageous, the court may find that the offending words could not be taken seriously by reasonable readers to represent an assertion of fact. In 2008, Elton John sued the Guardian News and Media Ltd for libel, for a claim relating to a spoof that appeared in the Weekend section. The fictitious diary entry of the renowned musician and composer related to an HIV/AIDS benefit ball; it asserted the claimant was insincere and hosted the ball as just another opportunity for self-promotion, knowing only a fraction of money raised would go to good causes. The judge agreed with the newspaper's submission that reasonable readers would expect so serious an allegation to appear in the news pages and to be made without humour. It was "obviously a form of teasing". [42]

It is not easy to predict when a court will say, oh well, no one could possibly take that seriously, or that the barb is serious and damaging. Decisions have gone both ways. Judges are not easily amused.

FALSE BUT NOT DEFAMATORY

The law of libel does not correct false statements. A statement could be untrue and not be libellous in the least. To say a man wears false teeth when he doesn't might be embarrassing but it certainly won't make reasonable people shun him. To be defamatory, the statement must have some sting to it. Defamation protects people's reputations, not their feelings. Mere words of abuse, indicating that the writer dislikes the claimant and has a low opinion of him, but without suggesting specific factual charges against him, are not defamatory.

ORDINARY READER TEST

The intention of the writer of the offending remarks is irrelevant. The test is the effect on the ordinary reader, who is wise to the ways of the world and is endowed with considerable common sense and knowledge. He can read between the lines and grasp hidden meanings, so cleverly wrapped in humour, innuendo and satire. The ordinary reader is not a literal-minded simpleton. He can take a joke, even one in bad taste, and he is not overly suspicious or so avid for scandal that he sees corruption and conspiracy behind every headline.

In *Lewis v. Daily Telegraph*,[43] the House of Lords described the ordinary reader in this way:

> The ordinary man does not live in an ivory tower and he is not inhibited by a knowledge of the rules of construction. So he can and does read between the lines in the light of his general knowledge and his experience of worldly affairs. Ordinary men and women have different temperaments and outlooks. Some are unusually suspicious and some are unusually naive. One must try to envisage people between these two extremes and see what is the most damaging meaning that they would put on the words in question.

In that case, the claimant sought damages for libel as a result of an article published on the front page, stating that Fraud Squad detectives were inquiring into the affairs of a company and the investigation was requested after criticisms of the chairman's statement and the accounts by a shareholder at the recent company meeting. It was argued that the words used meant that the firm was actually guilty of fraud. The House of Lords disagreed and media managers can now rest a little more comfortably.[44]

For example, to say a man is "helping police with their enquiries" is not defamatory. The ordinary reader, not being avid for scandal, will not assume that he is guilty of a crime – unless, the journalist goes further and suggests that the police have every reason to suspect the person is involved in the crime.

In the Belize case of *Lawrence v. Lightburn*,[45] the claimant was a politician who complained of an article published a few days before Belize City Council elections. It reported that the politician was the prime suspect in the stabbing of an opponent Bobby Smith shortly after a political rally. The defendant was the editor, printer and publisher of the *Reporter*.

The Court of Appeal stated: "Unless an allegation of grounds for suspicion necessarily imports an allegation of guilt the article was not capable of bearing the interpretation that Bobby Smith had been bashed and stabbed by the respondent. Accordingly, the trial judge erred in holding that it did."[46]

Had the publication stopped there, the newspaper would have escaped liability. But the writer added that the claimant and his "gang of paid henchmen" were on the scene shortly before the "bash and juk" incident. The Court of Appeal held that in the overall context of the article, such reference bore a criminal connotation and was libellous in relation to the politician.

The overall meaning and tone of the article are assessed. It is not necessary to analyse each word in detail but rather to consider the overall impact of the article. As stated in *Hayward v. Thompson*, it was a matter of impression to an ordinary person on first reading, not later analysis.[47]

DEAD OR ALIVE

The dead have no reputation to protect – and no one can be sued for defaming the dead, except in Barbados.

In Barbados, if a publication defames a person who has died, the relatives of the deceased can sue within three years of the death. But they cannot collect damages. The claimant can only obtain a declaration that the material published was untrue, an injunction and compensation for pecuniary damage likely to have been suffered by the deceased or his estate as a result of the defamation. The only relatives who can commence an action are spouse, parents, brothers and sisters.[48]

In the absence of such provisions, journalists still have to tread carefully. Be wary of cross-fertilization. In writing about a deceased person, you may accidentally make defamatory remarks about relatives even though the focus of your publication was the deceased.

Families of celebrities and famous people keep trying to get around the "dead cannot be defamed" rule – usually unsuccessfully. In 1981 Charles Higham wrote a biography of Errol Flynn in which he alleged the actor, known for his swashbuckling roles and love of Port Antonio, Jamaica, was a spy. Flynn's daughters sued for defamation – and lost.

Justice Hanson stated:

As a matter of sound public policy, the malicious defamation of the memory of the dead is condemned as an affront to the general sentiments of morality and decency, and the interests of society demand its punishment through the criminal courts, but the law does not contemplate the offence as causing any special damage to another individual, though related to the deceased, and, therefore, it cannot be made the basis for recovery in a civil action.[49]

WORDS MUST REFER TO THE CLAIMANT

The claimant must show that the offending words referred to him. It is no defence that you have not named the claimant in the article. A person will have a cause of action for libel if others can correctly identify him or her as the target, whatever literary devices have been used in camouflage. Asterisks, blanks, initials and general descriptions will not avail, if evidence proves that readers have solved the puzzle correctly. In Grenada, a report alleging sexual impropriety towards young girls seeking employment was held to contain sufficient reference to Prime Minister Eric Gairy, although it did not mention his name.[50]

The *Barbados Advocate* published an article under the headline "Little Help for Junior Doctors" and alleged that junior doctors at the Queen Elizabeth Hospital were forced to make decisions regarding the treatment of patients without the benefit of consultation with senior medical practitioners, who preferred to play golf rather than attend to their duties.[51] The plaintiff was a senior consultant physician and also a keen amateur golfer. The only other consultant who played golf was attached to the department of radiology and not likely to be involved in the medical care of patients. The plaintiff, therefore, successfully claimed that ordinary, sensible readers would understand the words to refer to him.

Great difficulty arises, though, when several people bear the same name or fit the same general description. Take the case of Harold Newstead.[52] The *London Express* reported, correctly, that Harold Newstead, a resident of Camberwell, had been jailed for bigamy. The court held that another Harold Newstead, a hairdresser, from Camberwell, had been libelled. This decision has been widely criticized as unsatisfactory but it is used as a warning to court reporters to include addresses and occupations of defendants and witnesses to avoid confusion.[53]

Generally, there is strength in numbers. A large group or class of people cannot be defamed unless the plaintiff can be identified. "Facetious exaggerations" or "vulgar generalizations" are not actionable.[54] Call all lawyers charlatans, if you like. No lawyer would be able to sue over it. But if you say all senior counsel members are crooks, may God have mercy on your soul. The narrower the class and the more specific the allegation, the more dangerous the territory. To say, for example, that the police service is corrupt will not attract a libel action, unless the report goes further and attributes corrupt practices to the commissioner of police. Or, to refer to the canine unit in derogatory terms could invite a libel suit if only a handful of police officers are assigned to that unit. Each of those officers could seek redress in the courts. In the American case of *Neiman-Marcus v. Lait*,[55] a statement calling "most" of the salesmen who worked in the Neiman-Marcus store in Dallas "faggots" gave rise to a claim by all twenty-five salesmen who worked there. In the Cayman Islands, a report that referred to the elected government as dictators and communists was held to be defamatory of each member of the Executive Council, which consisted of only four people.[56]

The approach to large, indeterminate groups was settled in *Knupffer v. London Express Newspaper*,[57] where the respondents published a newspaper article from a correspondent abroad adversely commenting on the activities of an association of certain Russian political refugees called Mlado Russ or Young Russia, in terms which, it was admitted, would have been defamatory if written of a named individual. The association had a very large membership in other countries, but the branch in the United Kingdom was only some twenty-four members. The appellant who resided in London was the active head of the UK branch of the association, and it was contended that the article reflected upon him personally. The respondents contended that the article was an attack on the general character and activities of the association and not on the appellant. There was, in fact, no reference in the article to the appellant or to the branch of the association in the United Kingdom. The plaintiff claimed that because of his prominence, readers would immediately think the words referred to him.

Viscount Simon LC, in delivering the judgment of the House of Lords, stated:

> Where the plaintiff is not named, the test which decides whether the words used refer to him is the question whether the words are such as would reasonably lead persons acquainted with the plaintiff to believe that he was the person referred to. There are cases in which the language used in reference to a limited class may be reasonably understood to refer to every member of the class, in which case every member may have a cause of action.

In the Mlado Russ case, the House of Lords held that nothing in the words referred to one member of the group rather than another.

Here is a tricky issue that has perplexed judges: One publication is defamatory but does not identify the claimant. Then, a subsequent item does. Is the claimant entitled to link the two and maintain a cause of action?

A rigorous rule that says "Never!" would not accord with justice and common sense.[58] A lot depends on the particular facts. If the articles are part of a series or saga and are published close in time, one is more likely to say yes, there is sufficient connection to support a claim.

In *Simon and Others v. Lyder and Others,*[59] the Privy Council remarked that the legal conundrum had no satisfactory conclusion.[60] But suffice it to say that for two statements (where one is defamatory and the other identifies the claimant) made by the same person to be aggregated for the purpose of giving rise to a cause of action in defamation, there must be in the mind of the reasonable reader a sufficient "nexus, connection or association" so that the claimant is identified in the mind of the reader.

In that case, the *Express* daily in Trinidad and Tobago published articles about the police killing of four occupants of a car and a woman nearby in her home in Wallerfield, Arima. The gist of the publications was that a police assassination squad had opened fire on the car, mistakenly believing an underworld target was one of the occupants, thereby killing innocent citizens. Six months later an inquest into the killings was concluded and the newspaper published a further article, naming the nine police officers involved in the shooting.

The trial judge decided in favour of the newspaper, concluding that more than likely readers would have forgotten the tenor and purport of the first articles. The trial judge weighed several factors: the passage of time between the publications; the notoriety of the incident in a small society; and the newspaper's urging to readers to pay attention to the inquest. He also considered that the subsequent report concerned the inquest and made no sufficient reference to the earlier articles. The Court of Appeal overturned his decision. But the Privy Council stated that the trial judge had weighed the relevant factors and was entitled to reach his finding. Merely because the Court of Appeal disagreed with his factual conclusion was no reason to overturn his decision. For that reason, the Privy Council advised that the newspaper's appeal should be allowed.

WHO CAN SUE

Anyone who has been made the subject of a defamatory attack may take legal action. The only qualification is that the person be alive. The dead cannot sue for libel, Barbados being a notable exception.[61] In most other jurisdictions, if the claimant dies one day before the completion of the trial, the action dies with him. Attorney General Selwyn Richardson of Trinidad and Tobago sued the *TnT Mirror* after it alleged he had AIDS. Shortly before the close of the trial, he was gunned down outside his home on the night of June 20, 1995. The action died with him.

A company can sue but only in respect of statements that damage its business reputation, such as allegations that its cheques bounce.[62] Lord Reid in *Lewis v. Daily Telegraph*[63] (where both the managing director and company were defendants) said at page 262: "A company cannot be injured in its feelings, it can only be injured in its pocket. Its reputation can be injured by a libel but that injury must sound in money. The injury need not necessarily be confined to loss of income. Its goodwill may be injured."

However, Lord Reid's speech was made decades ago and as noted by Bereaux J in *Pan Trinbago Inc., TC and Owen Serrette v. Sat Maharaj and Indra Maharaj*: "We now live in an era in which the non-natural person is described as a 'corporate citizen'. It has civil rights. Marketing and advertising contribute significantly to the burnishing of the corporate image. Companies including those set up for charitable or altruistic purposes depend on their goodwill for reputability."[64]

In that case, the claimant was a corporate body, involved in the development and promotion of the steel band. As an entity having an image and identity of its own, it was capable of being libelled. Bereaux J stated an article that imputed improper action and motives to it is bound to be damaging to its goodwill and reputation and may affect such things as sponsorship and other forms of assistance in promoting its objects.

In *Derbyshire County Council v. The Times,*[65] a local authority, brought an action for damages from libel against the defendants in respect of two newspaper articles that had questioned the propriety of investments made for its superannuation fund. The Court of Appeal held that the authority had no such right.

A publication attacking the activities of the authority will necessarily be an attack on the body of councillors that represents the controlling party, or on the executives who carry on the day-to-day management of its affairs. If the individual reputation of any of these is wrongly impaired by the publication, any of these can bring proceedings for defamation. Further, it is open to the controlling body to defend itself by public utterances and in debate in the council chamber.

It is unclear whether this rule prohibiting government bodies from suing for defamation also extends to wholly privatized companies carrying out functions of the state. It seems much will depend on the functions of the body and the degree of control exercised over it by government. In *Duke v. University of Salford*,[66] Eady J held that a university was entitled to sue for libel: universities receive substantial public funding and are subject to statutory controls but they do not provide a service on behalf of the government and are not to be equated with central or local government.

WHO CAN BE SUED

Everyone in the defamation chain can be sued – the person who first uttered the remark, the reporter who wrote it, the newspaper or media house that published it, the printer who printed the newspaper and the distributors who sell it.[67] Journalists, their editors and their newspapers or broadcast stations are usually named as co-defendants. Any person who contributes to the publication of the defamatory statements is liable. In reality, claimants focus on the big fish who can pay the damages. That means the media house but if the newspaper, for example, barely has a penny to its name, the aggrieved may also go after the printer.

Journalists can avoid responsibility by proving that the error was added to their copy without their knowledge or consent. When the media house decides to cut its losses and make a public apology, the innocent journalist can take action. An apology defames the writer of the article by suggesting the writer has been careless. The journalist so injured can sue the paper or media organization. (Then again, that might be career suicide.)

CRIMINAL LIBEL

This is an ancient common law provision, which is rarely invoked, but it is still on the law books and is not to be taken lightly, because the guilty can be sent to prison for up to five years in some instances.[68] The law says this type of libel is so serious it cannot be compensated by money and deserves to be punished as a crime.

The offence of criminal libel can be traced back to thirteenth-century England as a means of protecting the government from stories that might arouse the people and lead to breaches of the peace. In France, in 1898 the novelist Émile Zola was convicted of criminal libel after his cataclysmic newspaper article "J'accuse", in which he exposed the massive cover-up in the treason trial of a Jewish army captain, Alfred Dreyfus.

Generally, this offence is now considered to be an unnecessary relic of the past with no place in modern jurisprudence. Nevertheless, it is resurrected from time to time.

In Trinidad, in the 1970s, Irwin Sandy, editor of the *Bomb* weekly, was charged with the offence but died before the case could ever come to trial. In the Cayman Islands, a thirty-five-year-old woman was unsuccessfully prosecuted in 2009 for four counts of criminal libel after it was alleged she wrote letters to the chief immigration officer saying that her ex-lover had terrorist links.[69]

In Grenada, George Worme, editor of *Grenada Today*, a weekly newspaper, was prosecuted in 1999 for the criminal offence of intentional libel, after publishing an open letter in two issues of the paper that accused the prime minister of Grenada of winning the election by bribing voters in disregard of the law.

The defendants contended the law was inconsistent with the constitutional right to freedom of expression. In a 2004 ruling, the Privy Council disagreed, stating that the "objective of an offence that caught those who attacked a person's reputation by falsely accusing him of crime or misconduct in public office was sufficiently important to justify limiting the right to freedom of expression".[70] Further, it was held that the crime was reasonably required in Grenada to protect people's reputations and did not go further than was necessary to accomplish that objective.

However, after vigorous lobbying by the Association of Caribbean Media Workers and the International Press Institute, in 2012, Grenada became the first Caribbean state to abolish the provision. Jamaica, Trinidad and Tobago, and Antigua and Barbuda soon followed.

Despite abolishing criminal libel, Antigua and Barbuda, Grenada, and Trinidad and Tobago still maintain seditious libel provisions that criminalize libel and slander with the intent of exciting disaffection against the government and stirring up discontent among inhabitants. St Lucia and Dominica have similar provisions.[71] Also, in Trinidad and Tobago, a newspaper that publishes seditious libel can be suspended from publication for a year.[72]

In St Vincent and the Grenadines, in *Commissioner of Police v. Ordan Graham*,[73] the director of public prosecutions unsuccessfully prosecuted a speaker who, at a public meeting, criticized the leadership of the prime minister for using seditious words:[74]

Ralph Gonsalves feels he is the only man with some savvy in this country. We have to reverse that trend. If we do not reverse that trend in this country, you know what would happen here? You know what would happen? Blood would run on the streets of the country. And don't take that for a joke because what would happen, after all those lands are gone this would cause riot in this country. It would cause riot in this country.

The magistrate found that the speaker's words were highly emotive, wild and ill considered but it was not for the court to "ensure responsible speech writing". Without more, the words did not constitute sedition.[75]

In Trinidad and Tobago, Yasin Abu Bakr[76] was prosecuted under Sections 3 (1) c and (d) of the Sedition Act for statements made during an Eid al-Fitr sermon, with the alleged purpose to "raise discontent or disaffection" among the people and engender "feelings of ill will or hostility" between members of his own Jamaat al Muslimeen and other Muslim leaders and groups. The broadcast media published excerpts of the sermon in news programmes.[77] At his trial in 2011, the jury was unable to reach a verdict and a retrial was ordered.

MALICIOUS FALSEHOOD

False statements that are not defamatory may be categorized as malicious falsehood. An example would be a claim that a seller of goods or land is not the true owner. Another example would be a false assertion that a person has closed down his business.

The defendant must have published about the claimant, words that are false, and published them maliciously. Damages are recoverable only on proof that the claimant has suffered special damage as the direct and natural result of the publication. Successful actions are uncommon.

The *Today* newspaper in England displayed malice when it published an article alleging that a maid had stolen the Princess Royal's intimate letters and sold them to a newspaper. The Court of Appeal found that the publication was capable of being malicious because the defendants published the police suspicions as if they were gospel and did so without taking any steps to verify them.[78]

Avoid falling into the following traps:

1. **"It's not us saying it. We're just quoting him."** One of the most common causes of libel actions is repeating statements made by people you interview and not being able to prove the truth of what they told you.

2. **"We're only denying a rumour."** It is dangerous to repeat a defamatory rumour in any circumstances unless the newspaper is in a position to prove it is true. It is even dangerous to repeat the rumour for the bona fide purposes of contradicting it. (See Reynolds defence, chapter 6.)

3. **"We gave both sides of the story."** Not enough – you still printed a libellous statement even if you let the person give his or her side of the affair. The only safe way is not to print the libel unless you can prove it is true.

4. **"We printed a correction immediately."** This, combined with an apology, may help soothe angry claimants but it does not erase liability. The claimant can still pursue libel action but the timely correction and apology will mitigate damages.

5. **"It's a satirical piece."** Writers sometimes think they can shred public figures, change their names, call it satire and they are safe. Spoofing public figures is a form of commentary and more power to the talented writer who can be humorous, provocative and insightful, all at the same time. But beware, if you go too far, libel lawyers will see through all your clever disguises. Journalists sometimes go as far as to adopt the disclaimer usually run at the end if films: "This work is entirely fictitious and any similarity between the characters and any other person is entirely coincidental." But that fig leaf will not protect the news organization if readers and viewers can identify the claimant from the work.

6. **"We didn't call any names."** That won't work. The claimant will have a cause of action as long as he can be recognized or identified.

PREPUBLICATION CHECKLIST

1. Are you saying precisely what you mean to say? Is the article clear and unambiguous in its meaning?

2. Is it actual "fraud" or really "financial mismanagement"? Did he really "lie" or was he making an innocent mistake? Was it actual "corruption" or an "unusual payment", possibly involving "financial irregularities"?

3. Can you prove what you have said is true? Are the sources of the information relied upon prepared to give evidence in support of the story?

4. Have you safeguarded your notes? Are they coherent, with dates and time recorded? Do you have documents, ledgers, letters that support your allegations?

5. Is the publication of legitimate public interest or concern?

6. Have you interviewed the subject of the article? Have those likely to be defamed by the publication been given a reasonable opportunity to respond to each and every allegation in the item concerned? If so, has that person's response been properly incorporated in the article?

7. Has every effort been made to ensure that none of the sources of information relied upon for the purposes of the item are actuated by malice?

8. Does the publication of the item breach any duty of confidentiality?

9. Is there a hidden or inferential meaning? Example: the reverend was seen at 101 Lovers Lane (a well-known brothel).

10. If no one is named, is someone still identifiable and therefore able to sue? Will a number of people know the claimant is the person referred to?

11. Is the story perishable? Can it wait another day so you can verify details?

12. Not sure of some statement, allegation or detail? If in doubt, leave it to hell out.

CHAPTER 4

CYBERLIBEL

In this age of social media such as Twitter, Facebook and Skype, the publication of information which is in the interest of the public to know cannot and should not be restricted to newspapers and news producing media.

—Skyes J, in *Matalon v. Jamaica Observer*[1]

And then came the Internet.

With about four billion users worldwide,[2] this borderless telecommunications network, which came into popular use in the 1990s, has created accelerated means of publishing worthwhile information – and of spreading defamatory and harmful material.

In *Dow Jones and Company Inc. v. Gutnick*,[3] Kirby J, of the High Court of Australia, portrayed the Internet in these terms:

The Internet is essentially a decentralized, self-maintained telecommunications network. It is made up of inter-linking small networks from all parts of the world. It is ubiquitous, borderless, global and ambient in its nature. Hence the term "cyberspace". This is a word that recognizes that the interrelationships created by the Internet exist outside conventional geographic boundaries and comprise a single interconnected body of data, potentially amounting to a single body of knowledge. The Internet is accessible in virtually all places on Earth where access can be obtained either by wire connection or by wireless (including satellite) links. Effectively, the only constraint on access to the Internet is possession of the means of securing connection to a telecommunications system and possession of the basic hardware.

Anyone, at the click of a button, can become a "publisher", and be sued for defamation if the material damages someone's reputation.[4] Bad-mouthing someone online will get you into water of the same temperature, just as if you published the statements in traditional media. *Halsbury's Laws of England*[5] explains: "An individual who posts defamatory material on the Internet is a publisher of that material if it is subsequently accessed and read by a third party."[6]

In a defamation claim, there must be proof that the statements were published or communicated to someone other than the claimant. With newspapers and books, there is a presumption that the defamatory statement was so communicated. With material posted on the Internet, however, there is no such presumption that the material was downloaded by anyone. Rather, it is a matter of inferences.[7] This was discussed by the Eastern Caribbean Court of Appeal in the Dominica case of *Lennox Linton v. Pinard-Byrne*,[8] in which the claimant was defamed on a radio broadcast as well as in an article posted on a website. It was necessary for the claimant to bring proof that the article had been downloaded in Dominica.

A hyperlink, by itself, in an online article, without endorsement or adoption of the content of the linked material, would not usually amount to publication, even where the hyperlink is followed and defamatory material is accessed.[9]

Online defamation is considered libel (not slander) because of the permanency of the form, and so claimants do not have to show they suffered specific loss. Potentially, damages can be greater for Internet libel because of the wide reach of the worldwide web.[10] Also, Internet publishers or social media users may find themselves being sued in foreign jurisdictions where their posts were accessed and read.

In *Dow Jones and Co. Inc. v. Gutnick*,[11] a claimant who resided in Australia brought a defamation claim against Dow Jones, an American corporation, for statements made in articles published by Dow Jones on its website, which was maintained on servers located in New Jersey, in the United States. The High Court of Australia[12] rejected the argument by Dow Jones that the Australian court did not have jurisdiction.

All seven justices of the High Court held:

> In the case of material on the World Wide Web (web), it is not available in comprehensible form until downloaded on to the computer of a person who has used a web browser to pull the material from the web server. It is where that person downloads the material that the damage to reputation may be done. Ordinarily then, that will be the place where the tort of defamation is committed.[13]

This principle was followed *King v. Lewis*,[14] when the English Court of Appeal upheld flamboyant American boxing promoter Don King's right to sue boxing champion Lennox Lewis and other defendants in an English court, over texts stored in a website in California but accessed in England where King had a reputation to protect.

Newspapers and magazines can be sued for articles on their websites as well as in the paper itself. Each "hit" is considered a new publication of a defamatory statement. It is, therefore, essential to remove an offending statement from the electronic archive as quickly as possible. Newspapers and other publications that allow readers to post defamatory comments on their websites will also be held responsible.[15] Apologies should be published in the online edition of the newspaper as well.

In the English case of *Loutchansky v. Times Newspapers Ltd*,[16] an allegedly defamatory story had appeared both in the printed version of the newspaper and in its online edition. The limitation period for bringing an action had expired in respect of the printed copy but it was held that the online copy was republished every time a reader downloaded it and so an action in this respect was not time-barred.

The legislature in Jamaica, however, may have intervened to stop the clock from the first publication on the Internet. Section 33 (a) of the Defamation Act 2013 provides that an action for defamation must be brought within two years of when the statement is "first published" on the Internet or it is first capable of being viewed or listened through the Internet, whichever is later. Antigua, in Section 36 of the Defamation Act 2015, without specifying online statements, provides that an action for defamation must be brought within three years from the date the defamatory statement is first published.[17] However, this interpretation will have to be tested by a court.

Tweets and email messages can be defamatory. Even if all you do is forward a defamatory email message or retweet a post, you are publishing the statement and can be sued for libel. In 2008, a Trinidadian journalist received and forwarded to twenty-six people a defamatory letter about Calder Hart, the then chairman of the Urban Development Corporation of Trinidad and Tobago Ltd and a prominent public official who was under public scrutiny for his use of funds in several large-scale government construction projects. The public official threatened to initiate a libel claim. The journalist eventually apologized and the matter did not go to court.

In England, Sally Bercow, wife of the Speaker of the House of Commons, published a statement on Twitter about Lord McAlpine, who was a close aide to Margaret Thatcher when she was prime minister. The tweet, which read, "Why is Lord McAlpine trending. *Innocent face,*" was rooted in innuendo, but followers of Twitter would have been familiar with the context, and the court ruled that the statement was defamatory because readers would understand it to mean that the claimant was a paedophile who sexually abused boys.[18]

The tweet had appeared two days after a *Newsnight* report that had wrongly implicated the former Conservative Party treasurer in a sexual abuse scandal at a children's home in the 1970s and 1980s. Bercow apologized for her "irresponsible use of Twitter" and agreed to pay damages and legal costs. She also withdrew the remarks and promised never to repeat them. The peer also received damages from the BBC and ITV, and from comedian Alan Davies, who had retweeted the defamatory Twitter post.[19]

In Canada, in *Fantino v. Baptista*,[20] Julian Fantino, the police chief of London, Ontario, brought a lawsuit against a self-described government critic who made defamatory remarks in electronic messages. The police chief obtained judgment in the amount of CA$40,000. The defendant pleaded that he was an "Internet god" and "at war with the Canadian government", and that he liked bothering civil servants by distributing critical information through his computer.

Although people tend to be spontaneous and impulsive with online comments, it is no defence to say the post was made in haste, or jest or was meant as a prank. Bloggers, vloggers, Facebook activists, Instagram gurus and "citizen journalists" have no special immunity and can be sued for defamatory remarks – just like professional journalists or any Internet user. They will have recourse to the same defences as professional journalists, including truth or justification, honest comment on a matter of public interest, apology and offer of amends. (See chapter 5, "Defences".)

And why should it be any different?

The power of the Internet means that a careless remark can go viral in seconds and reach a wide audience. In the Canadian case of *Barrick Gold Corp v. Lopehandia*,[21] Justice of Appeal Blair discussed the power of the Internet to harm reputation: "Communication via the Internet is instantaneous, seamless, interactive, blunt, borderless and far-reaching. It is also impersonal, and the anonymous nature of such communications may itself create a greater risk that the defamatory remarks are believed. The Internet has greater potential to damage the reputation of individuals and corporations as a result of these features than does its less pervasive cousins."[22]

In Trinidad and Tobago, in *Child A and Child B v. Jenelle Burke*,[23] Seepersad J urged Internet users to exercise extreme caution:

Words in any form or on any forum, matter and must be used carefully and not impulsively. Within the public purview there is a misguided perception that the interaction over social media with flagged friends whether on Facebook, Twitter, WhatsApp, Viber, is private. This notion has to be dispelled. Such communication once uploaded becomes public and the said communication enjoys no cover of privacy protection. The advent and continued use of social media now results in a circumstance where the rules, regulations, rights, and responsibilities which govern traditional media must be applied. Social media ought not to be viewed as an unregulated media forum and anyone who elects to express views or opinions on such a forum stands in the shoes of a journalist and must be subjected to the standards of responsible journalism which govern traditional media.

The *Jenelle Burke* case raised for the first time in Trinidad and Tobago issues relating to liability for publication via social media, in that case Facebook. The claimants and defendant were next-door neighbours and they had a falling-out that involved the words *raperman* and *whore* being exchanged. Further allegations of a sexual nature ended up on Facebook. The defendant, who agreed she used the profile "Jenelle Burke", was ordered to pay damages.[24]

INTERNET SERVICE PROVIDERS

Internet service providers (ISPs) are usually not held liable for defamatory material posted by third parties because the ISP has no means of viewing the material before it is posted. The ISP is usually regarded as akin to a newsstand vendor, library or bookstore. However, if after being notified of defamatory material, the ISP allows the material to remain for an unreasonable period, the court may hold the ISP responsible as a publisher.[25] An ISP that exerts control or undertakes a gatekeeper role for bulletin boards, newsgroups or other websites it hosts may be considered an editor or publisher and be deemed responsible for posts. This was the outcome in *Stratton Oakmont Inc. v. Prodigy Services Co,*[26] which concerned defamatory posts on a bulletin board provided by Prodigy. Prodigy described itself as a family-oriented computer network and as exercising editorial control over message content. The New York Supreme Court held that Prodigy published the defamatory material.[27]

The Jamaica Defamation Act 2013[28] reflects this position under the defence of "innocent dissemination", which protects providers of service consisting of the "operation of or provision of any equipment, system or service by means of which the matter is retrieved, copied, distributed, or made available in electronic form" and the "operator or provider of access to a communications system by means of which the matter is transmitted or made available by another person over whom the operator or provider has no control". The Antigua and Barbuda Defamation Act 2015 is in almost identical terms, adding the word *effective* before *control*.[29]

Internet service providers can be ordered to disclose identities of users. In England, an ISP was ordered to provide disclosure of the identity of a website user known as Zeddust. In *Totalise plc v. Motley Fool Ltd*,[30] Totalise sought disclosure of Zeddust's identity from Motley Fool who operated a website.[31] Justice Owen said that disclosure was necessary in the interest of justice; to find otherwise would be to give the "clearest indication to those who wish to defame that they can do so with impunity behind the screen of anonymity made possible by the use of websites on the Internet".

CITIZEN JOURNALISM

Social media use is so pervasive that, more and more, traditional as well as digital journalists are relying on posts and tweets for tips and leads on their own reports. But unlike traditional or digital journalists, "citizen journalists", who use social media platforms such as Facebook and Twitter, have no editor to answer to and can publish with little or no restriction.

Greater vigilance is needed when republishing information obtained online; don't let the sheer ubiquity of the information fool you into thinking there is fire behind the smoke. Mainstream journalists who collaborate with citizen journalists[32] should remember that a claimant may very well choose to take action against them rather than the person behind the post, because the blogger may be someone of few assets and difficult to identify.

Despite the unstructured nature of citizen journalism, this type of publishing is growing in respect. Laura Dowrich, a Trinidadian digital media journalist, in a presentation entitled "Netizens and Citizen Journalism",[33] noted several advantages of citizen journalism: it helps resource-strapped news media houses get information; provides new and unique angles and leads; offers real-time reporting; and widens the range of topics being reported.[34] For example, in the aftermath of 2017 Hurricanes Irma and Maria, Linda Dias, an architect in Montserrat, posted on Facebook an essay about building codes in the Caribbean and the best way to construct roofs. Dowrich was able to republish the material (with permission) on Loop news service.

Historic examples of "citizen journalists" include Salam Pax, an Iraqi blogger who provided "on-the-ground" details of the US invasion in 2003, while mainstream journalists were embedded in the army; George Holliday, in 1991, who, using his Sony Handycam, captured the beating of Rodney King at the hands of the Los Angeles Police Department, and sold the tape to Los Angeles television station KTLA for US$500; and Abraham Zapruder, who, in 1963, with his home camera, captured the assassination of US President John F. Kennedy and sold the footage to *Life* magazine for US$150,000.

More recently, in the United Kingdom, an investment fund manager from New York who was passing through London on the day of the G20 protests in 2009 captured on video a police constable striking newspaper vendor Ian Tomlinson with a baton. Tomlinson was not part of the protests but was making his way home. He was struck from behind and died at hospital.

The *Guardian* obtained the video and published it on its website. Until then, the official version was that Tomlinson had died of a heart attack and had no physical contact with the police. Video from a freelance journalist also showed that police claims of rioters throwing bottles while the police tried to help Tomlinson were false.

A criminal inquiry was opened. The policeman was dismissed for gross misconduct and the pathologist was struck off the medical register.[35]

CHAPTER 5

DEFENCES

The local society is by and large a society which believes what it reads.
What is in the papers must be true or at the least, have a grain of truth.

—Justice Deyalsingh in *Basdeo Panday v. Blast Publications Ltd and others*[1]

Sometimes, claimants in defamation matters do a lot of sabre rattling to see if you will blink. On occasion, a robust response might be enough to end all hostilities.

In the celebrated case of *Arkell v. Pressdram*,[2] *Private Eye* magazine received a letter from Mr Arkell's solicitors, which ended with the usual legal demand for a full retraction at the earliest possible date and costs to be paid: "His attitude to damages will be governed by the nature of your reply."

To this the magazine replied, "We note that Mr Arkell's attitude to damages will be governed by the nature of our reply and would therefore be grateful if you could inform us what his attitude to damages would be, were he to learn that the nature of our reply is as follows: f**k off."

Except that *Private Eye,* never coy, spelt out the F-word.

Few defamation clashes end so satisfactorily and spectacularly.

The cost of defending a libel action, even if one is successful, can be enormous. Senior counsel may have to be retained and they do not appear without a learned junior; neither comes cheaply. Also, the stress of getting into a witness box, taking an oath and being cross-examined by grim lawyers in black robes is not to be taken lightly. So much better to ensure one is on safe ground before publishing material that taints a person's reputation. Whatever the defects in libel law, there are several weapons and shields at your disposal.

The main defences used by media defendants are:

- truth or justification
- fair comment on a matter of public interest

- unintentional defamation
- privilege
- innocent dissemination
- consent
- apology
- limitation

TRUTH OR JUSTIFICATION

This is an absolute defence. It means you are justified in publishing the defamatory remarks because they are true. Once a news organization can show that the article complained of is true or substantially so, it will have a complete, ironclad defence. It does not matter what motive led to the publication, or whether the newspaper or journalist was acting out of malice, ill will or revenge.[3]

Once the claimant shows that the statement is defamatory (let's say he has been called a thief), it is presumed, at that point, that the statement is not true. It is then up to the newspaper to prove that the words complained of are indeed true or substantially true. Each and every statement must be proved to succeed in this defence. The court may ignore statements of a minor nature that do not "materially injure" the claimant's reputation, although they have not been proved.[4]

Example: The *Daily Blah* reports that Miss X, a former beauty queen, is a drug mule, who, despite her illegal income, shoplifts at the grocery and writes bad cheques. She also throws cuttings from her trees on the public road. The newspaper can prove the first three allegations but not the third about her littering. A court is unlikely to punish the paper for that, because being called a litterbug is not going to do any further damage to this creep's reputation.

It is not sufficient to establish that many people widely believe the statement to be true. As Lord Devlin has explained, you cannot escape liability for defamation by putting the libel behind a curtain such as "I have been told that ..." or "it is rumoured that ..." and then asserting that it was true that you had been told or that it was in fact being rumoured.[5]

The *Bomb* unsuccessfully tried that feeble excuse after it published a report that a popular singer, Charmaine Forde, had died of complications related to HIV/AIDS. It pleaded justification, saying it was true that it had received reports of her death, although it had not a shred of proof. It was easy to defeat that ludicrous defence, because the lady walked into the courtroom very much alive – and with the negative result of an HIV test.

The task of proving statements are indeed true can be extremely challenging. Witnesses, who were so forthcoming before publication of the article, may back down at trial, and the newspaper may find itself without enough evidence to convince a judge that the statement is true. So even a lying claimant can succeed in his defamation suit against a newspaper.

Claimants have reputations to protect and may be prepared to go to all ends to maintain their position in society, even if it means committing perjury. In 1987, in a successful libel action, multimillionaire novelist Jeffrey Archer, a former deputy chairman of the Britain's Conservative Party, extracted £500,000 in damages from the *Star* tabloid after it reported that he had hired a prostitute. Although the prostitute herself gave evidence of their relationship and described Archer's "spotty back", the jury, clearly, did not believe her. But in November 1999, a friend of Archer's admitted that he had given Archer a false alibi to help him win his defamation case. Archer was convicted of perjury and sentenced to four years in prison.

In 1995, Jonathan Aitken, a former journalist, war correspondent and Conservative member of Parliament, sued the *Guardian* and Granada television for alleging that his £1,500 hotel bill at the Paris Ritz was paid by a businessman who was a close friend of the Saudi royal family, at a time when one of Aitken's jobs was to see through a defence deal with the Saudis. Aitken self-righteously declared he intended to "cut out the cancer of bent and twisted journalism with the simple sword of truth". The libel trial collapsed dramatically when the defendants proved Aitken was lying when he testified that his wife had paid the bill – because she had been in Switzerland that weekend. Aitken was sentenced to eighteen months in prison for perjury and perverting the course of justice. He declared bankruptcy and was stripped of his Rolex and cufflinks by debt collectors.

Aaah, if only newspapers could count on such a comeuppance for dishonest claimants at every libel trial.

In his novel *QB VII*, writer Leon Uris, gives a gripping account of a libel trial in England, where a revered Polish doctor is accused by a Jewish writer of performing thousands of experiments on Jews without the use of anaesthesia, in a Nazi concentration camp. This novel was inspired by the real-life experience of Uris, who named a Polish doctor in Nazi camp atrocities in *Exodus*, his sweeping account of the creation of the Jewish state of Israel. Although the doctor is haunted by the truth, he is driven to take action to defend his honour and secure his family's respect.

The defendant's attorney comments on why the doctor risked a trial: "You'd think a man who has done what Adam Kelno did would shut up and consider himself lucky and try to get along with his conscience, if he has one, and not rake it all up again after almost 25 years. He did it because he thought he could get away with it."

Indeed, claimants are not always guided by truth but by what they think they can get away with. Do not make it easy for them. Make sure you have the substance to back up your thunder. A heartfelt belief in the honourable nature of your cause will not save you. Ensure you have solid evidence before launching into publication. Get documents, tape interviews, keep impeccable notes, maintain a log of phone calls.

Before a plea of truth or justification is entered as a defence, the following criteria must be satisfied:

- The defendant should believe that the words complained of are true;
- The defendant should intend to support the defence of justification at trial;
- The defendant should have reasonable evidence to support the defence or reasonable grounds for supposing that sufficient evidence to prove the defence would be available at trial.

A cautionary tale: In the Canadian case of *Munro v. Toronto Sun Publishing Corp,*[6] a federal Cabinet minister was accused of making stock market trades using insider information obtained through his Cabinet position. The story was based on "evidence" on a microfiche that a reporter frequently held up for his editors but never actually let them or anyone else see. After the story was published and the minister sued the paper, its editors and reporters, the paper discovered it had no proof. The reporter said he had lost the microfiche. The court awarded damages of CA$100,000 to Munro and emphasized that the editors were just as responsible as reporters for the accuracy of the story. One reporter was fired and the other allowed to resign.

FAIR COMMENT

Sometimes called the "critic's defence", this defence should be renamed "honest comment" because to succeed, the writer does not have to be fair at all. He can be as obnoxious and imbalanced as he pleases – as long as he can back up his opinion.

The defence of fair comment will attach to:

- a statement
- in the form of an opinion
- which is based on "true facts"
- and which is made with fairness
- on a matter of public interest
- and without malice.

The comment must be one of opinion but it must be based on facts or on statements made on privileged occasions, such as during parliamentary or court proceedings. So, you may say someone is unfit to hold public office because he assaulted a rival on election day, but if it has not been proven that the official did in fact commit the offence, the defence of fair comment will be of no avail. The facts on which the opinion is based must be stated in the article.

Where a bald defamatory remark is made ("She's a disgrace to the medical profession") without reference to any fact from which the comment could be inferred, it is not likely to be defensible as comment, especially if it imputes dishonourable conduct or dishonesty. Merely inserting the phrases "In my opinion" or "It seems to me" will not necessarily transform a criticism into comment. Always remember that the comment is like a picture that needs something on which to hang – a provable fact.

In St Kitts–Nevis, an article published under the headline "Simmonds You Better Talk Fast: Where the ½ Million Gone?"[7] alleged that the prime minister had given away a ferry boat, purchased on behest of the government, to a party activist. Robotham CJ said that although "robust and intemperate language" may be used, the article was unprotected by fair comment because the allegations could not be substantiated.

By contrast, a prominent attorney sued the *Trinidad Guardian* when a letter writer commented that he did not deserve the title of senior counsel. The paper was vindicated because one could detect the facts upon which the comment was based, whether or not one agreed with the comment.[8]

A radio station in Nevis and a caller were both sued by a public official for defamation after the caller said, "She needs to be removed from that office, she's unfit, she's in my opinion indecent to be there, she is corrupt and she is one who worked hand in hand, day and night to help the change of government come to this island." He gave reasons for his opinion – that the official had registered non-nationals as voters. The judge dismissed the claim because the defendant, who was the executive officer in charge of the electoral sub-office in Nevis, admitted that she had indeed done so, though in error because she was new to her job and learning new duties. The judge also found that although the caller came across as pompous and arrogant, he bore no malice to the official and both he and the radio station took a serious interest in the politics of the country.

The official said she was humiliated and embarrassed but as stated by Eady J in *Branson v. Bower*:[9] "In a modern democracy all those who venture into public life, in whatever capacity must expect to have their motives subjected to scrutiny and discussed. Nor is it realistic today to demand that such debate should be hobbled by the constraints of conventional good manners – still less of deference. The law of fair comment must allow for healthy scepticism."

Sometimes, it is difficult to separate fact from comment in an article. The context and not merely the words must always be considered. There is no hard and fast rule. The test will be that of the ordinary reader. Will the ordinary reader, on digesting the article, say, "Well, that's how she feels about the matter" or "So that is the fact of the matter"? It is important to know the difference. An assertion of fact must be justified or proved to be true. That is a far more difficult exercise than establishing that a defamatory comment was an expression of opinion that a fair-minded person could honestly infer from the facts on which it is based. Phillips J in *Spiller v. Joseph*[10] described this defence as one of the most difficult areas of defamation law.

FAIRNESS

"Fair" is probably a misnomer in the defence of fair comment. Fairness here does not mean evenly balanced. Journalists and columnists have no duty to play Miss Mary Sunshine. The law does not insist they be pleasant, inoffensive or balanced in their views. As stated by Lord Nicholls in *Tse Wai Chun Paul v. Albert Cheng*,[11] a writer is entitled to dip his pen in gall for the purposes of legitimate criticism.[12] But the court also frowns on sensationalist name-calling. In *Douglas v. Jamaica Observer and Another*,[13] the newspaper was examining the poor state of the fire services and interviewed one fire officer who laid the blame at the feet of the chief technical officer and called him a "quashie", a derogatory term meaning a fool. The judge considered the use of the term may have been unprofessional and in poor taste but not enough to deprive the commentator and the newspaper of the defence of fair comment.

So you can call someone an overbearing buffoon or you can demand that a particular official resign. *Newsday* columnist Donna Yawching once described the head of the Trinidad and Tobago teachers' union as a "self-important blow-hard".[14] American comedian John Oliver in 2015 bought airtime in Trinidad and Tobago to poke fun at former FIFA vice president Jack Warner. "Right now, Jack, everybody hates you," Oliver said. "I mean, literally everybody. I think it's something to do with you seeming like an absolutely terrible human being." Rudeness is no offence in law.

The *Daily Chronicle* in 1940s British Guiana published a review of a piano recital under the headline "London Pianist Disappoints Canje Audience".[15] The writer remarked that it did not take a musical genius to detect the mistakes the pianist made, and members of the audience sulked and expressed disgust.

Verity CJ ruled in favour of the newspaper and said: "I am yet to learn . . . that a newspaper report is actionable because it does not preserve due balance in its terms or that a person who sets out to criticise . . . the public act of another is to be liable in damages if he does not at the same time catalogue the other's virtues or good deeds."

For the comment to be fair in law, the court must hold it to be an opinion that someone could honestly hold. It is not necessary for the court to find that the comment is one that could be reasonably held by a right-thinking person or that the journalist himself honestly held the belief. The court will consider whether an honest man, however prejudiced he might be or however exaggerated or obstinate his views, could have written the criticism in question.[16]

Where the comment is made maliciously, the defendant will be unable to rely on the defence. Malicious motive is notoriously difficult to establish, however, and the burden of proving that allegation will lie with the claimant. Malice would arise where the writer knew the allegations were incorrect but persisted in publishing.

PUBLIC INTEREST

The defendant must establish that the comment concerned a matter of public interest. A comment will be so defined if it concerns a subject that affects people at large, so that they may be legitimately interested in, or concerned at what is going on or what may happen to them or to others. So, it will include criticism of the conduct of public officials, local and national government and public and private companies insofar as it affects people and the administration of justice. The affairs of churches, hospitals, universities, schools, prisons and anything that invites comment or public attention is grist for the mill. Anyone who places himself or herself in the public arena – sports stars, beauty queens, newspaper editors, judges, novelists, artists, performers – are subject to scrutiny and robust criticism. People who hold no public office and have done nothing to place themselves in the public eye are off-limits.

In Canada, the *Victoria Times* was ordered to pay the minister of human resources for British Columbia CA$3,500 for libelling him in a cartoon, in which he was depicted gleefully pulling the wings off flies. The minister contended that the cartoon made him out to be sadistic and cruel but the Court of Appeal reversed the decision, ruling that the minister had made several provocative statements (including that aboriginal youth should return to their reserves), which led to a public response, and the cartoon was defensible as fair comment.[17]

However, journalists do not have any licence to attack public figures, whether or not they are politicians. In *Craig v. Miller*,[18] a speaker at a public meeting, during electioneering in Barbados, made devastating attacks on a government minister. The chief justice stated:

> It is said that the plaintiff who was a public figure and that men and women in public life must expect criticism which in their case is apt to have less impact than criticism of others. It is also said that the statements were uttered at a political meting which was part of the political campaign and held three months before the general election. In such circumstances there is a charged atmosphere and things are said which would not be said in normal times.
>
> These are imputations of criminal activity, and I know of no law which places public figures in a worse situation that other members of the public for protecting their reputations against charges of serious breaches of the criminal law, nor do I know of any provision which abrogates the rule of law during the conduct of political campaigns.

There is no wholesale public interest defence as in the United States, where journalists escape liability for libel on a matter of public interest, even if the report turns out to be untrue, as long as the journalists acted without malice. The movie *Absence of Malice*, starring Paul Newman as a crime suspect, and Sally Field as the overzealous reporter, illustrates the double-edged nature of that defence. (See chapter 6, "*Reynolds* Defence".)

Malice

In everyday use, malice means ill will or spite. But malice, in libel law, generally refers to dishonest reporting or writing. It means the writer reported material known to be false or opinions not genuinely held. The writer and the subject of the criticism may have a history of antagonism, but that does not defeat a fair comment defence, as long as the publication is an honest opinion. In *Tse Wai Chun Paul v. Albert Cheng*, Lord Nicholls in the Court of Final Appeal in Hong Kong, 2001, said the defence is not defeated by the fact that the writer is actuated by spite, animosity, intent to injure, intent to arouse controversy – even if that is the dominant or only motive.

UNINTENTIONAL DEFAMATION

The law makes some allowance for defendants who make seemingly innocent statements but accidentally defame someone. For example, a journalist may write an accurate report about a person being convicted for a criminal offence, only to be sued by someone who has the same name and who has never even had a traffic ticket. The ridiculous case of *Hulton v. Jones*[19] illustrates the point. The defendants published a fictional story about a Peckham church warden named Artemus Jones who was at a fair with a woman who was not his wife "and so she must be the other". A real person who had the misfortune of being christened Artemus Jones, who was a barrister-at-law, sued for libel, and his action succeeded.

The law provides an escape for newspapers caught in such a trap. The defendant can plead that the libel was inserted in the paper without malice and without gross negligence and that before the commencement of the action or at the earliest opportunity afterwards, the newspaper inserted a full apology for the libel.[20]

Absolute Privilege

Statements made on certain occasions are privileged, which is to say, defamatory statements arising from them cannot be made the subject of a successful libel action. Privilege is either absolute or qualified.[21] The common law has provided such protection at least since the nineteenth century. Statutory provisions reflect and supplant the common law. However, because the common law provisions have not been abolished, they still exist and may be relied upon.

Absolute privilege is justified on the ground that without it, people with a public duty to speak out might be threatened with vexatious actions for slander and libel. Thus politicians can call anyone a liar, a thief or worse in Parliament or at the proceedings of select committees and not be sued for defamation.[22] Parliamentary privilege also extends to Hansard, the official printed record of debates. Similarly, judges, lawyers and witnesses may not be held accountable for any statement uttered in court or before a commission of enquiry. The ombudsman's reports are absolutely privileged.

For example, in the parliamentary debate on the police reform bills, in Trinidad and Tobago, then Prime Minister Patrick Manning told off the former education minister in these terms, "I would like to tell the member for Siparia . . . at least, the country now has a minister of education who goes to work every day, who is sober when she goes to work, who does not drink on the job and who could account for all the furniture that she uses, she could account for all." The member for Siparia was outraged but could take no legal action against either the prime minister or the news media. But she did respond robustly in the news media.[23]

Hardly a better illustration of the defence of absolute privilege and the rudiments of libel can be found than in Frederick Forsyth's short story "Privilege". A newspaper suggests that Chadwick, a businessman, is involved in fraud. The poor fellow gets no redress from the newspaper editor and he cannot afford a long, costly libel action. So, he goes to the home of the reporter and punches him in the nose, knowing he would be charged with assault. On the day of the trial, he gives a stirring plea in mitigation, and, in the process, describes the reporter in scurrilous terms. At the end of the case, the discredited reporter angrily confronts the businessman:

> "You bastard," said the journalist. "You can't bloody get away with what you said in there."
>
> "I can actually," said Chadwick. "Speaking from the dock, yes, I can. It's called absolute privilege."

News organizations, however, do not enjoy absolute privilege. Instead, they can claim qualified privilege based on the accuracy and fairness of the reports.

QUALIFIED PRIVILEGE (COURT PROCEEDINGS)

When giving evidence in courts, witnesses make all manner of allegations against other people. Some of these remarks are extremely damaging. Police officers are accused of faking confessions and beating up prisoners;

politicians are accused of corruption, and men and women from all walks of life are called murderers, robbers, rapists. No action may be taken against a journalist reporting such testimony, as long as the publication gives a fair and accurate report. Some statutes, such as Trinidad and Tobago's, protect only newspapers and also require the report be published contemporaneously.[24] Broadcast media would rely on the common law protection, and only malice would defeat it.

The rationale for such privilege is that justice must not be dispensed in secret and the public must be allowed to follow proceedings, even though the unfolding evidence may be embarrassing or painful for some individuals.

In *Kimber v. Press Association*[25] Lord Esher MR stated:

> The rule of law is that, where there are judicial proceedings before a properly consti-
> tuted judicial tribunal exercising its jurisdiction in open court, then the publication
> without malice of a fair and accurate report of what takes place before that tribunal
> is privileged. Under certain circumstances that publication may be very hard upon
> that person to whom it is made to apply, but public policy requires that some hard-
> ship should be suffered by individuals rather than that judicial proceedings should
> be held in secret. The common law, on the ground of public policy, recognises
> that there may be greater danger to the public in allowing judicial proceedings to
> be held in secret than in suffering persons for a time to rest under an unfounded
> charge or suggestion.

Comments of bystanders and outbursts from the public gallery (which would amount to contempt of court) should not be included in court reports. Care must be taken when writing "colour stories" that one does not defeat the protection of privilege. So to write, "When the accused was giving evidence, members of the public gallery 'steupsed' loudly and one woman grumbled that she didn't believe a word he was saying" would bring down fire and brim-stone upon the reporter's head. Even a seemingly innocent comment, such as "The witness seemed nervous before answering", could get you into trouble, because it implies a reluctance on the part of the witness to tell the truth.

Be especially careful when including background material. In 1998, four police officers sued the Trinidad *Express* over a court report in which the final paragraph was background material, not an account of what took place in court during a coroner's inquest into the death of three men. The plaintiffs were all members of the Anti-Kidnapping Squad and were involved in a gun battle in which the three occupants of a red Nissan Sunny all died. The reporter wrote: "Police reported that the men opened fire on them, but some members of the public claimed the men were executed by the police."

The trial judge Jamadar J found the words were not capable of the meaning propounded by the policemen and dismissed the claim. In 2004, the Court of Appeal upheld the decision, finding that the report was not defamatory of the plaintiffs, but Hamel-Smith J, in delivering the judgment of the appellate court, offered these words of caution:[26]

> Where an article in a newspaper, or a report on radio or television, purports to be a report of judicial proceedings, then great care should be taken if the author wishes to introduce other material into the article, whether that material be described as background, narrative or otherwise. If that is done, then great care must be taken to make it plain and obvious that this is what is being done, since a failure to do so may lead to difference of interpretation which does not redound to the benefit of the author or publisher.

Hamel-Smith J also rejected the *Express* newspaper's defence of absolute privilege and qualified privilege because the report was not accurate of the proceedings and the reporter made no attempt to confirm the events from a reliable source.

Only proceedings in public will attract privilege. Proceedings held in camera and in chambers will not be so protected. Reporters should also be aware of restrictions regarding matters involving youth offenders, sexual offences, divorce proceedings, preliminary inquiries. (See chapter 7, "Court Reporting".)

AFFIDAVITS AND PLEADINGS

Documents, such as an affidavit or pleadings in a civil matter, are not privileged until they are used in court. In the English case of *Stern v. Piper*,[27] a newspaper published in its financial pages a report culled from an affirmation prepared in connection with a pending High Court debt matter. In the ensuing libel action, the judge held that it is no defence to a libel action to say one was merely repeating what one had been told, and, further, the protection of qualified privilege did not extend to court documents that had not been brought into the public arena and allegations that had not been tested in a "forensic joust in open court".[28]

In one Trinidadian case, a newspaper reported that a woman had sued a nursing home and doctor for negligence after undergoing a hysterectomy.[29]

The report relied on the filed statement of claim, which alleged that the plaintiff was subjected to treatment that was "inexpert, unskilful and unprofessional". The judge held that the defendants could not rely on qualified privilege or justification.

The problem for the newspaper is that it referred not only to the writ but also to allegations made in the statement of claim filed in the action. Mendonca J stated: "Privilege, however, protects only reports of proceedings taking place in open court." With respect to the defence of justification or truth, the judge added that "it would be totally unsatisfactory if a publication of a defamatory statement said to be made by someone or appearing in a document on an occasion which is not privileged can be justified simply by pleading and proving that the statements were in fact made by someone or that they in fact appear in the document".

However, in Bermuda, where statute requires the keeping of a register of court documents, and the register was open to public inspection, a newspaper was in the clear when it published documents that had not been ventilated in court.

In *White and Royal Gazette Ltd v. Hall,*[30] a newspaper requested and obtained, from the court registry, certified copies of transcripts of two tapes containing recorded conversations between prison inmates. The transcripts contained material defamatory of an attorney who was also a member of Parliament. In February 1993, the newspaper published the transcript of the first tape. The attorney initiated a legal action in which he claimed damages and an interim injunction preventing further publication of the transcripts. The newspaper argued that the transcripts were covered by qualified privilege. The injunction was granted. The newspaper appealed on the grounds that the trial judge incorrectly interpreted and applied the law of qualified privilege.

The Court of Appeal held that qualified privilege attached to the publication of a true copy of any extract from a register that, by statute, is required to be kept and may be inspected by the public. The transcripts constituted records of the Supreme Court within the meaning of the Supreme Court (Records) Act 1955 and the term *records* was defined in that act to include a "register" maintained by the court.

Publication of accurate extracts was therefore held subject to qualified privilege. Although the tapes and transcripts were never admitted in evidence, they were deposited with the registrar in connection with the exercise of the criminal jurisdiction of the Supreme Court. The injunction restraining further publication was therefore set aside. In reaching its decision, the court accepted that the effect of the 1955 act was to extend the range of documents to which the principles of qualified privilege apply. If this was not intended, then it was for the legislature, not the courts, to address that issue.

The court in that case cited the earlier Supreme Court decision in *Hector v. Royal Gazette Ltd*,[31] in which a letter containing material defamatory of a magistrate was included in the record of an appeal, although it need not have been. The Supreme Court held that the letter fell within the wide ambit of the Supreme Court (Records) Act 1955 and was therefore part of the record. Therefore, publication of the letter was privileged and the application for an injunction to restrain the newspaper from publishing the allegations was refused.

FAIR AND ACCURATE

The privilege is not lost if the inaccuracy is trifling, although it may get some lawyers and politicians hot under the collar. In one court matter, a man accused of murder denied the charge and was later acquitted. A newspaper report in which the denial was omitted was held not to be fair and accurate.[32]

The courts do not judge a news report with the same standard of accuracy as a law report of a trained lawyer. It is to be regarded from the standpoint of someone giving the public a fair account of what happened in the court. You can report the decision or judgment of the court without including the evidence. The report does not have to be verbatim; a summarized account is sufficient, as long as the report does not convey an impression that is substantially different from the impression that would have been gained if one were present in court.

When court reporters commit more than trifling errors, attorneys may visit the judge in chambers and point out the inaccuracy. The judge will usually give leave to the attorney to raise it in open court and the judge may also weigh in. Usually, it ends there, but it can get worse.

In England, Winchester Crown Court's Judge Griffiths launched a libel claim against a south coast news agency that released a distorted report of his handling of a sex assault trial. He also targeted national papers that carried and sometimes elaborated the agency's report. In the case reported, Griffiths ordered a sex offender to pay £500 to his victim and £950 costs. His comments to the defendant were widely reported throughout the national and local media and led to calls from a women's pressure group that he immediately resign. The agency report included the headline-grabbing passage: "A sex attacker was told by a judge today he would not be in the dock if he had sent his victim a bunch of flowers."

However, the report omitted to say that the assault victim had made it clear to the judge that she would probably have forgiven her attacker if he had apologized, that she had resumed an earlier sexual relationship with the man, had sought to have her complaint withdrawn and had emphasized she did not want the man jailed.

The reports of the judge's handling of the case, in the words of the statement read at the High Court before Mr Justice French, gave an "entirely false characterisation of Judge Griffiths as a judge who was wholly unfit to sit on the bench". So, although the report was accurate and contemporaneous, it fell short of being fair.

One common complaint is that reporters highlight one dramatic aspect of the case but do not stick around long enough to see the witness retract his statement in cross-examination. Another issue is that the opening day of the trial may be reported, when the allegations are spread out in all their malignancy, but if there is an acquittal, the news organization may fail to report that or may not give the acquittal the prominence accorded to the prosecutor's opening address. The principle is that a journalist is "entitled to report on the proceedings or that part of it which he selects in a manner which fairly and faithfully gives an impression of the events reported and will convey to the reader what he himself would have appreciated had he been present during proceedings".[33]

In 1993 the *Sunday Sport* in the United Kingdom paid substantial out-of-court damages to a police officer found not guilty of indecent assault. The paper had reported the opening statement by the prosecution and the main evidence of the alleged victim but did not include her cross-examination by the defence that began the same day. During the cross-examination, the alleged victim was discredited, and she made a number of admissions that weakened the evidence she had given earlier and that the paper had reported. The *Sunday Sport* then briefly reported the policeman's acquittal. The paper should also have reported the admissions that effectively neutralized much of the adverse publicity the policeman had endured.

CONTEMPORANEOUS

There is no precise time frame in which a report must be published, because there is no legal definition of *contemporaneously*. *Gatley on Libel and Slander*[34] defines contemporaneously "as nearly at the same time as the proceedings as is reasonably possible, having regard to the opportunities for preparation of the report and time of going to press or of making the broadcast". The time frame in which a report is published will depend on the schedules of the publication or news organization. In the Trinidad and Tobago case of *Gabriel v. Manmohan, Grant and the Trinidad Express Newspapers*,[35] contemporaneity was satisfied when an article was published seven days after the newspaper obtained the Industrial Court judgment. Some statutes, as in Antigua and the Cayman Islands, do not include contemporaneity as a condition for the defence of qualified privilege to apply to reports of legal proceedings.

Even where the report is not published contemporaneously, the defence of qualified privilege may still be invoked. The journalist can rely on the common law provision, a safety net for reports that fall outside the statutory protection because they were not published as soon as practicable after the event, as long as the report is not actuated by malice.

So if a court matter involving Mr X is ignored for a year and then unleashed when he is contesting a seat in the general election, dredging up desultory remarks by witnesses who testified, the court may infer malice – especially if the reporter and Mr X had an earlier falling out.

QUALIFIED PRIVILEGE (PARLIAMENT)

Everything said in the House of Representatives and the Senate is protected by absolute privilege, sometimes known as parliamentary privilege. This is an ancient common law protection that has existed since the nineteenth century, as established in the case of *Wason v. Walter*,[36] in which the *Times* had published a House of Lords debate. During the debate, a Law Lord was accused of having lied to Parliament. The newspaper successfully defended the libel action.

If journalists write or broadcast what is said in Parliament, they have qualified privilege. No action for libel can be sustained as long as the report is fair and accurate, and written without malice. Sketches and commentaries, which can be humorous or cryptic and focus on particular contributions or aspects of the debates, are also protected, as long as they give a fair and honest reflection of the events as they impressed the journalist. It would not be fair to omit the rebuttal to an allegation.[37] Journalists should be careful not to adopt the allegations as their own and not commingle extraneous material with material for which privilege is claimed.[38]

Example: A member of Parliament calls the prime minister a liar during a debate in the House of Representatives. After the close of proceedings, outside the Parliament chamber, the member of Parliament repeats the allegation and adds further details. The allegation uttered during the debate attracts absolute privilege and a journalist would be free to report it, accurately and fairly. If the journalist goes further and includes defamatory material offered by the politician afterwards, say, in a follow-up newspaper interview, the publication would not attract privilege. The journalist may, however, be able to plead the Reynolds defence or reportage principle. (See chapter 6.)[39]

FAIR AND ACCURATE

During parliamentary debates, accusations can fly back and forth, often erupting in much uproar. To ensure a report is fair and accurate, journalists must take great care to report the replies to defamatory accusations. Remember that where a remark is withdrawn, it may not be reported. Failure to include a denial would probably mean that the report will lose the protection of qualified privilege and a libel action could follow. Barbados specifically included this condition in its Defamation Act 1977.[40] Section 11(2) provides that in an action for defamation in respect of a report, the defence of qualified privilege shall not apply if it is proved that "(a) the defendant has been requested by the plaintiff to publish at the defendant's expense and in such manner as is adequate or reasonable in the circumstances a reasonable letter or statement by way of explanation or contradiction; and (b) has refused or neglected to do so or has done so in a manner not adequate or not reasonable in the circumstances".

LIVE BROADCASTS

Are live broadcasts protected by absolute or qualified privilege?

Not all countries that permit televised proceedings have modern legislation that refers to such technological advancements. But, in effect, any live broadcast of Parliament attracts qualified privilege and probably absolute privilege because it is the same thing as proceedings themselves, which are open to the public.

In contrast to older statutes, the Barbados Defamation Act 1977 makes it clear that live broadcasts or transmissions of the words spoken by any member of either house shall be protected by absolute privilege; where the transmissions are not live, they shall be protected by qualified privilege.[41]

The law accepts the practicalities of production schedules. A political programme or article published or broadcast once a week, reviewing what happened days earlier, would still qualify as a contemporaneous report. However, if material is saved to be used specifically much later, say during an election campaign to create fireworks, the news organization would have lost its protection of qualified privilege.

QUALIFIED PRIVILEGE (OTHER OCCASIONS)

The common law provides protection for fair and accurate reports of a range of public occasions and so do our statutes. The protection extends to fair and accurate reports of:

- any lawful public meeting for the furtherance of discussion of a matter of public interest;
- any meeting of a council, board or local authority, unless the public is excluded;
- any meeting of any committee appointed by any of these above-mentioned bodies;
- notices published at the request of any government office or department for the information of the public;
- extracts of any register or document required by law to be open to public inspection; and
- any government or court-appointed public inquiry.

The protection afforded by such provisions will be lost if it is proved that an aggrieved person asked the newspaper to publish a reasonable letter or statement by way of contradiction or explanation of such report or other publication and the paper has refused or neglected to do so.

Is a media conference a public meeting that attracts qualified privilege? The Barbados Defamation Act expressly protects fair and accurate reports of any press conferences "convened to inform the press or other media of a matter of public concern".[42] Similarly, Jamaica protects fair and accurate reports of proceedings at a "press conference anywhere in the world for the discussion of a matter of public interest".[43]

This is in accordance with the common law position. The issue arose in Northern Ireland, after paratrooper Lee Clegg was convicted of murdering a teenage joyrider and spent two and a half years in prison before being cleared.

In January 1995, the *Times* reported on a press conference organized by a group campaigning for Clegg's release. The newspaper's front-page article included comments in a press handout from the group that criticized the law firm's handling of the soldier's defence.

McCartan Turkington Breen sued for libel and was awarded £145,000 after the courts ruled the press conference was not a "public meeting" and the journalist did not have "qualified privilege", which protects the press. The House of Lords unanimously disagreed, finding that a press conference was a public meeting, with the reporters acting as the eyes and ears of the public.[44] They could not therefore be sued for providing a fair and accurate account of the meeting. Lord Bingham remarked: "The proper functioning of a modern participatory democracy requires that the media be free, active, professional and inquiring."

Also attracting qualified privilege are notices issued by government departments and offices that do not include material leaked from such sources, nor unauthorized comments made by junior officials. To be protected, the material must be issued or approved by someone in authority. Bear in mind, though, that the privilege will not extend to meetings of councils, boards or local authority where neither the public nor any newspaper reporter is admitted.

The Barbados statute[45] also specifies that qualified privilege will cover fair and accurate reports of the findings or decisions of any association for the promotion of any game, sport or pastime; of any association for the promotion of interest in any religion, art, science or learning; any association for the promotion of interest in any trade, business, industry or profession; any report or document circulated to shareholders or stockholders with the authority of the board of a corporation that is not a private company;[46] and publication in a scientific or technical journal of an article of a scientific or technical nature.

Extracts from public registers include registers of bills of sales, list of bankrupts, companies registers and registers of court documents. If the newspaper publishes the list but it turns out that the list contains errors, the newspaper is immune as long as it published without malice. This common law protection has existed as far back as the nineteenth century as illustrated by *Searles v. Scarlette*[47] where a hotel keeper contended he was portrayed incorrectly as insolvent when his name appeared in a trade protection journal that had published an extract from a register of county court judgments as a warning list of sorts to merchants. The publication may have been libellous but the journal enjoyed the protection of privilege.

QUALIFIED PRIVILEGE (RIGHT OF REPLY)

Victims of attacks deserve the right to reply and can make honest, if defamatory, replies to criticisms. A newspaper can carry the response of someone who has been attacked on a privileged occasion, as in Parliament, even if the response contains defamatory material. In the absence of malice, neither the newspaper nor the victim would be liable. In such a reply, the defendant is allowed some latitude in protecting himself. The defence only extends to such facts as are necessary "to repel the charges brought against him – not to bring fresh accusations against his adversary".[48]

Although the defender is entitled to some considerable latitude in the defence, unnecessary allegations or charges wholly irrelevant to the attack are not covered by the privilege.[49]

Lord Oakley put it this way:

> There is, it seems to me, an analogy between the criminal law of self defence and a man's right to defend himself against written or verbal attacks. In both cases he is entitled, if he can, to defend himself effectively, and he only loses the protection of the law if he goes beyond the defence and proceeds to offence. That is to say, the circumstances in which he defends himself, either by acts or by words, negative the malice which the law draws from violent acts or defamatory words. If you are attacked with a deadly weapon you can defend yourself with a deadly weapon or any other weapon which may protect your life. The law does not concern itself with niceties in such matters. If you are attacked by a prize fighter you are not bound to adhere to the Queensberry rules in your defence.[50]

The defence was successfully invoked by a member of Parliament in Trinidad and Tobago after a radio talk-show host maligned all members of Parliament of the United National Congress political party. George "Umbala" Joseph in December 2004 hosted a morning talk show, *The Today Show,* on radio I 95.5, which discussed current affairs and politics.[51] On one such instalment of the show, Joseph called all United National Congress members of Parliament "malicious", and on numerous prior occasions had made highly derogatory and insulting remarks about the United National Congress and its members, using such terms as "United Nasty Canesuckers" and "United Nasty Coolies".

United National Congress member of Parliament Harry Partap had had enough and sought to defend himself and his colleagues by sending a letter to the editor of the daily newspapers. The *Newsday* published Partap's response in which he called Joseph an "ungrateful Grenadian who sought refuge from poverty and degradation in his land coming here to pass judgement on the UNC", and contended that Joseph might have felt committed to defend the People's National Movement, which was then in government, because "he came here as part of Dr Eric Williams' vote bank in the 60's to keep the PNM in power".

Joseph then had the gall to claim that Partap's letter represented brutal lies and serious libel against him. The judge, however, found that the words complained of in Partap's letter were not defamatory and that Partap was entitled to enjoy the protection of qualified privilege to answer the attack. Further, he found that Partap's reply was "connected, relevant and reasonably germane to the subject matter of the occasion; he offered a rational two-fold interrelated explanation for the claimant's attack".

QUALIFIED PRIVILEGE (SOCIAL AND MORAL DUTY)

The law recognizes that there are occasions when people have a social or moral duty to speak up, even when they may not be able to prove the accuracy of their remarks. Communications between people who share a common interest in the subject matter of the communication will attract qualified privilege (for example, reference by an employer, a circular published to shareholders of a company, an inter-office memorandum). To be protected, the communication must be made to a person who has a duty to receive and act upon it, such as a police officer investigating a crime or a public health official.

But to what extent are journalists under a social and moral duty to communicate unproven allegations of wrongdoing to the world? What if they are warning the public that there might be contaminated milk or unsafe drugs on the shelves?

In 1999, a beacon appeared on the distant horizon with the landmark decision of the House of Lords in *Reynolds v. Times Newspapers Ltd.*[52] Journalists learned that they could defend themselves even when they get it wrong. The limits and strengths of this defence are discussed in the next chapter.

INNOCENT DISSEMINATION

"Why me?" the printers and distributors of defamatory material may cry because they did not write or create the material. There is protection for them, as well as newsvendors, booksellers and libraries, in both the common law and statute.

According to *Gatley on Libel and Slander:*[53] "The common law gives some degree of protection to the person who publishes but who is not the author, printer, or the 'first or main publisher of a work which contains a libel', but has only taken 'a subordinate part in disseminating it' e.g. by selling, distributing or handing to another a copy of the newspaper or book in which it appears."

Such a person will not be liable if he succeeds in showing that

- he did not know that the book or paper contained the libel complained of;
- he did not know that the book or paper was of a character likely to contain a libel; or
- such want of knowledge was not due to any negligence on his part.

Internet service providers are viewed on the same footing as distributors and not the first or main publishers of a work. Jamaica and Antigua have included the "innocent dissemination" defence in their reformed statutes that define "distributors" as booksellers, news agents, newsvendors, librarians, wholesalers, retailers, providers of postal services, broadcasters of live programmes on radio or television, providers of processing or copying services relating to any electronic medium on which defamatory matter is recorded, and operators of communication systems by means of which defamatory matter is transmitted.[54] Barbados refers to people not primarily responsible for publication including "such other person as satisfies the court that he is not the author of the publication and that his involvement in the publication extends only to conversion of material into a readable form, or the transmission or reproduction of that material".[55]

TRIVIALITY

Barbados provides a defence of triviality in Section 6 of the Defamation Act 1996, which states: "It is a defence in an action for defamation that the circumstances of the publication of the matter complained of were such that the person defamed was not likely to suffer harm to his reputation."

"Circumstances" include the readership of the publication but not the reputation of the claimant. In *Marshall v. The Nation Publishing Co. Ltd*,[56] the newspaper incorrectly inflated the criminal charges the claimant was facing, reporting that he was charged with a series of robberies and burglaries when in fact he was in court for criminal damage to a laptop. The defence of triviality did not succeed. The court held that the paper had a very wide readership around the globe, and so the claimant was likely to suffer harm to his reputation.

The common law position is different. Defamation is actionable without proof of actual harm to the reputation. Triviality is not a defence. In fact, Jamaica expressly rules it out by Section 19 (2) of the Defamation Act 2013.[57] In common law, where the court finds the degree of harm to be minimal, it will reflect that view in the amount of damages awarded. So the claimant will have his victory but it may be hollow.

CONSENT

People who willingly expose the skeletons in their closets cannot thereafter complain to the court. Consent to publication is a complete defence. The consent must relate to specific libellous statements, not merely to the grant of an interview in which the offending topic was not canvassed. Bear in mind, though, that when interviewees see their lives in print, they may then insist that they were misquoted or taken out of context. Keep scrupulous notes, tapes, email messages. As soon as you have returned from the interview, convert your scribblings into proper notes but please, keep the original jottings, even if it is on a napkin or back of a grocery bill. Record the time and place of interviews. Sometimes, in circumstances where the interviewee is expected to be prickly, journalists take along a colleague, not directly involved in the matter, so as a witness to what takes place.

APOLOGY

Liability for libel can be mitigated by a timely correction, a full apology and offer of amends. Antigua and Jamaica specifically provide for the court to make a "correction order" and dictate the content, time of publication of the correction and prominence to be given to it in the particular medium.[58] A correction or a declaration that the defendant is liable for defamation may satisfy the claimant and no damages will be sought or awarded, although the defendant may still have to pay costs.

The offer of apology should be made before commencement of the action or at the earliest opportunity afterwards. The apology is usually placed prominently in the newspaper, and it may be necessary to publish it more than once to appease the injured party. Similarly, broadcast stations would have to air the apology on or around the same time of day as the defamatory broadcast. The media house must plead the libel was inserted in the newspaper or broadcast

© Mike Baldwin / Cornered

"Something that says I'm sorry without admitting liability."

CartoonStock.com

without actual malice and without gross negligence. The media house will pay into court a sum of money by way of amends.

Sometimes, this is all it takes to placate a claimant and the lawyers. If, however, the injured party is still insistent on continuing with the suit, the defendant can usually expect the amount of damages to be lowered by virtue of having made a prompt apology.[59]

The court may also order an apology be tendered and published.[60] In *Geeta Ragoonath v. Ancil Roget*[61] in Trinidad and Tobago, the judge remarked that a simple "I'm sorry" might be more valuable to the claimant and would give a sense of relief and vindication. In that case, the claimant had been wrongly accused of writing to the head of the state to have the president of the Industrial Court removed because she was dissatisfied with the decision of the court. Kokaram J ordered that the defendant tender an unconditional apology to the claimant within twenty-eight days and if he did so, the exemplary damages of TT$60,000 would be reduced by 50 per cent.

LIMITATION

The action by the claimant must be brought within a particular period, which varies among jurisdictions, ranging from one year to six.[62]

CHAPTER 6

THE *REYNOLDS* DEFENCE

The press discharges vital functions as a bloodhound as well as a watchdog.

—Lord Nicholls of Birkenhead[1]

The right to get it wrong.

That is one way of summing up the *Reynolds* defence or "public interest" defence.

It essentially protects journalists who publish statements that they believe to be in the public interest, even though they may have got the story or parts of it wrong.

It is not a licence to publish untruths.

The Antigua Defamation Act 2015 now incorporates this common law principle, whereby it is a defence for a defendant in an action of defamation to "show that the statement complained of was or formed part of, a statement on a matter of public interest; and the defendant reasonably believed that publishing the statement complained of was in the public interest".[2]

The *Reynolds* defence arose out of an article in the British edition of the *Sunday Times* concerning the collapse of the coalition government in Eire in 1994. It accused Albert Reynolds, who only days before had resigned as Taoiseach (prime minister of the Republic of Ireland), of deliberately misleading the Dail (lower house of Parliament) and his coalition partners.

The House of Lords decided that, in certain circumstances, the media did have a duty to impart information to its readers and that the public at large had a legitimate interest in receiving certain information. The *Reynolds* judgment clarifies the application of the common law defence of qualified privilege.[3]

Lord Nicholls, delivering the leading judgment, said: "The court should be slow to conclude that a publication was not in the public interest and therefore the public had no right to know, especially when the information is in the field of political discussion."[4]

The House of Lords laid down the criteria (the list is not exhaustive) by which a judge presiding over a libel trial would decide whether the story was protected by common law privilege. So, if a newspaper prints an allegation against a person that is untrue and the newspaper is sued and pleads this type of qualified privilege as a defence, the court will take into account the following before granting or withholding the defence:

- The seriousness of the allegation. The more serious the charge, the more the public was misinformed and the individual harmed if the allegation was not true.
- The nature of the information and the extent to which the subject matter was a matter of public concern.
- The source of the information. Do informants have direct knowledge of the events? Or do they have their own axes to grind, or are they being paid for their stories?
- The steps taken to verify the information.
- The status of the information. The allegation might already have been the subject of an investigation that commanded respect.
- The urgency of the matter. News is often a perishable commodity.
- Whether comment was sought from the plaintiff. He might have information others did not possess or had not disclosed. An approach to the plaintiff would not always be necessary.
- Whether the article contained the gist of the plaintiff's side of the story.
- The tone of the article. A newspaper could raise queries or call for an investigation. It need not adopt allegations as statements of fact.
- The circumstances of the publication, including the timing.

In practical terms, this means that the newspaper can flag the public interest on a particular point, such as the investigation of crime, exposing corruption, public health issues, and the incompetence, hypocrisy or misdeeds of public officials. The journalist should adopt a neutral tone, rather than embracing the allegations as gospel. The newspaper can push for a response or fuller investigation from the relevant authorities.

Most importantly, the newspaper must be able to demonstrate that it made serious efforts to obtain a full response from the person being spotlighted, and that it had done its best to verify the information obtained. All supporting documents must be in the possession of the newspaper before publication.

Material based on rumour, suspicion and conjecture or from a single source who may have an axe to grind should be excluded.

The *Times* actually lost the libel action in *Reynolds*. Although the matter was undoubtedly of public concern in the United Kingdom, the paper made serious allegations without mentioning the public official's version. Shorn of his considered explanation, the allegations were not information that the public had a right to know, and thus the publication was not one that should, in the public interest, be protected by privilege in the absence of proof of malice.[5]

The *Reynolds* defence was clarified in *Jameel v. Wall Street Journal* (Europe),[6] where the House of Lords pointed out that the ten factors listed in *Reynolds* were not hurdles that journalists had to scale along an obstacle course, but rather each case ought to be assessed on its own facts. Judges had been applying he *Reynolds* principles in an overly restrictive manner.

Lord Hoffmann set them aright when he said that judges, with "leisure and hindsight", should not second-guess editorial decisions made in busy newsrooms. "That would make the publication of articles which are . . . in the public interest too risky and would discourage investigative reporting," he added.[7]

In *Jameel*, the *Wall Street Journal Europe* had stated that Mohammad Jameel's family and their businesses (Jameel's family owned Harwell Motors in Oxford) had been monitored by the Saudi government on request of the United States to ensure no money was siphoned off to support terrorists. The thrust was to inform the public that the Saudis were cooperating with the United States. It could not be proved true because it would have been impossible to prove covert surveillance material in open court.

The newspaper successfully relied on *Reynolds* with the House of Lords holding that the defence should not be withheld simply because the newspaper did not delay publication of its allegation to allow the subject of the article to comment. The paper had reported that the claimant "could not be reached for comment". The journalist had also adopted a neutral, investigative tone and sought to verify the information.

By contrast, the *Sun's* campaign against former Liverpool goalkeeper Bruce Grobbelaar is an example of how not to get on the right side of the qualified privilege defence.[8] The newspaper had secretly filmed Grobbelaar talking to Chris Vincent in a sting operation set up by the paper with his former business partner. The newspaper filmed him receiving an initial payment of £2,000, and Grobbelaar told Vincent on tape that he would throw the game between Southampton and his former club, Liverpool. The tape also showed Grobbelaar talking about throwing three other games. In 1994, two reporters approached Grobbelaar at Gatwick Airport and put to him a number of allegations. The following day the paper ran a series of articles charging the player with corruption. Grobbelaar and his alleged co-conspirators were charged by police, leading to two criminal trials in which they were acquitted.

The paper pleaded the defence of qualified privilege but the Court of Appeal, considering *Reynolds,* held that the paper had deprived itself of that defence by adopting the roles of police, prosecuting authority, judge and jury. The paper's actions focused not only on Grobbelaar but also were calculated to embarrass and hound his wife and children. However, it was an empty victory for Grobbelaar. In 2002, a jury had awarded him £85,000 in damages but the House of Lords reduced it to the derisory sum of one pound.[9] Their Lordships' distaste for the way the paper conducted its investigation was exceeded only by their scorn for Grobbelaar.

PUBLIC INTEREST

To qualify for the *Reynolds* defence, a defendant must show the publication of the statements was in the public interest. This is not accomplished by merely showing that the topic was in the public domain. One cannot put any old thing on the six o'clock news without bothering to verify accuracy and then shout, "Public interest!" As Lord Hobhouse in *Reynolds* explained: "There is no human right to disseminate information that is not true. No public interest is served by publishing or communicating misinformation.... There is no duty to publish what is not true: there is no interest in being misinformed."[10]

In *Loutchansky v. Times Newspapers Ltd,*[11] it was held that to talk of a public right to know, without more, was facile and misleading. This was applied in *Abraham Mansoor and Others v. Grenville Radio and Others,*[12] where a caller to an Antiguan radio show made defamatory remarks about the claimants who were businessmen. The defendants, claiming qualified privilege, stated that the public was legitimately interested in the grant of duty-free concessions at a time when the government's policy was to curtail such concessions. Blenman J stated that the public had no right to know untrue defamatory matter about which the broadcaster made no sufficient inquiry before deciding to publish it. The defendants were obliged to adhere to the standards of responsible journalism.

In *Flood v. Times Newspaper*,[13] Lord Brown said:[14]

> In deciding whether *Reynolds* privilege attaches . . . the judge, on true analysis, is deciding but a single question: could whoever published the defamation, given whatever they knew (and did not know) and whatever they had done (and had not done) to guard so far as possible against the publication of untrue defamatory material, properly have considered the publication in question to be in the public interest? In deciding this single question, of course, a host of different considerations are in play.

You could almost hear the clash of the cymbals when the Privy Council reiterated this fundamental factor in the Dominican case of *Pinard-Byrne v. Linton*.[15] The defendant Lennox Linton was a journalist who commented on a controversial development project in Dominica, which involved the granting of economic citizenship to investors. He made defamatory remarks on a radio call-in programme and also published on a website. The claimant was a chartered accountant Kieron Pinard-Byrne who was appointed "owners' representative" for the Layou River Project and also liquidator of a hotel whose operating assets were sold to an investor in a luxury hotel project.

As a result of contract problems, construction fraud and natural disaster, the Layou River Project was never completed and the shareholders in a luxury hotel development project lost the funds they had invested.

The defendant made remarks to the effect that Pinard-Byrne, mockingly described as "this paragon of Irish virtue", knew of the "squandermania" and deception and had benefited personally from the siphoning of funds and corruption.

The Privy Council said the Court of Appeal had got it wrong, by focusing on the underlying circumstances pertaining to the controversy over the economic citizenship programme and the Layou River Project, and it was not sufficient to say that the project was a matter of public interest or public importance. Before making allegations that the claimant was guilty of wrongdoing, the journalist had a duty to carry out a reasonable investigation to ascertain whether the allegations were true: "The problem is that LL did not carry out an investigation to that end. The Board[16] accepts that, as the Court of Appeal concludes, he made some investigations into the Project. There is however no evidence that he investigated whether KPB was guilty of the kind of wrongdoing alleged in the words complained of."

Cottle J, the trial judge, was therefore entitled to decide as he did, that the defendant could not avail himself of the "public interest *Reynolds* defence"

because he did not provide a shred of evidence to support his allegations of wrongdoing; the defendant himself had no expertise in accounting or any of the aspects of the matter, and called no witnesses relevant to the issues; the claimant was not asked to respond to specific allegations before the defamatory remarks were published; and the defendant's demeanour in the witness box was "more consistent with personal animosity towards the claimant rather than an unbiased search for the truth. The overall tone of the offending publications also reeked of rancour rather than even-handed reporting".

RESPONSIBLE JOURNALISM

Each case is to be assessed on its own circumstances. And as underscored in *Jameel*, the guidelines in *Reynolds* are examples of factors that would signal the defendant exercised due care and skill, notwithstanding some inaccuracies. Such factors as failing to verify accuracy; relying on hearsay sources or those with axes to grind; failing to contact claimants for their side of the story;

and adopting a sensational tone will be inconsistent with the standards of responsible journalism.

Quite often, a simple rewording of a few sentences can keep a publication within the bounds of responsible journalism. West Indies cricketer Augustine Logie successfully claimed damages for defamation against the National Broadcasting Network in Trinidad and Tobago, which demonstrated "carelessness at its highest" in a television broadcast on the publication by the Indian government on match fixing in cricket.[17]

The Indian government report had stated that Logie had refused to have anything to do with Mukesh Gupta, a bookmaker and punter who had carried on a business in India, and Logie had never even spoken to him.

Instead of stating just that in plain language, the sports announcer reported that Logie had to "clear the air"; was "forced to defend his name"; and "had his name linked to match-fixing now that the Indian Government has published its report". Through careless and sensational wording, the radio station failed the test of responsible journalism.

In *Bonnick v. The Gleaner Co. and Ken Allen*,[18] the Privy Council gave guidance on what is meant by responsible journalism:

> Responsible journalism is the point at which fair balance is held between freedom of expression on matters of public concern and the reputations of individuals. Maintenance of this standard is in the public interest and in the interests of those whose reputations are involved. It can be regarded as the price journalists pay in return for the privilege. If they are to have the benefit of the privilege, journalists must exercise due professional skill and care.

In the epic battle between the *Times* newspaper and Grigori Loutchansky,[19] the Court of Appeal grappled with the issue of just where to set the bar called "responsible journalism". It could not be too high or too low, and judges must be careful not to apply too stringent a test.

The *Times* portrayed the claimant as a Russian mafia boss involved in money laundering and smuggling nuclear weapons. The newspaper did not seek to prove the allegations were true but pleaded qualified privilege. The newspaper contended that the subject matter of the articles in question was of the greatest general interest and importance to the public at large and to the readers of the *Times* in particular, that is to say the corruption and criminalization of Russian society since the breakup of the USSR, the involvement of Russian organized criminal groups in money laundering through western banks, the smuggling of nuclear weapons and the activities of such groups, including the acquisition of businesses in the West and in the United Kingdom in particular.

The *Times* investigation was extensive, and its journalists relied on various information, which they contended they were entitled to treat as reliable, responsible and authoritative. That comprised media reports of the involvement of the Bank of New York in laundering the proceeds of criminal activity in Russia; media reports of suspicions about and investigations into serious crimes allegedly committed by Loutchansky, which have resulted in his exclusion from various jurisdictions including the United Kingdom; a statement by the then director of the CIA about the respondent's company, Nordex, being associated with Russian criminal activity; the respondent's conviction by a Latvian court in 1983 of offences of dishonesty; and various reports by intelligence services.

In addition, the *Times* relied on information provided to Mr Lister, the author of both articles, by three unidentified sources and a fourth source (eventually named as Jeffrey Robinson, author of a book about organized crime) who asserted among other things that Loutchansky either had been or was being investigated by various law enforcement agencies in connection with money-laundering offences.

The *Times* failed because the documents it relied on were obtained after publication of the articles. Judges have to assess whether the paper behaved responsibly at the time of publication and so can only look at what the journalists knew then – not what they uncovered later. (Leave to appeal to the House of Lords on this point was refused in May 2004.)

The Court of Appeal summarized the correct approach to be adopted. In determining whether the standard of responsible journalism had been satisfied, the following considerations are likely to feature prominently in the court's thinking:[20]

First, a holding that a publication was privileged would, to all intents and purposes, provide the publishers with a complete defence since, in such a case, a finding of privilege would effectively pre-empt a finding of malice. Secondly, setting the standard of journalistic responsibility too low would inevitably encourage too great a readiness to publish defamatory matter. Journalists should be rigorous, not lax, in their approach. It was in the interest of the public, as well as the defamed individual, that, wherever possible, truths and not untruths should be told. That was also in the interests of the media. Once untruths could be published with impunity, the public would cease to believe any communication, true or false. Thirdly, however, setting the standard too high would be no less damaging to society because it would deter newspapers from discharging their proper function of keeping the public informed. When determining whether any given article should attract qualified privilege, the court had to bear in mind the likely impact of its ruling not only upon the case in hand but also upon the media's practices generally. Qualified privilege ordinarily fell to be judged as a preliminary issue before the truth or falsity of the communication was established. Accordingly, the question to be posed was not whether it was in the public interest to publish an untruth, but whether it was in the public interest to publish the article, true or false. Even when the untruth of the article was established, or where it was not formally disputed, it was important to remember that the defence of qualified privilege tolerated factual inaccuracy for two purposes, namely in order not to deter either the publication sued upon (which might have been true) or future publications of truthful information. In the instant case, the judge had applied too stringent a test. Its application merely as a "cross-check" would be unexceptionable in a case where the test had been satisfied: the publisher's claim to privilege would be indisputable if a failure to publish would have laid him open to legitimate criticism. The converse, however, was not true. Not all journalists could or should be expected to reach an identical view in every case. Responsible journalism would in certain circumstances permit equally of publication or of non-publication.

VERIFYING ACCURACY

To what extent must journalists go to verify accuracy of reports?

Telephoning someone minutes before publication deadline and then reporting the subject was "unavailable for comment" will not be a proper attempt at verification.

Neither would sticking a microphone in someone's face as they open the front door, when there has been no other attempt at contacting the interviewee.

When interviews are granted, journalists must put the most serious allegations to interviewees for their reaction or comment.

When reporting on police investigations, journalists may not be able to verify the truth of the complaints, but the status of the investigation and the allegations themselves may be the heart of the story. In such situations, when applying *Reynolds*, the journalist must tread carefully, taking a balanced approach, without asserting the truth of the allegations or assuming the guilt of the suspect.

Such was the scenario in *Flood*, in which the *Times* successfully relied on the *Reynolds* defence.

The claimant was a detective sergeant in the Metropolitan Police who was suspected of taking bribes from Russian exiles, selling to them highly confidential Home Office and police intelligence about attempts to extradite them to Russia to face criminal charges.

The journalists were concerned that the police might not be properly conducting an investigation into the detective sergeant. Their enquiries triggered an investigation and several weeks later, *The Times* published an article headed "Detective Accused of Taking Bribes from Russian Exile". The claimant sued for libel over both print and website publications. The investigation eventually concluded there was no evidence to sustain the allegations.

Although the article was damaging to the detective sergeant, it was balanced in tone; it did not assert the truth of the allegations; and it gave him the opportunity to respond. The decision to publish the details of the allegations and identify the policeman was justified, and the appeal judges stated that editorial judgment had to be respected. In that case, the allegations themselves and the status of the investigation were the whole story.

The Supreme Court reiterated, however, that the public interest defence does not mean journalists do not have to verify. Responsible journalists have to satisfy themselves that the allegation is true and their belief in the truth has to be the result of a reasonable investigation. Journalists are entitled to draw reasonable belief from information gleaned from reliable sources or such may be inferred from the fact of a police investigation. In *Flood*, there was strong circumstantial case against the detective sergeant.

Reynolds, therefore, holds journalists to a high standard. And although sensible journalists have always known they need to get all sides of a story and they must be suspicious of sources who have axes to grind, the process by which journalists put together a report has been placed under intense scrutiny.

Attorney-at-law Faarees Hosein, who represents a news media organization in Trinidad and Tobago, likens the *Reynolds* "responsible journalism" standard to doing maths. You may not always arrive at the correct answer but you get points for showing your working.[21]

REPORTAGE

This is a term used to describe the neutral reporting or republication of unproven allegations rather than the journalist adopting the allegations. Reportage may also be defined as a special and rare form of *Reynolds* privilege. *Reynolds* generally requires some attempt by journalists to verify the truth of allegations published. But this is not so for reportage, where only the fact that the allegations have been made needs to be verified. Failure to verify allegations in such situations would not be fatal to a defence.

Alarm bells are probably going off in your head right now. This seems to fly in the teeth of everything you have been reading so far. But there are rare situations where the ten *Reynolds* principles would be an uncomfortable fit, yet the court will uphold the public interest defence. The reportage doctrine has been successfully invoked in instances where there is an ongoing dispute and the fact of the allegations and counter-allegations are of legitimate public interest.

In *Al-Fagih v. HH Saudi Research Marketing (UK)*,[22] the English Court of Appeal upheld a plea of *Reynolds* qualified privilege on the basis of reportage. In that case, the defendants' newspaper published a series of articles in the context of an ongoing political dispute between two members of the Saudi Arabian community, Al-Fagih and Al-Mas'aari. One article, written by Al-Khamees, repeated defamatory allegations that were made by Al-Mas'aari against Al-Fagih – essentially, that Al-Fagih, the claimant, was a liar and "purveyor of malicious sexual gossip".

Even though the allegations were not from a reliable source and the journalist did not take steps to verify their accuracy, the majority of the Court of Appeal held that the publication was nevertheless protected by *Reynolds* qualified privilege. The publication did not adopt or endorse the allegations and, importantly, because the allegations were attributed to Al-Mas'aari and were made in the context of an ongoing political dispute, it did not matter that the defendants' newspaper did not delay publication to get a response from the claimant.

Importantly, Latham LJ said it is "the fact that the allegation of a particular nature has been made which is in this context important, and not necessarily its truth or falsity".

The Court of Appeal followed *Al-Fagih* in *Roberts v. Gable*.[23] In that case, an investigative journalist wrote an article published by *Searchlight* magazine concerning allegations made in an ongoing row between two factions of the British National Party. The claimants (brothers and active members of the British National Party) brought suit, stating that the article meant one brother had stolen money collected at a political rally and both had threatened to "kneecap" and torture their rivals.

The journalist and the magazine pleaded the doctrine of reportage, saying the public had a right to know what was going on within a political party that had regularly presented itself for consideration by the electorate.

The Court of Appeal agreed with the defendants, underscoring that the journalist was not adopting but reporting. The readers would be able to appreciate that allegations and counter-allegations were being exchanged, and many of them would be sceptical of both sides. Eady J stated: "the readers know who is making the accusations on either side. Readers of *Searchlight* are unlikely to accord much 'status' to allegations being made in such circumstances and may indeed be sceptical about both. A significant proportion is likely to say 'A plague on both your houses!'"

The Court of Appeal highlighted the following points:

1. Reporting both sides in a disinterested way is an important element of the reportage doctrine.
2. Journalists will not be deprived of the defence because they have a particular personal or political stance, though the defence will be scrutinized carefully in such instances.[24]
3. Failure to verify will not be fatal, where the fact of the allegation being made is what is important.
4. The source of the story is of less significance in a reportage case, because it is not the reliability of either side that matters so much as the nature of the quarrel.
5. Although there is no special category of *Reynolds* privilege attaching to political speech, it is nonetheless obvious that the political significance of a publication will often be an important factor in determining the merits of a privilege plea.[25]

In *Charman v. Orion Publishing Group*,[26] the claimant was a former member of the Metropolitan Police, and the defendants were the authors and publishers of a book called *Bent Coppers*, describing Scotland Yard's attempts, at times unsuccessful, to uncover police corruption. The offending passages suggested there were cogent grounds to suggest the informant had made corrupt payments to the claimant in exchange for his protection in relation to a large theft.

The defendants pleaded both reportage and *Reynolds* privilege as defences. The reportage defence failed because the author did not simply report published material in a neutral manner but mixed that material with other information that his own considerable research had revealed.

The Court of Appeal decided that the case was miles away from the confines of reportage properly understood. A defining characteristic of reportage was missing: the book was not written to report *the fact* that allegations of corruption were made against the claimant and *the fact* that he denied them and in turn accused the investigating officers of plotting against him. The author went further to write his own story – the inside story of corruption in the Metropolitan Police.

Ward LJ, helpfully, put it this way: "This was a piece of investigative journalism where McLagan was acting as the bloodhound sniffing out bits of the story from here and there, from published material and unpublished material, not as the watchdog barking to wake us up to the story already out there."[27]

However, the Court of Appeal held that the book was a work of "responsible journalism" and upheld the *Reynolds* defence, reiterating that a fair balance has to be struck between the freedom of expression and the reputations of individuals, bearing in mind that the court should suffer no greater limitation of press freedom than was necessary to hold that balance.[28]

The limits of the reportage category of *Reynolds* are still unclear but as *Gatley on Libel and Slander* advises, it certainly contemplates the situation where a journalist in an even-handed manner reports an accusation and counter-accusation in an ongoing dispute. However, it would be going too far to give a general automatic media privilege for repetition of accusations originated by others.[29]

Do note, however, that reportage does not require the publication be bland or dry. You can be hard-hitting and also show delight in reporting the matter. What it means is that you cannot treat matters that would call for investigation as proof of guilt.

CASE STUDIES

An examination of how the *Reynolds* defence was applied in the Jamaican case of *Bonnick* is necessary reading, though the result achieved produces some brow furrowing. Other cases from Jamaica and Trinidad and Tobago are also good studies in what to do and what to avoid.

Hugh Bonnick was the managing director of a government-owned company that was involved in a dispute with a Belgian milk exporter over certain payments. Bonnick was dismissed shortly before the company entered into a second contract with the exporter. Bonnick contended that the article imputed a connection between his dismissal and irregularities in the company.

The defendants did not plead justification but relied on qualified privilege as set out in *Reynolds*. The reporter had only an anonymous source who did not provide a factual basis for the allegations of irregularities, and she did not include Bonnick's versions of events regarding his dismissal in the article. But, overall, the article was even-handed, leaving readers to make up their own minds, and the defamatory imputation was not high up on the scale of gravity. Had the article expressly stated that Bonnick had been dismissed because of the irregularities, the defence of qualified privilege would have been unavailable.

The Privy Council described *Bonnick* as a case "near the borderline"[30] but on the balance, the defence of qualified privilege was available to the publisher because the subject matter was in the public interest and the newspaper had satisfied the standards of responsible journalism.

In *Seaga v. Harper*,[31] the board held that the defendant's publication of the words was not protected by qualified privilege because the defendant had failed to take sufficient care to check the reliability of the information he had disseminated.

Another Jamaican case, *Patterson v. Nationwide News Network*,[32] is a good example of two points: the danger of relying on a source who is repeating hearsay; and how inappropriate on-air jokes and comments by radio journalists and talk-show hosts can defeat the defence. In this case, the radio morning news alerted listeners to a "major incident" at the airport involving Cuban diplomats and senior politicians arriving on a private jet containing a diplomatic pouch with US$500,000. The news broadcast said that police and customs were investigating, and that former Prime Minister P.J. Patterson was on the flight. The broadcast added that things got heated among officials and the diplomats reboarded the flight with the pouch of cash.

The imputation was that the former prime minister had used his diplomatic passport to try to circumvent airport security and was associated with illicit cash.

The police investigated and discovered no such incident, neither major nor minor. The government issued a news release clearing the claimant of any wrongdoing. The claimant said there was no incident, no Cuban diplomats, no cash and no police questioning him about the source of any money.

The defendants accepted that there was no airport incident; that the first broadcast contained falsehoods; and it was not in the public interest to publish such an item. But they contended they had exercised due diligence, and had relied on an "impeccable source", a senior officer within the Office of the Director of Public Prosecutions. The defendants had then confirmed with the solicitor general what the source had told them.

But the sources on whom the defendants relied to break the story were not at the scene of any alleged incident and therefore had no firsthand knowledge of the matter. The broadcast did not make it clear that the impeccable source was only repeating what the source had been told via a telephone call. The sources could only confirm the fact of the call, not the truth of what they had been told.

The court also found that the tone of the reports was aimed at being sensational and the comment, "What a prekeh"[33] accompanied by laughter at the end of the broadcast did not add an air of professionalism to the report.

The *Reynolds* defence was rejected by the Court of Appeal in Trinidad and Tobago in *Ramdhan and Others v. Trinidad Express Newspapers Ltd*[34] for the following reasons:

- The information came from hearsay sources, people who had not witnessed the shooting.
- There was no evidence the reporter tried to confirm the information from reliable sources.
- No evidence had been given by a named police superintendent as stated in the article.
- The reporter admitted she did not know whether any evidence had been given by the superintendent.
- The reporter had sufficient time prior to publication to ascertain the accuracy of the statements included in the article.
- The reporter's actions could not be considered to have been of sufficient standard to qualify as responsible journalism and so the *Reynolds* defence was not open to the newspaper.

In another Trinidad and Tobago case, *Kayam Mohammed and Others v. Trinidad Publishing Co,*[35] the *Reynolds* defence was successfully pleaded, although the judge found the first claimant would have suffered pain and hurt over the untrue allegations. And so too the board members, though to a lesser extent. The newspaper report concerned allegations that the chairman of a board was corrupt and other board members were incompetent and weak, which led to a million-dollar loss when a faulty crane was purchased.

The judge said it fell within the ambit of responsible journalism – but not by a wide margin. The journalist relied on one source who did not provide the crucial document because he was fearful it would be traced back to him. Instead, he read out over the telephone an excerpt of the report that was supposed to contain the evidence. Attempts to contact the chairman were minimal and non-existent in the case of board members.

What saved the reporter – barely – is that she did contact one of the people mentioned in the article and he declined to comment but he told the chairman that the newspaper was working on a story. The chairman sent a warning letter, saying he would get an injunction unless the newspaper gave an undertaking that the article did not allege corruption or impropriety. And the judge found that such a letter meant the journalist would not have obtained any useful information from the claimant anyway – and there was no point in delaying publication.

The Court of Appeal concluded:[36]

> Critical to this case is the status and source of the information and steps taken to verify it. The source is one that was believed to be reliable and this was a belief that the third Respondent was justified in holding. The third Respondent had done what she could to verify the information. The information was a matter of public interest. It concerned a public company and one in respect of which the Government was a major shareholder. The matters contained in the article were matters of public interest. The Respondents had a duty to publish such information and the public to read it.

By contrast in another action, the *Reynolds* defence failed although the journalist did considerable research and conducted a lengthy interview with the claimant before publication. Conrad Aleong,[37] who was contracted in 1993 to restructure the failing Trinidad and Tobago national airline BWIA, sued the *Express* over eight articles. The journalist interviewed Aleong for four hours but the judge found that the most serious allegation against the CEO was not put to him. The judge also was concerned that the sources of the information were people who had their own interest to serve.

Similarly, in *Ken Julien v. Trinidad Express Ltd,*[38] the judge refused to accept the defence of responsible journalism. The series of articles concerned the affairs of the University of Trinidad and Tobago and its accountability for how it spent public funds. The claimant Dr Kenneth Julien was a chartered engineer and president of the university, as well as chairman of the board of governors. He had garnered numerous national and international accolades and was a "giant in the landscape of the republic".

The thrust of the articles was that the claimant had expended millions from the public coffers in an unethical, corrupt or improper manner. "The University Untouchable" was one headline.

The journalist did many things correctly. She searched numerous documents from registries concerning the claimant's business interests and directorships. She made repeated attempts to get a response from the claimant, resorting to camping out in a waiting room for over an hour without an appointment. When she made contact, the claimant cooperated and replied promptly to a list of questions she had submitted in writing. University of Trinidad and Tobago's senior manager in charge of business development also submitted answers to queries. The journalist sought the views of the relevant government ministry by making repeated calls to the permanent secretary but got no reply.

The journalist's downfall was that she made no attempt at verification of some of the most serious allegations, such as a "web of companies" with cross-directorships and contracts linked to Julien companies; the lease of a luxury apartment; and million-dollar scholarship grants. After the first article appeared, an attorney representing the claimant had sent a comprehensive statement with respect to several matters raised by the journalist but subsequent articles made no mention of that statement.

Also, the source for some of the allegations was an employee who had been terminated, and the tone of the article was sensational and overheated. The judge remarked that the journalist's motivation seemed to be to "get the proverbial scoop from a disgruntled employee rather than to produce a balanced professional article".[39]

QUALIFIED PRIVILEGE (POLITICAL EXPRESSION)

Is there a special defence of privilege covering publication of political expression?

Are members of the media and the general public free to criticize politicians and other public figures without liability for libel even if they get some of the statements wrong or cannot prove them to be true?

The short answer is no. There is no special dispensation when it comes to political material. The *Reynolds* defence is generally available, but you must adhere to the standards of responsible journalism.

The courts of England, Australia and New Zealand have each tackled this issue and have come up with different answers. For a full understanding of the issue, you need a world view.

England rejected the proposition, Australia says yes but defendants must pass the test of reasonableness and New Zealand also says yes within certain parameters. In arriving at its decision, the New Zealand Court of Appeal reviewed decisions about publications on political matters given by courts in

Canada, the United States and Europe, as well as those of Australia and the United Kingdom. To this can be added decisions from South Africa,[40] India[41] and Pakistan.[42]

Those cases demonstrate two things among others: the first is the critical importance accorded to freedom of speech in respect of political matters in many countries, and the second, the different balances that are struck in different countries according to different assessments of the competing principles, rights and interests.

The issue began gathering greater force in the 1990s, when David Lange, former Labour Party prime minister of New Zealand, sued two news organizations. Lange brought an action in New South Wales against the Australia Broadcasting Corporation over the televising of a New Zealand programme dealing with his time in office. In 1997, the High Court of Australia held that the defence of qualified privilege could extend to political expression, because each member of the Australian community had an interest in disseminating and receiving information, opinions and arguments concerning government and political matters that affect the people of Australia. But defendants would have to pass the test of reasonableness of conduct.[43]

Lange also sued Dr Joe Atkinson, a political scientist at the University of Auckland; the monthly current affairs magazine *North and South;* and the publisher, Australian Consolidated Press NZ Ltd. In an opinion column, published in October 1995, Atkinson was generally critical of Lange's performance as a politician and prime minister. He cast doubt on his recollection of certain events and said that Lange found the job of premier "too much like hard work". An accompanying cartoon showed Lange seated at a table, breakfasting on "Selective Memory Regression for Advanced Practitioners". Lange contended that the article meant he was irresponsible, insincere, manipulative and lazy. At the time the articles were published, Lange was a senior member of the opposition in Parliament.

Elias J in the New Zealand High Court ruled that defendants could use the qualified privilege defence (a few months before the Australia Broadcasting Corporation judgment) and Lange appealed. The New Zealand Court of Appeal dismissed his appeal, for substantially the same reasons as Elias J, ruling that the defendants were indeed entitled to rely on the defence of qualified privilege but within certain boundaries. The defence applied to generally published statements about those elected or seeking election to Parliament, so far as one was commenting on those people's capacity to meet their public responsibilities.

Their Lordships declared: "We hold that the defence of qualified privilege applies to generally-published statements made about the actions and qualities of those currently or formerly elected to Parliament and those with immediate aspirations to be members, so far as those actions and qualities directly affect or affected their capacity (including their personal ability and willingness) to meet their public responsibilities."

Lange then took his fight to the Privy Council. In 1999, the Privy Council set aside the decision of the New Zealand Court and remitted the appeal from the judgment of Elias J for rehearing.[44] Their Lordships considered that New Zealand should take into account the decision of the House of Lords in *Reynolds,* delivered on the same day and by the same judges as those who sat in the Privy Council in the present case. Their Lordships found that the New Zealand court was best placed to assess *Reynolds* in the political, social, constitutional and legislative context of its own country. *Reynolds* had rejected the proposition of a special category of qualified privilege for political expression.

So, the New Zealand Court of Appeal duly reviewed *Reynolds* but reaffirmed its earlier decision that political statements may be protected by qualified privilege and drew the following conclusions about the defence of qualified privilege:

1. The defence of qualified privilege may be available in respect of a statement that is published generally.
2. The nature of New Zealand's democracy means that the wider public may have a proper interest in respect of generally published statements that directly concern the functioning of representative and responsible government, including statements about the performance or possible future performance of specific individuals in elected public office.
3. In particular, a proper interest does exist in respect of statements made about the actions and qualities of those currently or formerly elected to Parliament and those with immediate aspirations to such office, so far as those actions and qualities directly affect or affected their capacity (including their personal ability and willingness) to meet their public responsibilities.
4. The determination of the matters that bear on that capacity will depend on a consideration of what is properly a matter of public concern rather than of private concern.
5. The width of the identified public concern justifies the extent of the publication.

The New Zealand Court of Appeal quoted a rousing passage from *Towards More Open Government* (1980), a report of the Committee on Official Information, which reflects important considerations that would be familiar to Commonwealth Caribbean territories:

> New Zealand is a small country. The Government has a pervasive involvement in our everyday national life. This involvement is not only felt, but is also sought, by New Zealanders, who have tended to view successive Governments as their agents, and have expected them to act as such. The Government is a principal agency in deploying the resources required to undertake many large scale projects, and there is considerable pressure for it to sustain its role as a major developer, particularly as an alternative to overseas ownership and control. . . . Our social support systems also rely heavily on central government. History and circumstances give New Zealanders special reason for wanting to know what their Government is doing and why.

After the Court of Appeal reaffirmed its decision, Lange ended his libel action against Atkinson and the co-defendants, saying he could no longer afford to stick with it. Then in 2017, in *Hagaman v. Little*,[45] the High Court held that qualified privilege could be available to the leader of the opposition for statements made in pursuance of a duty to hold the government to account. In that case the leader of the opposition gave several media interviews in which he was critical of the award of a hotel management contract to the claimant who had made a sizeable donation to the ruling party. The categories of qualified privilege are not closed. Clark J decided that the communication attracted qualified privilege because the opposition leader had a vital role in a representative democracy, and protection of communications on a matter of demonstrable public interest facilitated discussion about the exercise of government power and official conduct.

So the dust has not quite settled on this issue, but watch out – there is no special protection for journalists reporting on political issues.

Politics generates plenty of fodder for journalists. In election season, journalists often do not have to go looking too far for headlines – stories practically fall on their doorsteps. Therein lie the dangers. Don't get carried away; don't become tools for those with their own interests to serve.

CHAPTER 7

COURT REPORTING

Publicity is the very soul of justice.

—Lord Bentham[1]

One pillar of free speech is the open justice principle. This means that every court is open for the public to see justice being done. The first newspapers in Britain consisted primarily of court reports, and the courts still provide rich sources of newsworthy stories.

Reporters are exercising their rights as citizens to witness proceedings. However, reporters are the eyes and ears of the public, and even where a courtroom is full and no other members of the public may be admitted, room is usually made for reporters. The principle is expressed by Watkins LJ in *Felixstowe Justices ex p Leigh:* "No one nowadays surely can doubt that [the journalist's] presence in court for the purpose of reporting proceedings conducted therein is indispensable. Without him, how is the public to be informed of how justice is being administered in our courts?"[2]

The court has no power to exclude the media merely for convenience. Where there is secrecy, there is suspicion, and the best antidote to irregularity or impropriety in the administration of justice is to publicize, publicize, publicize. However, the open justice principle must give way to other public interest considerations that demand a degree of privacy. Journalists must know the restrictions on reporting certain judicial proceedings.

SEXUAL OFFENCES

Generally, provisions in the Criminal Codes and Sexual Offences Acts seek to protect both the accused and alleged victims in criminal cases. The media are prohibited from identifying either party after an accusation has been made.

For example, Section 38 of the Dominica Sexual Offences Act prohibits the publication of "any matter that is likely to lead members of the public to identify a person as the complainant or as the accused in relation" to the charge. The breach is punishable by a maximum fine of EC$50,000 and imprisonment.[3]

The prohibition can be lifted on application by the complainant, if the court finds that such restriction is unreasonable and it is in the public interest to remove it. In some jurisdictions, the accused can also make the application if, for example, it is necessary to get witnesses to come forward.[4]

As has been discussed in chapter 3, it is possible to identify someone without naming names. After the accused has been convicted, you can use his name. In so doing, however, journalists must be careful not to also identify the victim by giving details of how and where the offence was committed. Particularly in incest cases, it is dangerous to say too much about the accused and the case because it would not take a lot of imagination for neighbours, relatives and schoolmates to figure out who the victim is. It is better to avoid using the term *incest* at all; it is sufficient to say the offender was convicted of "unlawful sexual intercourse" or a sexual offence. The ban on naming the victim exists as long as she is alive.

The constitutionality of such provisions was called into question in Trinidad and Tobago in the 1980s, when a popular Anglican priest, Fr John Sewell, was arrested and charged for a sexual offence. No newspaper named him but several divulged enough detail for readers to piece it together. Prosecution was initiated against the newspapers but Fr Sewell slipped out of the country before his trial and later died overseas. Later, the Sexual Offences Act 1986 was amended to remove the prohibition against naming the defendant. The Barbados Sexual Offences Act, by virtue of Section 35 (1) similarly protects only the complainant.[5]

In 2013, in Trinidad and Tobago, Ian Alleyne, the flamboyant host of the *Crime Watch* television programme showed three times during his programme a video of a teenager being sexually assaulted. He pleaded guilty to three charges of identifying a complainant contrary to Section 32 of the amended Sexual Offences Act and was fined a total of TT$30,000.

Preliminary Inquiries

Serious offences, such as murder, rape and kidnapping, are heard by a judge and jury (or judge alone in some jurisdictions) in the High Court. But, first, such matters are usually heard by a magistrate, who will see whether there is sufficient evidence to send the matter to the High Court. The magistrate will hold a preliminary inquiry and, at the end of the proceedings, will either commit the accused to trial or dismiss the charges.

A preliminary inquiry, therefore, is not a trial. To publish evidence of witnesses could seriously impair the trial before a jury, whose opinion might be tilted by the pretrial publicity. This would offend the *sub judice* rule and contempt proceedings may follow. Further, defence counsel usually reserves the defence, calling no witnesses at this early stage and so the public would receive a distorted view of the strength of the prosecution's case. Therefore, at preliminary inquiries, journalists are not allowed to publish evidence. Magistrates' reasons for refusing bail or prosecutors' for opposing bail may not be published. Journalists must restrict themselves to:

- names, addresses, occupations, ages of accused and witnesses;
- names of counsel, magistrate, police prosecutor;
- concise statement of the charges;
- submissions on points of law and the decision of the magistrate thereon;
- decision to commit or how the case was otherwise disposed of;
- date and place to which hearing was adjourned;
- arrangements for bail; and
- whether legal aid was granted.[6]

Antigua, Barbados, Jamaica and St Lucia have abolished old-style preliminary inquiries which require witnesses testifying and tend to be time-consuming.[7] Instead, judicial officers make the decision to commit entirely on the basis of written statements and exhibits. Reporting on such pretrial proceedings is similarly restricted, and journalists may not publish contents of the statements or evidence, either from the prosecution or the accused.

Coroner's Inquest

Magistrates sit as coroners to inquire into unexplained deaths and causes of fires when such is not clear from initial investigations. Witnesses are summoned and questioned and the coroner will render a decision. In many jurisdictions, including Jamaica, Grenada, St Vincent, St Lucia, Antigua, Dominica, Cayman, Guyana and Belize, the coroner sits with a jury.

Inquests are held in open court and do not follow the usual adversarial pattern of criminal proceedings. Rather, the coroner's role is inquisitorial. The parties and their lawyers are present more as guests of the court. A fair and accurate report of the proceedings published contemporaneously would be covered by privilege. Given the inquisitorial nature of an inquest, there should be no reason for media comment to be suppressed, although there have been decisions to the contrary.

In *Peacock v. London Weekend Television*,[8] six police officers obtained an interlocutory injunction to restrain a television company from broadcasting a reconstruction of the arrest and death of a Hells Angel member on the ground that the broadcast would amount to contempt of an inquest into the death being conducted by a coroner. The television company appealed, contending that the proceedings before the coroner were not "active" and media comment would be too remote from the proceedings. The inquest had been adjourned indefinitely while police investigation continued. The Court of Appeal disagreed with the television station and dismissed the appeal.

Because the objective of an inquest is to determine the cause of death, the news media may even be able to help the court discover the truth.[9] In the United Kingdom, at the inquest of Helen Smith, a nurse who died in suspicious circumstances during a party in Saudi Arabia in 1979, a Thames Television documentary that was aired the week before the inquest was viewed at the inquest because it featured interviews with important witnesses who had declined to travel to the United Kingdom to give evidence.

Also, the court granted a witness summons for Channel Four Television Corporation to produce documents relating to a programme it had aired about the circumstances of the car crash that killed Princess Diana and Dodi al Fayed.[10]

Indecent Material

Although reporters are shielded by privilege in court reporting, they must not release certain material in judicial proceedings, including "indecent", "obscene" or "blasphemous"[11] material.

For example, Section 13 (2) of the Libel and Defamation Act of Trinidad and Tobago prohibits publication of "any indecent matter or indecent material, surgical or physiological details being matter or details the publication of which would be calculated to injure public morals".[12]

This sounds quaint in today's society where anyone can see anything on cable TV without even looking too hard. The vulnerability of public morals must be judged by current standards. In any case, if a matter arises that a court thinks outrages public decency, most likely the judge will warn the media about it beforehand.

Juveniles

The law seeks to shield juveniles or children who are defendants from the glare of the public by clearing the courtroom during trials and preventing publication of their names or other details that may identify them.[13]

The term *juvenile* usually refers to someone under the age of 16 but in some jurisdictions the age limit is 18, as in the Bahamas, Dominica, Jamaica, St Kitts and Nevis and Trinidad and Tobago. In Guyana, a juvenile is a person under age seventeen. In Grenada, a child for the purposes of trial is defined in the Criminal Procedure Code as someone under the age of fourteen.

Juveniles are usually tried in special juvenile courts. In some countries, a court building separate from the regular magistrates' courts has been created, whereas in others the same court building is used but special days are dedicated to juvenile matters. Trinidad and Tobago created a Children's Court within the Family and Children Division[14] where defendants under age eighteen are tried in more user-friendly spaces, with appropriate support services.

Juveniles are generally tried summarily by a magistrate, except in homicide cases. Where the juvenile is being tried jointly with an adult, especially for a serious offence, he may be tried in ordinary court.

Only people directly concerned with the case are allowed in juvenile court. But bona fide representatives of the news media are allowed to attend though they are not allowed to publish. Publications of the court proceedings require special permission from the magistrate.

In the British Virgin Islands, for example, restrictions may be lifted in the public interest but this is on application by a police officer on the basis that such publication would assist in apprehending a young offender or on application of the child or young person himself, once the magistrate is satisfied the report would not be contrary to the best interest of the child or young person.[15]

Particulars, such as address and school, which could lead to the identification of a young offender should also be omitted. The same goes for juvenile witnesses in the matter. Photographs of juveniles are also prohibited. Breach of this prohibition could result in a fine and imprisonment.[16]

In Absence of Jury

During a jury trial, anything that is discussed in the absence of a jury is not to be published by the news media. Jurors are judges of the facts, not the law. So, when counsel wish to make legal submissions, the jurors are sent to the jury room. These submissions often have to do with the admissibility of evidence, so you will appreciate how prejudicial it would be for the jury to learn, through the media, about evidence that has been excluded. This would make a mockery of the courts and could cause the trial to be aborted, incurring great expense and hardship to parties. When a *voir dire* (trial within a trial) is being held, usually to determine whether a confession was voluntary, the media must not even mention that such proceedings are taking place. The most they can do is to state that legal submissions are being heard.

In Camera

Literally, this means "in a room". Proceedings held in camera are in private and the news media are not permitted to enter or to report on what takes place behind closed doors. This is the case with trials and preliminary inquiries of sexual offences and human trafficking. Only the magistrate's decision at the preliminary inquiry or the jury's verdict may be reported. If the verdict is guilty, the name of the prisoner may be reported but the victim must always be protected. The court has the power to prohibit the publication of any report or account giving details of any acts that the complainant was induced or compelled to perform.

In Chambers

Judges sometimes hear pretrial applications, such as injunctions, in chambers. But the privacy of chamber hearings does not mean they are secret. Sometimes, matters are held in chambers by convention or for administrative convenience, not for secrecy. If you can persuade parties to divulge details, you are free to publish without being in contempt. The danger is that you will not be shielded by privilege because the proceedings did not take place in open court. Judgments given in chambers may be freely published, because the concept of secret judgments is inherently abhorrent. Lord Woolf in *Hodgson v. Imperial Tobacco Ltd*[17] took the opportunity to outline principles of good practice for chamber hearings:

1. The public has no right to attend hearings in chambers because of the nature of the work transacted in chambers and because of the physical restrictions on the room available, but if requested, permission should be granted to attend when and to the extent that it is practical.

2. What happens during the proceedings in chambers is not confidential or secret and information about what occurs in chambers and the judgment or order pronounced can and, in the case of any judgment or order, should, be made available to the public when requested.

3. If members of the public who seek to attend cannot be accommodated, the judge should consider adjourning the proceedings in whole or in part into open court to the extent that this is practical or allowing one or more representatives of the press to attend the hearing in chambers.

4. To disclose what occurs in chambers does not constitute a breach of confidence or amount to contempt as long as any comment which is made does not substantially prejudice the administration of justice.

There are exceptions, of course, where publication of certain chamber matters, usually to do with children, would result in contempt. They are:

- wardship (where child is placed under protection of the court);
- adoption;
- guardianship;
- custody and rights of access;
- pretrial reviews; and
- bail applications.

Generally, it is appropriate to protect children from the glare of the public in family matters, which can be sensitive and emotionally explosive. Adoption legislation in the region includes provisions that proceedings be held in camera.[18] In Belize, under the Families Law and Children Act,[19] it is a criminal offence to publish any material that is intended to or likely to identify a child in any proceedings under the act. The non-publication provision includes the name or address of the school the child is attending. The Bahamas Child Protection Act[20] includes almost identical provisions. Similarly, Grenada relies on the Family Law Act,[21] which forbids publishing names and addresses of parties related to any proceedings concerning juveniles (under age eighteen).

Legislation, generally, does not expressly address non-publication of wardship proceedings, but the court can order that names be redacted or that material not be published. In so doing, the court will be acting in its role as *parens patriae*[22] to protect the child. Family and matrimonial proceedings legislation also address the court's power to forbid publication of names and details of proceedings concerning custody, rights of access and guardianship.

The danger in reporting pretrial reviews and bail applications is that material that could prejudice a fair trial may be revealed, such as previous convictions of an applicant, potential evidence and the availability of witnesses.

Jury Vetting

In 1996, for the first time in the region, a jury was vetted to see if they were suitable to serve, because of widespread negative pretrial publicity. This took place in Trinidad and Tobago during the trial of Dole Chadee (Nankissoon Boodram) and eight others for the murder of four members of a family. The media were allowed to be present during the questioning of jurors but not to report on what took place. To do so would have given rise to contempt of court proceedings. Jury vetting next took place in 2012 in the trial of Yasin Abu Bakr for sedition.[23]

Divorces

Divorces and separations have become so commonplace that proceedings have become much less interesting to reporters. The charges and counter-charges may tickle someone's curiosity but can only be reported if evidence is given in support of them. If the allegations are withdrawn, publication is prohibited. Such breaches will not be covered by privilege and could expose the journalist to libel action.

Generally, in relation to proceedings for divorce, separation or nullity, journalists should avoid lurid, unnecessary details but can properly report:

- the names, addresses and occupations of the parties and witnesses;
- a concise statement of the charges, defences and counter-charges, in support of which evidence is given;
- legal submissions; and
- ruling of the court and observations made by the judge.

Section 13 (2) of the Trinidad and Tobago Libel and Defamation Act[24] specifically contains such provisions. Additionally, the court may forbid publication of details of matrimonial proceedings. So, apart from becoming vulnerable to libel proceedings because one will not be protected by the defence of privilege, journalists and publishers who contravene court orders can be charged with contempt of court, which may result in a fine or imprisonment.

Section 22 (1) of the Trinidad and Tobago Matrimonial Proceedings Act[25] provides:

> The Court may at all times in any proceedings under this Act, whether heard and tried in chambers, in camera or in open court, make an order forbidding the publication of any report or account of the evidence or other proceedings therein, either as to the whole or any portion thereof; and the breach of any such order, or any colourable or attempted evasion thereof, may be dealt with as contempt of court.

In Barbados, Section 97 of the Family Law Act has similar restrictions on publication of proceedings. In jurisdictions with no such specific provisions, people can rely on data protection and privacy laws to prevent publication of unnecessary and lurid details. And judges still have an inherent jurisdiction to make orders to protect the integrity of proceedings and the administration of justice, which may include orders limiting publication of certain details.[26]

In the Public Interest

Are there exceptional circumstances in which a court can sit in private? Does the court have an inherent power to exclude both media and the public in the interest of justice? This important question has not received a definitive answer, although it has been considered. In *Scott v. Scott*, which concerned a divorce petition, the House of Lords was divided on the topic. Several judges said the court had no power to enforce secrecy other than that granted by statute. One thought that the public was to be excluded if "administration of justice would be rendered impracticable by their presence". Viscount Haldane put the test thus: "to justify an order for a hearing in camera it must be shown that the paramount object of securing that justice is done would really be rendered doubtful if attainment of the order were not made".

Trials in magistrate courts, as in the High Courts, must be held in open court unless there are special reasons to close the court and exclude the public. Such powers are dictated by statute.

In Trinidad and Tobago, for example, magistrates have wide powers to regulate their own affairs by virtue of Section 54(2) of the Summary Courts Act,[27] which provides that a magistrate "may on special grounds of public policy, decency or expediency, in his discretion exclude the public at any stage of the hearing; and in every such case shall record the grounds on which such order has been made".

Also, in Grenada, by virtue of Section 40 (1) of the Magistrates Act, magistrates can exercise their discretion to restrict the public in such proceedings as "bastardy or in relation to obscene, abusive or insulting language" or where an indictable offence is concerned.

Section 209 (1) of the Barbados Magistrates' Court Act 1996 provides that a summary trial must be in open court but is subject to the "provision of any law conferring power on a magistrate to sit in camera and to any enactment relating to domestic proceedings or affiliation proceedings or in juvenile court".[28] Section 23 of the Jamaica Criminal Justice (Administration) Act is similar in effect and applies to all criminal proceedings. Section 23 (1) specifies that the public shall "in the interest of public morality be excluded during the hearing of specified offences", which relate to sexual matters.[29]

Access to Court Documents

The Supreme Court civil procedure rules in various jurisdictions limit the documents that non-parties to legal proceedings can access through the court registries.[30] Non-parties are generally limited to claim forms, notices of appeal and any order or judgment on file. They will not be entitled to inspect or take a copy of statements and affidavits that detail the allegations or claims being made, except by leave of the court. If journalists obtain such documents and choose to publish the contents, they will not be able to claim the defence of privilege and may expose themselves to defamation suits.

Even where a document has been used or read to or by the court or referred to in open court, the judge can make an order restricting or prohibiting the use of the document. But such measures are to be rarely employed, and only in exceptional circumstances, such as the need to preserve national security or trade secrets.

In Bermuda in 2015, a newspaper successfully went to court to gain access to documents.[31] The *Royal Gazette* had sought copies of affidavits[32] used in a civil case that had garnered much public attention and involved allegations of government corruption. The registrar had refused access on the basis that she had no power to hand over documents in a pending or ongoing matter. But Chief Justice Ian Kawaley held that the common law principle of open justice meant that the registrar had a discretionary power in appropriate cases to provide a member of the public with copies of written evidence filed in court and referred to by parties or the court in the course of a public hearing.[33] Thereafter, the Supreme Court issued Practice Direction No. 23 of 2015 (published on its website) that widens the scope of public access to documents in civil matters.[34]

In the criminal arena, generally, the criminal procedure rules in the region do not furnish provisions on access to documents by the news media. However, given the principle of open justice, one is at pains to see why journalists, with legitimate purpose, should be refused documents that have been used in open court. Journalists are often rebuked for getting it wrong and so the courts should be the last place where their efforts to get it right are stymied. Justice thrives in air and light, not in dark, musty cabinets and lockers.

In *R (on the application of Guardian News and Media Ltd) v. City of Westminster Magistrates Court,* extradition proceedings were under way. The US government requested the extradition of two British citizens from the United Kingdom. Prior to delivery of the judgment, the newspaper wrote to the court, requesting copies of affidavits, skeleton arguments and witness statements that had been used in court. The district judge said she did not have the power to order the release of the documents. The claimant applied for judicial review of that decision. The divisional court dismissed the claimant's application, holding that the open justice principle did not extend to the media inspecting court documents.

The Court of Appeal set things aright. The divisional court had erred. The Court of Appeal stated that the "default position" was that media access should be granted where it is sought for proper journalistic purpose:

> In a case where documents had been placed before a judge and referred to in the course of proceedings, the default position should be that access should be permitted on the open justice principle. Where access was sought for a proper journalistic purpose, the case for allowing it would be particularly strong. However, there might be countervailing reasons, but it was not sensible or practical to look for a standard formula for determining how strong the grounds of opposition needed to be in order to outweigh the merits of the application. The court had to carry out a proportionality exercise which would be fact specific. Central to the court's evaluation would be the purpose of the open justice principle, the potential value of the material in advancing that purpose and, conversely, any risk of harm which access to the documents might cause to the legitimate interests of others.

The Judicial College of England and Wales has published a guide called *Reporting Restrictions in the Criminal Courts* for court officials and the media.[35] Also, media access to prosecution material is governed by a protocol between the Association of Chief Police Officers, the Crown Prosecution Service and the media entitled *Publicity and the Criminal Justice System* and published in October 2005.[36]

The protocol sets out the categories of material relied upon by the prosecution in court that should normally be released to the media. This includes maps and photographs (including custody photos of defendants), diagrams and other documents produced in court; videos showing scenes of crimes as recorded by police after the event; videos of property seized; sections of transcripts of interviews or statements as read out in court and videos or photographs showing reconstructions of the crime and CCTV footage of the defendant.

This is eminently a subject on which our regional media associations, law associations, the police and the judiciary can collaborate to ensure greater openness, accuracy and accountability, in the reporting of public proceedings.

CHAPTER 8

CONTEMPT OF COURT

I am and have always been satisfied that no judge would be influenced in his judgment by what may be said by the media. If he were, he would not be fit to be a judge.

—Lord Salmon[1]

Courts have the power to punish anyone who interferes with the proper functioning of the court system. That interference can take place in a number of ways, from swearing at the judge to threatening witnesses or jurors, to taking photographs, to commenting about the merits of a case during a trial.

Section 2 of the Guyana Contempt of Court Act 1919 describes contempt as anything "calculated to obstruct, interfere with, or improperly prejudice, the administration of justice in proceedings before the court". This is a reflection of the common law position, which generally applies through the region, unlike the United Kingdom, which has passed legislation.[2]

Contempt in the presence and hearing of the court, or "in the face of the court", includes insulting the judge; threatening violence, or using threatening or abusive language to a juror in or near the court building. Contempt also includes disobeying court orders, such as an injunction prohibiting a newspaper from publishing certain material or a witness anonymity order where the identity of a witness is withheld or concealed, usually for security reasons.[3]

Contempt risks by the news media usually arise when someone breaches the sub judice rule by publishing evidence before it is received in court or discussing the merits of the case while it is active. However, commenting inappropriately about a case, even after it has been completed, such as imputing improper motives to the judge or suggesting the trial is not fair could amount to contempt of court.

Contempt protects all bodies that exercise the "judicial power of the State",[4] so employment tribunals, liquor and gambling licence applications, and disciplinary councils of professional bodies would not be covered. But court martials would. Magistrates' courts have no power to punish the media for contempt on their own volition but High Courts have an overall power to protect the lower courts.

SUB JUDICE RULE

People are supposed to be tried by jury, not by the media. The law seeks to ensure an accused person gets a fair trial and that the jury is not contaminated by media reports about the person and the case. The Latin term *sub judice* means "under the judge", and the sub judice rule prescribes that once a case becomes active, journalists are to refrain from publishing:

- previous convictions of the accused or parties in civil matters;
- interviews with the accused or witnesses;
- opinion or speculation on whether the accused person is guilty or how likely it is that he will be convicted;
- photographs of suspects in matters where identification is in issue;
- interviews with any member of the jury (just speaking to a juror at all during a trial is ill advised);
- reporting evidence or legal submissions in absence of the jury; and
- any material that could cause a real risk of prejudice to the accused, in a criminal matter.

WHEN A CASE BECOMES ACTIVE

A case becomes active, generally, from the time of arrest in criminal matters and in civil litigation, after the action has been set down for trial. A case remains active until it has been dismissed or the accused has been sentenced. Sentencing sometimes comes a few days later, so a case can remain active even after the verdict is in. However, when the accused is found guilty, he usually appeals. Appeal proceedings begin from the time when they are launched by lodging a formal notice of appeal or application for leave to appeal.

Civil proceedings end when they are disposed of, discontinued or withdrawn. Most civil trials are conducted by judges sitting alone, and a judge is very different from a juror. As with appellate judges, it is presumed trial judges will not be influenced by what is published in newspapers or televised. In *R v. Duffy, ex p Nash*,[5] the chief justice had this to say about judges:

> Though in no sense a superhuman, he has by his training no difficulty in putting out of his mind matters which are not evidence in the case. This indeed happens daily to judges on Assize. This is all the more so in a member of the Court of Appeal, who in regard to an appeal against conviction is dealing almost entirely with points of law and who in the case of an appeal against sentence is considering whether or not the sentence is correct in principle.

IMMINENCE

By common law, contempt can be committed even before proceedings are active but merely imminent. The dictionary definition of imminent is "threatening" or "impending", but in the area of contempt, it remains an imprecise term that can cause enormous difficulty for investigative journalists. Judges have used the phrase "virtually certain".

Two examples illustrate the difficulties the imminence test presents. In *Beaverbrook Newspapers*,[6] a man was suspected of a recent murder. He was surrounded in a house by police. A reporter gained access and interviewed him. The reporter's newspaper published the interview before the accused was arrested but when it was obvious that he shortly would be. The article contained a denial of guilt by the accused but also details of his previous convictions that he himself supplied. The article was held to be in contempt because proceedings were "virtually certain" to take place.

In Australia, in *James v. Robinson*,[7] two people were shot dead and the assailant escaped. A newspaper published his name, photograph and accounts from eyewitnesses. The High Court ruled that it would be astonishing if the publisher were to be found guilty or not guilty according to the fortuitous circumstance of whether or not proceedings were subsequently commenced.

Contempt is unlikely to arise, therefore, where proceedings are speculative and remote. In *Attorney General v. Sport Newspapers Ltd*,[8] the publisher and editor of the *Sport* newspaper in England were prosecuted for contempt following a story about the rape and murder of a fifteen-year-old schoolgirl. The police had held a news conference, asking for the public's help in locating a suspect, David Evans, a convicted rapist. The police also warned the audience that to broadcast or publish anything about the suspect's record would be likely to prejudice legal proceedings.

The paper, nevertheless, published an article headlined "Evans Was Given 10 Years for Rape", in which Evans was described as a "vicious, evil rapist" with details of what he had done to other girls. Evans was arrested in France five days later and convicted the following year for the rape and murder of the fifteen-year-old girl. The Court of Appeal held that the intent to prejudice the administration of justice had not been made out, because it was wholly uncertain whether Evans would be caught at all.

RED FLAGS

So let's say proceedings are clearly active, what should journalists look out for?

Where criminal proceedings are concerned, avoid any publication that could influence a verdict or ruling or provoke a situation in which the jury would have to be discharged and a fresh trial ordered. Media houses that publish comments by readers, viewers or listeners will be held liable for those improper comments.

To publish a photograph of a suspect in a matter where identification is in issue may be found to be contempt. In 1994, the *Sun* in London published the photograph of a suspect just before he was about to take part in an identification parade. The newspaper and editor received heavy fines, and the prosecution was aborted.[9]

In the United Kingdom in 2011, the *Mail Online* published a photograph of the defendant in a current trial holding a gun; it was on the site for five hours. The *Sun* newspaper website also published the photograph. None of the jurors saw the photographs and the trial proceeded smoothly; yet the newspapers were found in contempt and fined £15,000 each.[10]

Publishing confessions of a defendant prematurely resulted in a Hong Kong newspaper and its editors being fined HK$550,000 in 2015, for their "foolish" and "reprehensible" decision in running a sensational interview with a murder accused while he was inside a detention centre, just two days after he appeared before a magistrate. The man was subsequently convicted and sentenced to life imprisonment for murdering and dismembering his own parents whose heads he kept in a fridge.[11]

Previous convictions of a defendant or "colour stories" that paint him in a bad light are likely to cause prejudice. Interviewing eyewitnesses to an incident is perfectly all right but once a suspect has been charged, no potential witnesses should be approached for an interview. See chapter 7 on court reporting for other restrictions, such as reporting on trial matters conducted in the absence of the jury.

INTENT

"Oops" is not a defence to a contempt action.[12] Otherwise, it would be ludicrously easy to defeat the law by merely claiming you didn't know some fact or you didn't mean to cause trouble. Or as Lord Erskine said in *Roach v. Garvan*,[13] "the ends of justice would be defeated by contrivance".

It does not matter whether the journalist intended the publication to have an adverse effect.[14] Neither does it matter whether the jurors were actually influenced or even read or saw the offending reports.

The New South Wales Court of Appeal in *A-G (New South Wales) v. John Fairfax Ltd*[15] defined contempt of court at common law as follows:

> Contempt will be established if a publication has a tendency to interfere with the due administration of justice in the particular proceedings. This tendency is to be determined objectively by reference to the nature of the publication; and it is not relevant for this purpose to determine what the actual effect of the publication upon the proceedings had been, or what it will probably be. If the publication is of a character which might have an effect upon the proceedings, it will have the necessary tendency, unless the possibility of interference is so removed or theoretical that the *de minimis* principle should be applied.

Where a criminal trial is concerned, the requirement of intent will be made out where it is obvious that the journalist or editor must have foreseen that the publication would create a real risk of prejudice to a fair trial.

In *Attorney General v. Sport Newspapers Ltd*,[16] Lord Bingham explained:

> Such an intent need not be expressly avowed or admitted but can be inferred from the circumstances, including the foreseeability of the consequences of the conduct, although the probability of the consequences taken to have been foreseen must be little short of overwhelming before it will suffice to establish the necessary intent. But it need not be the sole intention of the contemnor, and intention is to be distinguished from motive or desire.

One way of testing whether the prejudice is substantial is to consider whether it can be cured by the court itself, say, the judge giving a direction to the jury or asking jurors who have read the publication to stand down from the panel, rather than by a prosecution or an injunction against publication.[17]

In 1968, Black Power leader Michael X (Abdul Malik)[18] of Trinidad and Tobago was awaiting trial for incitement to racial hatred in the United

Kingdom. The *Times* published his photograph and referred to a previous conviction for brothel keeping. The paper was fined £5,000.

When Michael Fagan crept into the queen's bed chamber in Buckingham Palace in 1982 and perched on her bed like a cockatoo (an event immortalized in calypsonian Mighty Sparrow's "Phillip, My Dear") several newspapers got into trouble. The *Sun* described him as a junkie, a glib liar and a thief of palace cigars. None of those descriptions was held to be likely to cause substantial risk of prejudice. But the *Daily Express* referred to an alleged confession of Fagan to a theft of wine. That went to the heart of the case against him and was found to be contempt. The *Sunday Times* was found guilty of contempt because it exaggerated an unrelated charge against Fagan, publishing that he was accused of wounding his stepson when in fact he was charged with the less serious crime of assault occasioning actual bodily harm.

In 1997, the *Evening Standard* was fined £40,000 (plus £50,000 legal costs) for revealing that three of the six men on trial for an escape from Whitemoor Prison were convicted Irish Republican Army terrorists.[19]

If a news organization has published material about an active case, all is not lost. Much will depend on which court is trying the issue. Juries are assumed to be the most susceptible to media influence. But if a long time has elapsed between publication and trial (the fade factor) the journalist may be forgiven. Magistrates and judges, who sit without juries, are expected to be able to put out of their minds matters that are not evidence in the case.[20] The court's function is to secure a fair trial – not to keep journalists on a short leash or to prevent publication of articles that are merely objectionable or reprehensible.

The law balances the right of freedom of expression with the need to protect the integrity of the justice system. Lord Reid in *A-G v. Times Newspapers Ltd*[21] put it this way:

> The law on this subject is and must be founded entirely on public policy. It is not there to protect the private rights of parties to a litigation or prosecution. It is there to prevent interference with the administration of justice and it should, in my judgment, be limited to what is reasonably necessary for that purpose. Public policy generally requires a balancing of interests which may conflict. Freedom of speech should not be limited to any greater extent than is necessary but it cannot be allowed where there would be a real prejudice to the administration of justice.

In Trinidad and Tobago, in 2008, a television reporter, the head of news and the news agency itself were found guilty of contempt for airing a report during the trial of an accused for firearm and ammunition charges.[22] The report conveyed the impression that the accused was responsible for the issuing of death threats to a police witness and his wife, as well as the murder of his relatives.

During the report, the camera clearly showed documents on which the name of the case and the accused were visible. The journalist told the court he had instructed the video editor to blur or redact the names, but those instructions were not followed. The court did not fine or imprison the journalist or the head of news because the former was young and inexperienced and deserved a second chance and the head of news had devised an elaborate system of checks and balances. It was through human error that the objectionable report was aired. So the judge reprimanded and discharged them.

Not so fortunate was popular and colourful radio talk-show host Dennis "Sprangalang" Hall, in 2010, when his station was fined TT$25,000.[23] The judge found the talk-show host and the station were without contrition or remorse and offered little to purge the contempt. Hall and his co-host were discussing a newspaper report of a current murder trial; they focused on scandalous sexual details, dubbing a policeman "Constable Slackie", and suggesting that the police had set up the accused.

The judge held that the programme producers and directors were just as guilty of the contempt because they allowed the talk-show hosts great latitude in terms of content without clear guidelines as to what was permissible. It was no defence for the station that the programme was unscripted and management did not know what the hosts were going to say.

PRETRIAL PUBLICITY

Pretrial publicity can be so prejudicial that the only course is to abort the trial. But judges and the directors of public prosecutions tend to find measures to preserve the integrity of trials, including warnings to the news media, robust judicial directions, postponements and sequestration of juries.

In Trinidad and Tobago, defence counsel for Dole Chadee (also called Nankissoon Boodram), who was eventually hanged for murder in 1999, failed to have his trial stayed on the basis that a fair trial was no longer possible because of pretrial publicity. However, the Privy Council found that the pretrial publicity was prejudicial but commended the trial judge for the measures he took to protect the integrity of the trial and concluded that despite the prejudicial publicity, the trial had been fair.

Among other things, reports suggested he was a notorious drug smuggler who had been previously charged with murder, was involved in killing a state witness, and he and his brother were involved in systemic witness intimidation.

The Privy Council also stated that the directors of public prosecutions had a duty to "take measures to protect the administration of justice from abuse such as prejudicial pre-trial publicity. As the public authority in charge of prosecutions, he has the power and means to prosecute contemnors, those who are in contempt of court for adversely affecting the administration of justice by prejudicial pre-trial publicity".[24]

An infamous example of how wrong it can all go when the media are allowed free rein is the case of surgeon Dr Sam Sheppard who was convicted in 1954 of murdering his wife after a five-week carnival of a trial in Cleveland, Ohio. At one low point, a front-page photograph of the wife's bloodstained pillow was published after being "enhanced" to show more clearly an alleged imprint of a surgical instrument. His story was the inspiration for *The Fugitive* television series and movie.[25]

In England, the 1995 assault charges trial of Geoff Knights, the partner of the former *East Enders* actress Gillian Taylforth, failed to get off the ground at all because of what the judge described as "scandalous" reporting.[26] Another famous English case involved two sisters, Lisa and Michelle Taylor, who were convicted of murder but cleared on appeal in 1993 because of sensational reporting during their trial.[27]

In December 2003, Lord Goldsmith, the English attorney general, issued stern warnings and guidelines to the news media, following the trial and conviction of Ian Huntley and his girlfriend, Maxine Carr, who became the two most hated figures in Britain. Huntley, the caretaker at a Soham school, had abducted and murdered two girls, Holly Wells and Jessica Chapman.

Lord Goldsmith's office, in a statement, said:[28]

The attorney general agrees that journalists have a vital function in the administration of justice. This is supported by the right to freedom of speech. But journalists must bear in mind that the consequences of a prejudicial report can be high. Those consequences are felt by individuals, often those who are vulnerable, such as victims and witnesses, as well as defendants. And it is in the public interest that we have a fair, decent and effective system of justice.

The Soham trial media frenzy was of billowing proportions, beginning the day after the arrest of the couple. The *Mail on Sunday* published an article in which a woman gave vivid details of her underage relationship with Huntley. The *Star* said that the couple had "bizarre sex pasts" and that Huntley's mother had had a lesbian affair. When Carr made her first appearance, the *Mail* reported, "At least she had the decency to bow her head." People carried explicit details of Carr's past under the headline "Maxine's Twisted Sex Shame". The trial judge also rebuked the *Mail* for an article that read, "Holly's father stared intently at Huntley. The look in his eyes could have shattered stone."

The trial judge referred the reporters and the papers to the attorney general for contempt of court proceedings but allowed the trial to proceed because of the length of time that had elapsed because much of the adverse publicity and because the proceedings would focus the minds of the jury and because he could warn the jurors not to be influenced by what they may have read.

But two Beacon FM radio presenters, Mark Peters and Lisa Fraeme, did not get off easily. The presenters had mocked Huntley's defence while the trial was still in progress, describing it as the "most unbelievable made-up story in the world ever", and they invited listeners to share their views on air. One listener's text message was crisply to the point: "Do you idiots not understand the principle of sub judice?"

Following "discussions" with the radio station, both presenters left the station "to pursue opportunities elsewhere". For Peters, that meant returning to his roots as a deejay in a club.

JURY DELIBERATIONS

It is common to see jurors in the American media commenting about a case, giving lengthy interviews and appearing on talk shows. In the aftermath of the O.J. Simpson murder trial, several jurors wrote books about the controversial trial. In Commonwealth jurisdictions, this is heavily frowned upon. In England, it is specifically prohibited by the Contempt of Court Act 1981 to "obtain, disclose or solicit any particulars of statements made, opinions expressed, arguments advanced or votes cast by members of a jury in the course of their deliberations in any legal proceedings".

However, in England, there is no contempt where jurors merely give their opinion of the case, rather than what went on in the jury room, as decided in *AG v. News Statesman*.[29] In that case, an article was published following an interview given by a juror, without reward, to two reputable journalists. It contained an account of significant parts of the jury's deliberations in the course of arriving at their verdicts of acquittal in the much-publicized trial of a well-known politician and others for conspiracy to murder and other offences.

The article recorded the juror as saying that the jury could not accept the uncorroborated word of a prosecution witness who had agreed to accept money from a newspaper, the amount to be increased in the event of a conviction. The juror revealed those matters because he felt that certain aspects of the case ought to be made public, and the editor of the periodical agreed to the publication of the article because he honestly believed that nothing but good would result from its publication.

But in the course of his judgment, Lord Widgery CJ lamented the diminishing respect for the secrecy of the jury room:[30]

> We were reminded that, until a few years ago, it was accepted that the secrets of the jury room had to be treated as secret. The solemn obligation by jurors to observe secrecy was well maintained and breaches of the obligation were kept at an acceptable level. It had never been necessary to invoke the law of contempt in respect of such breaches, but that law had always been available for use in any case in which the administration of justice would have been imperilled. Recently, however, the solemn obligation of secrecy has been shown to be breaking down; a considerable number of publications involving jury room revelations, some more objectionable than others, has occurred. Accordingly, in view of the apparently diminishing respect for the convention of observance of jury secrecy and the risk of escalation in the frequency and degree of disclosures, it has become right for the Attorney-General to invoke the law of contempt in relation to this article in the *New Statesman* since it represents a departure from the norm and is a serious and dangerous encroachment into the convention of jury secrecy.

In the absence of statute similar to English legislation, what takes place in a jury room is nevertheless considered sacrosanct. No one, not even a judge, may peer into jury deliberations, even where a jury returns a perverse verdict. Such inquiries by journalists could be interpreted as being disruptive to the administration of justice. If jurors are tracked down for interviews, if jury deliberations are exposed, and therefore made subject to public criticism and probing, jurors would lose some of their protection and anonymity. The whole idea is for jurors in a criminal trial to feel safe and free to sit on a trial and to make up their own minds.

In New Zealand, in April 1989, two Swedish tourists were murdered and their possessions were stolen. After an intense police investigation and much public and media interest, a suspect, David Tamihere, was arrested. He was convicted in 1990. After the trial, a watch belonging to one of the victims was found in an unexpected location. Radio New Zealand tracked down jurors and asked them, had they known about the watch, whether they would have found the accused guilty beyond reasonable doubt. The radio station was held to be in contempt.[31]

Still, the Radio New Zealand judgment hints that if the jurors' revelations raise a matter of real public concern, publication might be permissible.

So the door to the jury room might be locked and bolted but sensible journalists might be able to interview jurors after the completion of trials on matters of real public concern without violating the sanctity of the jury room.

INTIMIDATING WITNESSES

Placing unfair pressure on witnesses or parties to proceedings also amounts to contempt – for example, a trade union paper castigating a member for taking a grievance to court, with hints of the retribution that would follow. There must be a real risk of the influence being felt or else there is no contempt. In 1975, a feud erupted between the millionaire Sir James Goldsmith and the satirical *Private Eye* magazine. Goldsmith brought about ninety libel actions against the magazine and its distributors in the 1970s, nearly bankrupting the magazine, which was founded in the 1960s with the purpose of opposing "cant and humbug".

In 1977, *Private Eye* was acquitted of attempting to prejudice an action brought by Sir James because the court agreed that the barbs and vitriol were intended to persuade the tycoon to drop the case but that was unlikely to have any effect on the final outcome of the action. Read all about the epic battle in the real-life comic thriller, *Goldenballs!* by Richard Ingrams, co-founder of the magazine.

Many newspapers and their journalists have risen to fame on the basis of public interest campaigns, seeking justice for the voiceless and oppressed. Do not let your compassion for the masses be diluted by fear of contempt proceedings. Trying to sting authorities into action – the police to investigate, the director of public prosecutions to initiate prosecution – is not prejudicial to the administration of justice. But to go further and threaten witnesses with ostracism or to call down a plague upon their houses is much more dangerous and might well constitute contempt.

It must always be remembered that the purpose of the law is not to stifle criticism of the workings of the courts after cases have been concluded. On 14 February

1997, the *Daily Mail* drew scorn and fury from the establishment and admiring gasps from colleagues, when it named five young men as murderers. The headline read "Murderers: If We Are Wrong, Let Them Sue Us". The headline was prompted by the verdict of an inquest jury that black teenager Stephen Lawrence, who had been knifed at a bus stop, had been unlawfully killed in a "completely unprovoked racist attack by five white youths". The *Mail* ran the headline although the five had never been convicted. Lord Donaldson, master of the rolls, called on the paper to be prosecuted for common law contempt. But the attorney general cleared the paper of contempt. The justice system had already run its course.

The men were free to sue for libel, which they never did.

SCANDALIZING THE COURT

This is an ancient type of contempt, invented in eighteenth-century England to punish radical critics of the establishment. In Scotland, it is known by the delightful term of "murmuring judges", which conjures images of cloaked figures whispering around a cauldron.

It is defined as publishing material so defamatory of a judge or a court as to be likely to interfere with the due administration of justice, by seriously lowering the authority of the judge or court.

It exists solely to protect the administration of justice, not the feelings of judges, and writers have been robust and trenchant in their criticism of the judiciary. Charles Dickens led a campaign of press criticism against one magistrate (Mr Fang in *Oliver Twist*), which resulted in his dismissal from the bench in 1838.

In a celebrated Bahamian nineteenth-century case,[32] the Privy Council gave similar advice to Chief Justice Yelverton, who got into a squabble with an editor of the Nassau *Guardian* and an anonymous letter writer. The judge had written two letters to the newspaper addressing health issues of the town, which provoked a reader's response that contained sarcastic comments about the judge, such as "Difficult as it is, Mr Yelverton has mastered the problem of being great in little things", and chiding him for spending too much time out of the colony.

The editor Alfred Moseley was summoned to the judge's chambers and ordered to hand over the manuscript of the letter and reveal the identity of the writer, who called himself "Colonist". The editor refused and was sent to jail, but the Privy Council held that although the letter may have been the subject of libel proceedings, it did not amount to contempt.

Their Lordships remarked: "A judge who descends into the arena of municipal strife must expect and be prepared to put up with a fair measure of rough treatment in the combat, and Mr Yelverton would have consulted his own dignity and that of his office better if he had passed over and been content to live down any imputations that his critic's letter conveyed."

On the other hand, in 1890, Howard Gray of the *Birmingham Daily Argus* was fined when he described Justice Darling as an "impudent little man in horsehair" who was a "microcosm of conceit and empty-headedness". And the unkindest cut of all: "One of Mr Justice Darling's biographers states that 'an eccentric relative left him much money'. That misguided testator spoiled a successful bus conductor."[33]

It is unlikely that such abuse would constitute a contempt today because although personally abusive of the judge, it could hardly be said to interfere with the administration of justice.

Nowadays, many judges prefer to ignore even outrageous insults to them, perhaps embracing the advice Lord Ackner once gave to newly appointed judges:[34] "I said that I thought that the soundest advice was to grin and bear it, that they should bear in mind today's newspaper is tomorrow's fire-lighter and that this was one of the occupational hazards of being a judge."

Judges seemed to adopt that approach when the *Daily Mirror* ridiculed the injunction the House of Lords issued in 1987 in the *Spycatcher*[35] case by exhibiting the inverted photographs of Law Lords below the headline "You fools", and the more sober *Economist* ran a blank page where a review was meant to be with a boxed explanation that concluded, "The law is an ass."

Lord Diplock, in *Secretary of State for the Defence v. Guardian Newspapers Ltd*,[36] described this type of contempt as "virtually obsolescent". Nevertheless, it is occasionally defrosted and applied in the Commonwealth. In an 1899 case, Lord Morris, in language typical in offensiveness for the period, found this type of contempt was necessary to keep order in "small colonies, consisting principally of coloured population".[37]

In Singapore, proceedings were instituted against the writer, editor, publisher, printer and distributor of an article that had alleged that senior politicians were bankrupting their opponents by bringing defamation actions with the assistance of a "compliant judiciary".[38]

In Trinidad and Tobago, Patrick Chookolingo, the irreverent, sometimes obnoxious, editor of the *Bomb* weekly, was imprisoned by Hassanali J for twenty-one days for publishing a thinly disguised "short story" about bribery in the judiciary, entitled "The Judge's Wife".[39]

In St Vincent and the Grenadines, in 1987, the editor of the *Vincentian* barely escaped contempt proceedings after a columnist opined that there was no longer any separation of powers between the judiciary and executive and that politicians were influencing the outcome of court cases.[40] Justice Satrohan Singh described the article as "highly contemptuous", but the writer and editor apologized and the solicitor general sought leave to withdraw committal proceedings against the editor.[41]

In an extreme and rare case, the *Oriental Daily News,* a mass-circulation paper in Hong Kong, published a series of articles that was so abusive of the judiciary that Chookolingo himself might have run a blue pencil through it.[42]

The newspaper had earlier lost a court case dealing with its publication of indecent photographs. The articles referred to judges as "judicial scumbags"; "British white ghosts"; "tortoises having retreated into their shells"; and "having to run for cover like a rat in the gutter". The newspaper accused the judiciary of bias and persecution and acting as implements of the British government. Judges were "white-skinned pigs and yellow-skinned dogs who are evil remnants of the former [British] government". The paper also stridently declared its intention to attack the judiciary in every possible way to destroy its authority.

Finally, there was an active campaign of harassment against a particular judge: a team of reporters pursued him around the clock, with photographs and articles detailing his movements to and from court, the cases he was involved in, the times he left the court building and when he returned from lunch. He was advised in the newspaper not "to take any false steps". The editors were given a sentence of four months' imprisonment and fined HK$5 million.

Still, journalists need not be mealy-mouthed in their criticism of the judiciary. The words of Lord Atkins in the famous *Ambard* case[43] has become the battle cry of journalists: "Justice is not a cloistered virtue: she must be allowed to suffer the scrutiny and respectful even though outspoken comments of ordinary men."[44]

In that case, the editor, manager and part proprietor of the *Port of Spain Gazette* was fined $25 for publishing an article, which commented on the inequality of sentences, while referring to two cases in particular. The Privy Council found no evidence in the article taken as a whole that the publisher had acted with untruth or malice or that he imputed improper motives to those taking part in the administration of justice.

Journalists seeking general guidelines are often referred to Lord Salmon (in *Blackburn*[45]) who remarked: "No criticism of a judgment, however vigorous, can amount to contempt of court if it keeps within the limits of reasonable courtesy and of good faith."

However, if a judge is truly corrupt or his conduct biased (and the newspaper has the proof), surely it is in the interest of the administration of justice that he be exposed, even if the language employed falls short of courtesy.

GAGGING ORDERS

The court has inherent power to control proceedings and to protect the due administration of justice. Therefore, when a judge concludes that the revelation of certain material would seriously interfere with the administration of judges, the judge can warn the media that to publish such material would amount to contempt of court. The judge can also choose to hear the evidence in camera or order that it be written down but not stated in open court.

In 1996, in Trinidad and Tobago, during the "trial of the century" of Dole Chadee and his gang of henchmen for murder, Jones J told the media to refrain from publishing that one of the accused, Levi Morris, had pleaded guilty, turned state witness, and in return, his death sentence was commuted to life. Four days later, during jury selection, the *Mirror* published three articles, one written by Sharmain Baboolal and two by Ken Ali, which, when taken altogether, made it clear one of the accused had turned state witness. The two journalists were hauled before the court, given a summary trial and found guilty of breaching the gag order. Baboolal was fined but Ali was sentenced to fourteen days' simple imprisonment.

The matter eventually went all the way to the Privy Council, which, in 2004, ruled that the trial judge's order was justified, because the jury was likely to be influenced by publication of the plea bargain. So, the journalists were in contempt, not because of the gag order (which the judge had no power to make) but because they published material likely to prejudice a fair trial.

The decision has been described as giving half the cake to the judiciary and the other to the news media.[46]

INJUNCTIONS

Sometimes, parties who get wind of a news organization's plan to publish a damaging article threaten to go to court for an injunction, preventing the publication. Or after an initial publication, the aggrieved may seek to prevent further publication, for example, the continuation of a newspaper or television series.

To disobey an injunction is a contempt. But injunctions are harsh measures, and courts do not grant them just for the asking. Courts generally will not grant injunctions on the ground of libel where the publishers indicate they intend to prove the truth of the statement. The court must balance the importance of the constitutionally guaranteed freedom of free speech with the individual interest of the aggrieved party.

In Jamaica, Prime Minister Andrew Holness obtained an *ex parte* injunction preventing the rebroadcast of an investigative feature about his property ownership entitled "Big House",[47] aired on 30 May 2016, on Television Jamaica and presented by journalist Zahra Burton.[48] Justice Chester Stamp granted the injunction on 3 June, but the defendants applied to have the injunction discharged. After hearing legal arguments, Justice Stamp upheld the journalists' submission that an injunction should be granted in a defamation case before trial, only if the defendants had no substantive defence. He discharged the injunction on 3 August.[49] And Holness remained free to pursue his million-dollar libel claim against the television station and Burton. (The parties eventually resolved the matter out of court.)

In democratic countries, which uphold freedom of expression, the media must be free to publish, and if it publishes material that is false, mischievous or illegal, then it will stand the consequences. This is known as the principle against "prior restraint", which was invoked in the United States when the government learned that the *New York Times* intended to publish a set of army research papers, known as the Pentagon Papers, on American involvement in Vietnam.[50] It tried to injunct the paper on the ground that the material contained military and diplomatic secrets. The Supreme Court agreed that publication would harm the national interest and might even make the newspaper guilty of a criminal offence, but it had the right to publish and face the consequences. In refusing to stop the presses, the Supreme Court stated, "For without an informed and free press there cannot be an enlightened people."[51]

The Duke of Wellington, the British military hero who scuttled Napoleon for good, was much more succinct in his views on freedom of speech. When a discarded mistress threatened to publish love letters he had written to her, his famous reply was: "Publish and be damned."

Although the common law rule is that an interim injunction will be granted only where there is no arguable defence,[52] the Court of Appeal in Trinidad and Tobago recently decided that the ancient rule should not be followed in that jurisdiction and a more flexible approach was necessary.[53] The appellate court stated that the defendant would have to do more than assert such and such defence and show a proper basis for the proposed defence (without going into a full analysis). Once that is done, "the question then becomes: where does the greater risk of injustice lie, in granting or refusing an injunction?"[54] In most cases, the appellate court concluded, the "extraordinary weight" to be attributed to the right to free speech and freedom of expression would produce the same result as if *Bonnard v. Perryman* were applied.[55]

So much for trying to bolt the stable doors before the horse gallops out. However, where a defamation suit is successful, the judge may also grant a final injunction prohibiting further publication of material similar to the offending statements.

On 24 September 2004, a High Court judge in Trinidad and Tobago granted an injunction restraining the *Mirror* from "further publishing any statements similar to those contained in the article captioned 'HCU on a Tumble' . . . which suggests expressly or by implication that there is any reason for concern about the financial stability or integrity" of the Hindu Credit Union Co-operative Society Ltd.

On 1 October 2004, while this injunction was still in force, the *Mirror* published an article entitled "HCU Terror Tactics", which asserted that the prior article "describes the current state of affairs" at Hindu Credit Union. The article also expressed the *Mirror*'s intention to continue its "high standard of reporting the news without fear or favour".

On the 8 October 2004, while the injunction was still in force, the *Mirror* published an article entitled "Dookeran Warned HCU", referring to statements attributed to the former governor of the Central Bank, Winston Dookeran, warning Hindu Credit Union that unless it paid close attention to certain measures, it was likely to become a failed financial institution.

The newspaper was fined TT$150,000 and the director TT$30,000.[56]

OTHER CONTEMPT RISKS

The chief justice[57] is in control of all courts and may issue directions from time to time. Pay heed.

Taking photographs, even with a cell phone, within the courtroom or its precincts constitutes contempt.[58] Even in the press-friendly United States, the idea of photographers roaming the courtroom shooting pictures has been considered contrary to courtroom dignity and the administration of justice.

The ban on cameras includes the lobby area. In Jamaica, it is a criminal offence to photograph defendants on their way to or from court, as provided by Section 33 of the Criminal Justice (Administration) Act. Some people do not want their photographs taken at all, but journalists are entitled to be persistent and intrepid to get the job done. Be careful that you do not cross the line into molesting or intimidating witnesses or defendants.

In the English case of Simon Runting[59] a press photographer ran after a defendant and persisted for about two minutes in taking his photograph. The defendant had blocked his face with a newspaper and the photographer tried to get a shot from below, by holding the camera low and pointing at the defendant's groin. The incident ended with the defendant, unable to see where he was going, bumping into some scaffolding and then making a dash for it with the photographer in hot pursuit. The Court of Appeal ruled that although the photographer's behaviour was "offensive, rude, uncivilised and wholly reprehensible", it fell short of acts that were capable of interfering with the administration of justice. Had the photographer snatched the paper away from the defendant or pushed him into the scaffolding, the decision would have been different.

Do not take photographs of jurors at all. Sometimes, jurors must visit the scene of the crime. Be careful that their faces are not shown in photographs of the event. Using tape-recording devices and making sketches are also prohibited. However, journalists are usually given permission to use laptop computers in court. There is no prohibition on someone drawing a sketch from memory, however.

Television coverage of trials is not allowed. TV cameras have been allowed in Scottish courts under strict supervision since 1992, and the BBC in 2002 was finally given permission to film the proceedings of the appeal by Abdelbaset ali Mohmed al-Megrahi against his conviction in the *Lockerbie* case[60] after a long discussion. The actual trial was not televised. Judges tend to fear that televised coverage will lead to soap opera melodrama, as takes place in high-profile American trials, such as the O.J. Simpson case.

You can whisper discreetly but the court is not the place for chatting, giggling, chewing, sleeping – or reading. A reporter from southeast London learned that the hard way when he turned the pages of a broadsheet in front of him as he sat in the front row of the Canterbury Crown Court in May 2003. The judge threatened to send him to jail for contempt but accepted a grovelling apology instead, but not after the reporter was hauled before the bench and questioned about his journalistic experience and training before a packed court.

But it would be hard to top the example of Paul Griffin, a freelance reporter in England, who, in 1996 escaped jail after he "borrowed" photographs, showing a victim's injuries, from counsel's file during a court recess and took them to an alleyway where news agencies copied them. The Court of Appeal called the incident "reprehensible".[61]

CHAPTER 9

REPORTING PARLIAMENT

Night after night, I record predictions that never come to pass, professions that are never fulfilled, explanations that are only meant to mystify.

> —David Copperfield, on being a parliamentary reporter
> in the novel of that name by Charles Dickens

Like the courts, Parliament is a place of special importance for journalists. Allegations, often of the most grievous sort, can be made right and left on any matter of all.

No member of Parliament can be brought before the civil or criminal court for what the member says in parliamentary proceedings or in a report to the House of Parliament of which he or she is member; or to any parliamentary committee. This immunity is guaranteed in the various constitutions.[1] Where constitutions do not expressly say so, legislation provides for freedom of speech in Parliament.[2] Even where the member of Parliament may have exceeded or abused his or her privilege, such misconduct falls entirely within the jurisdiction of the Parliament itself.[3]

The news media's fair and accurate reports of the allegations and war of words are also protected. In fact, journalists sometimes prod members of Parliament to ventilate in Parliament matters that they are restricted in reporting. The protection of privilege is discussed in chapter 5, on defences.

COURT V. PARLIAMENT

Journalists grow nervous when there is a conflict between Parliament and courts of law. For example, a judge may grant an injunction prohibiting further repetition of a libel but a member of Parliament may nevertheless repeat the contentious statements in Parliament to ventilate an issue of public interest.

Or, a matter may be pending before the courts and therefore sub judice. Is the member of Parliament in contempt of court for discussing the court matter in Parliament? Will the journalist who reports the member of Parliament's statements in Parliament enjoy the protection of privilege in such circumstances?

In *Attorney General v. Times Newspapers*[4] a national Sunday paper in the United Kingdom published articles on the devastating effects of the drug thalidomide (which caused babies to be born with malformed limbs) while civil claims against the drug company were pending. On the attorney general's motion, the court granted an injunction restraining publication on the basis that such would be a contempt of court.

Although the newspaper's appeal was pending, the thalidomide tragedy was debated in Parliament with speeches reflecting the substance of the banned reports. On appeal by the newspaper, the Court of Appeal held that the law of sub judice that restrained publication did not apply in the unique circumstances of the national tragedy. The public interest in a matter of national concern far outweighed the possible prejudice to a party.

The members of Parliament were never in jeopardy. What is said in Parliament cannot be inquired into in a court of law. But Lord Denning still uttered words of caution: "It is desirable that the convention of Parliament as to matters sub judice should, so far as possible, be the same as the law administered in the courts."[5]

Here is the rationale:

> for this very good reason: as soon as matters are discussed in Parliament, they can be, and are, reported at large in the newspapers. The publication in the newspapers is protected by the law. Whatever comments are made in Parliament, they can be repeated in the newspapers without any fear of an action for libel or proceedings for contempt of court. If it is no contempt for a newspaper to publish the comments made in Parliament, it should be no contempt to publish the selfsame comments made outside Parliament.

Notwithstanding the protection of privilege, journalists can get in trouble in other ways when covering Parliament. The experience of being hauled before the Privileges Committee can be even more dreadful than being named a defendant in a libel action.

CONTEMPT OF PARLIAMENT

Erskine May described this as "any act or omission which impedes either member or officer of such House in the discharge of his duty, or which has a tendency directly or indirectly to produce such a result". Indirect tendencies can include disorderly conduct and articles that "bring the House into odium, contempt or ridicule or lower its authority".[6]

In similar thunderous tone, the Trinidad and Tobago Parliament, for example, describes contempt of Parliament like this: "Any offence against the authority or dignity of Parliament, including disobedience to its commands or libel against it or its Members."[7]

This power of Parliament to punish publications for such behaviour resembles the court's power to punish for scandalizing the judiciary. Referring to members in unflattering terms is not enough to invoke this power. If judges can stand to be criticized robustly, parliamentarians should expect no better treatment. In 1957, English journalist John Junor was rebuked for not checking his facts when he attacked members of Parliament's petrol allowances during the Suez Crisis.[8]

The Speaker dressed him down: "You did not seek, so the committee have found, to establish the truth of the article, nor did you appear willing to admit its obvious implications. Although given every opportunity to express your regret, you made what the committee were only able to regard as an entirely inadequate apology."

In 1983, Junor was as rambunctious as ever, when he described in the *Sunday Express* members of Parliament who called for pay raises for themselves as hypocrites with "greedy snouts in the trough". No one threatened him with contempt – although the House got back at him by debating Junor's own salary and highlighting the tax perks of Fleet Street editors, with one member of Parliament calling them the "most proficient expense-account fiddlers in the country".[9]

Before live broadcasts of parliamentary proceedings, when a member of Parliament made an outrageous statement, the Speaker would order that the statements were not to be reported and were to be expunged from the records. To disobey could result in contempt proceedings. In the case of live broadcasts, there is no time to expunge anything and the statements are aired for all the world to gasp. The media would not be at fault for the live broadcast but they have a duty to publish the denials that usually follow when offended parties appeal to the Speaker to have their response read into the record at the soonest possible subsequent sitting. To fail to do so would also result in the loss of the protection of qualified privilege.[10]

In modern times, the power to punish for contempt is usually invoked to reprimand journalists for breaching embargoes, such as publishing committee reports before they are laid in Parliament, which is a breach of House rules.

Journalists who breach this rule may be fined or banned from the Parliament for a period; the penal power of Parliament is to be used sparingly in the most exceptional circumstances where no other measure could protect members or the House from substantial interference and obstruction. In the United Kingdom, no one has been locked up since atheist member of Parliament Charles Bradlaugh in 1880.

In Trinidad and Tobago, on 9 October 2009 *Newsday* reporter Andre Bagoo and editor in chief Therese Mills had to appear before the Privileges Committee and were questioned. Both Bagoo and Mills said they were not thoroughly familiar with the rule that prohibited such premature publications and there was no formal training for parliamentary reports. Both refused to divulge the source of the leak. The committee recommended that Bagoo be banned from the media gallery for the remainder of the session,[11] and the newspaper had to publish an apology.

ACCURACY

You can also be hauled before the Privileges Committee for inaccuracies, even "innocent" ones. In Trinidad and Tobago, in the 1990s, an *Express* columnist and his editor were once so summoned because of a typing error (not committed by the columnist) that conflated the contributions of two members of Parliament. They explained the error and escaped sanction, other than the temporary interruption of their peace of mind.

To minimize the margin for error, reporters should be well acquainted with parliamentary proceedings. Where proceedings are televised, journalists must observe the House rules. Make sure you know the names and functions of the various officers of the Parliament (e.g., Leader of the House, the Whip, Speaker).

Get to the Parliament chamber on time. Note any obscure points, and at the end of proceedings, contact the House Speaker or sponsor of the bill, for example, for clarification. The clerk of the House or Senate is also a good checkpoint. Chairmen of relevant standing committees may also be contacted for help as well.

If you are caught out in your parliamentary reporting, a sincere apology and truthful explanation will probably suffice. Vow never to repeat the transgression, and after you are done squirming and grovelling, get on with the job – covering Parliament is another opportunity to witness history in the making.

As the most famous parliamentary reporter Charles Dickens noted, through the voice of the hero of *David Copperfield,* "I had heard that many men distinguished in various pursuits had begun life by reporting the debates in Parliament."

CHAPTER 10

ELECTION REPORTING

A politician for his public conduct may be criticised, held up to obloquy: for that the statute gives no redress; but when the man beneath the politician has his honour, veracity and purity assailed, he is entitled to demand that his constituents shall not be poisoned against him by false statements containing such unfounded imputations.

—Justice Gibson[1]

During election campaigns, rivals taunt and tease and engage in lively and colourful double entendre and repartee. As the political temperature rises, extremely vicious and damaging accusations may be hurled back and forth among candidates and supporters.

Do journalists get to report, without restraint, whatever is said on the hustings?

The law of defamation is not suspended during election campaigns. But the law affords some shelter for reporters under the umbrella of qualified privilege, which protects fair and accurate reports of bona fide public meetings and press conferences. (See chapter 5, "Defences", qualified privilege.)

Other occasions, such as an interview with a political candidate or an advertisement, will not be so protected when published. Some jurisdictions expressly say so in their legislation. For example, Section 6 of the Cayman Defamation Act reads: "A defamatory statement published by or on behalf of a candidate in any election to a local government authority or to the Legislative Assembly shall not be deemed to be published on a privileged occasion on the ground that it is material to a question in issue in the election."

So if they have no legal defence, journalists and media organizations may still be successfully sued for defamation when they publish the allegations made by candidates and party supporters. However, a defamation suit is a poor remedy when the outcome of an election hangs in the balance. By the time the case is heard, the false statements already may have distorted the campaign and wrecked the fairness of the election.

Through the Representation of the People Act (and equivalent legislation), the law imposes criminal penalties on anyone who tries to win votes through dishonest and false statements during election campaigns. Although some allowance has to be made for the cut and thrust of politics, outright lies are another matter altogether.

REPRESENTATION OF THE PEOPLE ACT

The court recognizes that freedom of expression is particularly important in the context of elections. In *Bowman v. United Kingdom:*[2]

> Free elections and freedom of expression, particularly freedom of political debate, together form the bedrock of any democratic system. . . . The two rights are inter-related and operate to reinforce each other: for example, as the Court has observed in the past, freedom of expression is one of the "conditions" necessary to ensure the free expression of the opinion of the people in the choice of the legislature. . . . For this reason, it is particularly important in the period preceding an election that opinions and information of all kinds are permitted to circulate freely.

However, freedom of expression has to be balanced against freedom of election. The primary objective of the Representation of the People Act is to protect the electorate from acts and statements that would damage the freedom and fairness of the election. The main illegal practice for journalists to be concerned about is publishing false statements about the personal character or conduct of an election candidate.

PERSONAL CHARACTER OR CONDUCT

For example, Section 124(1) of the Guyana Representation of the People Act[3] provides: "Any person who, before or during an election, shall for the purpose of affecting the return of any group of candidates, make or publish any false statement of fact in relation to the personal character or conduct of the candidates of that group or any of them, shall . . . be guilty of an illegal practice."[4]

The purpose of making or publishing the false statement must be seen to affect how many votes the candidate will get. The statement must be one of fact as distinct from an expression of an opinion or comment about a candidate. Even if the statement is not defamatory, you may still be in breach of the Representation of the People Act, for example, in a constituency where temperance is an issue, a statement that a candidate enjoys taking a drink.

A defence to prosecution for this offence is that the defendant had reasonable grounds for believing the statement was true at the time of publishing it – even if the statement is shown to be false. This differs from defamation and libel actions, where the defendant has to prove the statement is in fact true. The penalty is a fine and imprisonment up to one year.

The publishing of false statements is not limited to news reports and editorials, but can be contained in letters to the editor, cartoons and advertisements placed for and by candidates, as in *Abbas v. Yousef*[5] in 2010, in which a political advertisement was placed in the *London Bangla* paper alleging a rival mayoral candidate was a wife beater.

In a prosecution under the Representation of the People Act, a court has to decide whether the statement is about the personal character or conduct of the candidate, or a statement as to the political position or public conduct of the candidate. The law does not restrict a false statement about a candidate's political or public conduct. One explanation for that distinction is that statements on personal matters are more likely to deceive voters. The administrative court in *Woolas*[6] stated that the Parliament "trusted the good sense of the electorate to discount" false statements on political matters, but then added: "However statements as to the personal character of a candidate were seen to be quite different. The good sense of the electorate would be unable to discern whether such statements which might be highly damaging were untrue."

Statements about a candidate's family, religion, sexual conduct, business or finances are generally likely to relate to personal character. However, a statement of that kind may also bear implications for his conduct as a candidate, and will fall within the provisions of the statute. So be careful of cross-fertilization.

In *The North Division of the County of Louth*,[7] an Irish election court had to consider a large number of challenges to the result of an election in North Louth, one of which concerned breach of Sections 1 and 2 of the Corrupt and Illegal Practices Prevention Act 1895.

Gibson J stated: "A politician for his public conduct may be criticised, held up to obloquy; for that the statute gives no redress; but when the man beneath the politician has his honour, veracity and purity assailed, he is entitled to demand that his constituents shall not be poisoned against him by false statements containing such unfounded imputations."

It is not always easy to distinguish whether the statement is about the personal character or public conduct of the candidate. In deciding the matter, the court will ask the following questions:

- What is the meaning of the statements of which complaint is made?
- Do the statements amount to statements of fact?
- Are any such statements of fact in relation to the petitioner's personal character or conduct?
- Are such statements false?
- Did the respondent believe them to be true and have reasonable grounds for believing them to be true?

For example, a statement made simply about a candidate's conduct as a businessman might imply he is a hypocrite, as in *Bayley v. Edmunds*[8] or *Storey v. Doxford*.[9] As his conduct as a businessman relates to his personal conduct, such a statement is within the statute, subject to possible issues of proportionality to be determined in relation to the seriousness of the allegation.

However, a statement about a candidate's political position may well imply that he is a hypocrite or untrustworthy because of the political position he is taking. That is not a statement in relation to his personal character or conduct. It is a statement about his political position, though it might cast an imputation on his personal character.

In *R v. Eli Hanna*,[10] in Jamaica, the appellant was convicted by the resident magistrate in Kingston of making a false statement of fact on 17 July 1959, in relation to the personal conduct of Florizel Augustus Glasspole, a candidate during an election for the House of Representatives for the purpose of affecting the return of the said Florizel Augustus Glasspole, contrary to Section 105 (c) of the Representation of People Law.[11]

The statement was:

When you hear Mr Glasspole talking a lot of bulls over the radio why don't you write him a letter and question him as residents of this constituency what happen to the $8,000 that was entrusted to him by people in the United States for the people in Jamaica. Ask him what happen to that $8,000 and why it never reach to its destination, and see if as an intelligent people you are satisfied with his reply.

The appellant made this statement while addressing a public political meeting in support of his own candidature, and his speech was recorded by a tape-recording machine operated by the police.

At the trial, evidence was given by the Hon. Florizel Augustus Glasspole, who was returned as the successful candidate for the constituency, to the effect that the statement made by the appellant concerning him was false in several material particulars. Glasspole stated that in 1949 he visited the United States of America on a speaking mission on behalf of the People's National Party, of which he was a member, and that he collected from donors there the sum of $8,000 for this party. On his return to Jamaica, the money was left in his coat pocket, from which it was stolen by a man working at a dry-cleaning establishment to which the coat had been sent. On discovering the loss of the money, he made a report to the police, who recovered the full amount. The thief was arrested, tried and convicted by the resident magistrate in Kingston. The crown tendered in evidence a certified copy of the indictment and conviction.

Glasspole further stated that as soon as the police returned the money to him, he handed it over to the People's National Party. He emphatically denied that people in the United States had ever entrusted him with US$8,000 for the people in Jamaica and swore that any statement to this effect was false. The amount he had received was US$2,100, and it was not donated to "the people in Jamaica", but was given to him for his political party. The statement that the money had never reached its destination was also completely false.

Duffus J, in delivering the judgment of the appellate court, said there could be no doubt that the appellant's statement "assailed the honour, veracity and purity" of his rival, Glasspole. Merely placing the allegations in the form of questions did not deprive the false statements of their sting. The words used were in relation to the personal character and conduct of the candidate and were not "a mere argumentative statement of the conduct of a public man", as the appellant had contended. As the false statements were clearly made during an election for the purpose of affecting the return of a candidate at such election, the offence was proved as charged and the appeal failed.

In the United Kingdom, in 1992, there was a conviction under the Representation of the People Act after an individual published a leaflet that claimed that Jack Straw (who became Home Secretary in 1997 and Foreign Secretary in 2001) "hated Muslims". In 2007 Miranda Grell, a Labour candidate, was convicted after making allegations that her gay opponent, a Liberal Democrat candidate, was a paedophile and having sex with teenage boys. She was elected in the May 2006 local elections for the Leyton ward, but in September 2007 she went on trial for charges under the Representation of the People Act 1983 of making a false statement of fact about a candidate's personal character or conduct for electoral advantage. In addition to losing his seat, the opponent was verbally abused in the street, spat at and was forced to relocate to the North of England as a result of the false allegations, fearing for his life.

Grell admitted to outing her opponent and falsely claiming he had a nineteen-year-old Thai boyfriend (his partner was actually thirty-nine and Malaysian), though she denied making the false allegations of paedophilia to four residents. On 21 September 2007, she was found guilty on two counts, fined £1,000 and ordered to pay £3,000 towards the prosecution costs. On 30 November, Grell's conviction for making false statements about another candidate to gain electoral advantage was upheld. She vacated her seat and was banned from holding public office for three years. Liberal Democrat Winnie Smith won the by-election for Leyton ward on 14 February 2008.

Following the appeal verdict, Grell resigned from the Labour Party, her job working for the deputy mayor of London and her seat on the management committee of the Compass pressure group – but still pleaded her innocence.

In November 2010, an electoral court found Labour member of Parliament Phil Woolas to have breached the legislation by publishing false statements about the personal character or conduct of his rival that he had no reasonable grounds to believe to be true.[12] The false statements of fact were published in three election leaflets sent to voters shortly before the election. Members of the respondent's election team drafted those election leaflets, and he approved them. The false allegations linked the rival with Muslim extremists and suggested he obtained overseas funding. The judges ruled that a by-election for the seat should be held. Woolas said that he would apply for a judicial review into the ruling. In a statement released through his lawyer, Woolas stated that "this election petition raised fundamental issues about the freedom to question and criticise politicians" and that it "will inevitably chill political speech". But the judicial review failed to overturn the ruling of the election court.

LIBEL OR CRIMINAL SANCTION

The publisher of a false statement about an election candidate may, of course, face a libel action in the civil courts if it is believed to be defamatory. However, it is much easier to get an injunction against the repetition of false statements through criminal law than through a libel action, because the criminal sanction of the act allows a quicker remedy. Election candidates worried about their reputation will most likely choose this route to deal with any false allegations made about them. Candidates who can prove a *prima facie* ("at first sight") case that they have been maligned by such a false statement can obtain such an injunction. In a libel action, it could take months or years to resolve at trial or through settlements, owing to the legal rule against "prior restraint", which makes it difficult to get an injunction this way.

FALSE STATEMENT OF WITHDRAWAL

This offence is easy enough to spot and avoid. Section 74 of the Trinidad and Tobago Representation of the People Act provides: "A person is guilty of an illegal practice who, before or during an election, knowingly publishes a false statement of withdrawal of a candidate at the election for the purpose of promoting or procuring the election of another candidate."

Legislation throughout the region is in similar terms. The provision takes effect from the time formal notice is given that the election is to take place to the time the election ends.

EXIT POLLS

In the region, unlike the United Kingdom, there is no specific provision prohibiting the publication of exit polls before the polls are officially closed. However, such publication could be interpreted as seeking to influence voters during the hours when polls are open; it is also forbidden to ask people how they voted within one hundred yards of a polling station. For example, Section 87 of the Representation of the People Act (Grenada) stipulates that "during the hours that the poll is open upon polling day no person shall in, in any polling station or upon any road or in any public place within one hundred yards of any polling station, seek to influence any elector to vote or to refrain from voting for any candidate or political party or to ascertain from whom any elector intends to vote or has voted".

INCITING VIOLENCE

In the heat of an election campaign, parties and candidates often resort to vicious and offensive language against their opponent. Journalists should be careful when reporting speeches and other material produced by extremists, who may be treading into sedition.[13] And inciting violence. Guyana makes specific provision for this type of misconduct, and under Section 139D of the Representation of the People Act, it is an offence to commit any act or publish any statement that results or can result in racial or ethnic violence or hatred. The maximum penalty is two years imprisonment.

ELECTION TOOLBOX

Reporters Without Borders,[14] an international nonprofit organization, had published an online toolbox, entitled *Handbook for Journalists During Elections,* which provides practical responses to the multiple issues that arise during elections. It offers the following guidelines:[15]

> The dissemination of false rumours and allegations is another frequent tactic designed to weaken foes.
>
> A journalist often has no choice but to report these developments because they can help the voting public understand candidates' personalities. The responsibility for hateful, abusive rhetoric does not lie with a journalist but with the politicians whom a journalist quotes.
>
> All the same, a journalist is professionally obliged to:
>
> Report these quotes with strict accuracy and attribute them accurately.
>
> Seek a response from the target of the remarks in order to produce a balanced account.
>
> Offer no judgment, positive or negative, on what was said or on the response. But a journalist can include the comments of prominent independent figures and/or officials of human rights organizations in order to raise the issue of harm done to the community at large by hateful, abusive or defamatory political rhetoric.
>
> Note that a journalist's sense of social responsibility requires him to take the political environment fully into account. In extremely volatile socio-political situations, when reporting on hate speech that could endanger individuals, communities or the entire nation, one ethical option is to refrain from reporting such comments.
>
> Nevertheless, a journalist can use other professional approaches, such as editorials or columns, to warn politicians and citizens of threats to social peace, and of the divisions that generate conflicts and violence.

CHAPTER 11

THE BROADCAST JOURNALIST

In the new era, thought itself will be transmitted by radio.

—Guglielmo Marconi[1]

Radio and television journalists are subject to the same rights and restrictions as the rest of their profession. The law governing defamation, copyright, breach of confidence, contempt and other aspects of expression and communication applies to the broadcast media too.

Radio, in particular, has given rise to a proliferation of talk-show hosts, many of whom lay no claim to being journalists, but offer comments and opinions as well as statements of fact on many matters of public interest. They, too, have no immunity from those legal provisions.

However, the broadcast media must also operate in an environment of licences and codes that impose restrictions unknown to the print media.[2] Given the power of the broadcast media, these restrictions should be consistently reviewed and debated to ensure freedom of expression is not being eroded regulation by regulation, even in the smallest way.

Telecommunications authorities and broadcast commissions in the various Caribbean territories are responsible for regulating and monitoring licences to radio and television stations. They are also empowered to issue broadcasting codes or policies for licensees, although in some states, such as Trinidad and Tobago, no code has been implemented.[3]

Governments are not entitled to arbitrarily withhold licences – to silence critics, for example; denial could only be on constitutionally justifiable grounds.[4] Sometimes, licences are not renewed, though the stations are permitted to remain on air but then they can be abruptly closed.

In Trinidad and Tobago, for twenty years, the government and a broadcasting service fought over a radio licence. Central Broadcasting Services Ltd, operated by a Hindu organization led by a dyspeptic and controversial general secretary,[5] applied for a licence in 1999. The application was not refused – neither was it granted. The Privy Council, in July 2006, found that the government had breached the appellant's fundamental rights to equality of treatment and freedom of expression and described the government's behaviour as arbitrary and capricious. The licence was granted in September and the broadcasting service claimed damages for the delay. Boodoosingh J awarded the broadcasting service about TT$3 million, which triggered another costly court battle. The Privy Council upheld the award of damages in 2018.[6]

Where licences are granted, conditions or concessions are attached. Where licensees contravene the conditions, the commission or authority may require a licensee to justify its actions or specify remedial action, failing which, it may direct that an apology be issued. Ultimately, a failure to comply with directions given by the commission or authority may result in suspension of the licence by the relevant government minister upon the commission or authority's recommendation. Anyone who contravenes the regulations may also be liable to a fine and imprisonment.

Generally, licensees are prohibited from transmitting malicious, indecent or defamatory content or content that is derogatory of any race, colour, ethnicity or religion or in breach of any law of the land. For example, the Jamaica Broadcasting Commission administers the Television and Broadcasting Regulations, Section 31, which empowers the commission to issue directives to licensees. These directives prohibit licensees from transmitting:

- any statement or comment concerning race, colour, creed, religion or sex of any person that is abusive or derogatory or a pictorial presentation thereof except where same is contained in a news report or in a programme on matters of public interest or is an objective report;
- any malicious, scandalous or defamatory matter;
- any indecent or profane matter (with exception for adult programming between the hours of 11 p.m. to 4 a.m.); or
- any portrayal of violence that offends good taste, decency or public morality.

The Barbados Broadcasting Regulations[7] additionally prohibits transmitting any programme "presenting, promoting, advocating or endorsing a person, group or institution who claims, for the purpose of or during the programme, supernatural or psychic powers or the ability to foretell the future or to analyse the character of any person by supernatural or psychic means".[8]

In Grenada,[9] St Kitts and Nevis, St Lucia, and St Vincent and the Grenadines, no message that appears "dangerous to the security" of the state or "contrary to public order or decency" shall be accepted for transmission. In Trinidad and Tobago, Section 22 requires the concessionaire upon request by the Minister of National Security to "collaborate with the Ministry in all matters of national security".

POLITICAL AIRTIME

This is often a contentious issue, especially during general elections. Licensees are required to ensure fair and reasonable airtime for the broadcasting of political matters. For example, Section 7 (1) of the Barbados Broadcasting Regulations 2000 stipulates that the licensee shall ensure that there is "fair and reasonable allocation of time for the broadcasting of religious or political matters and matters relating to any industrial controversy".[10] Section 32 (2) of the Guyana Broadcasting Act 2011 states that in election time licensees in consultation with the Election Commission should afford political parties airtime.

In Trinidad and Tobago, an opposition politician successfully challenged the refusal of the only television station that was government owned to air a political broadcast.[11] In that case, the judge stated that the exercise of political broadcasting must be conducted openly and fairly, and "with maturity and in an attitude of willingness to assist political parties rather than hinder them".[12]

In states, such as Barbados and St Vincent and the Grenadines, where there is only one television station that is government owned, the station must nevertheless allow political parties airtime and abide by the constitution that guarantees freedom of expression.

Often, radio stations are aligned to or owned by political parties, and so the concept of "fair and reasonable airtime" is not a live one for radio. In St Vincent and the Grenadines, in 2000, an agreement was made between then Prime Minister James Mitchell and Leader of the Opposition Dr Ralph Gonsalves while walking along the beach in Grenada. Under the "Grand Beach Accord" the government-owned National Broadcasting Corporation radio station offers access to free airtime to the political parties during election time, but the offer is hardly taken up.

In Barbados[13] "government-reserved time" must not exceed more than 10 per cent of total broadcasting time and is not meant for political party campaigning or electioneering. The regulations provide: "Government-reserved time or additional time . . . shall not be used for any matter which is likely or is intended to further the interest of any political party or to promote the election to any public office (including election to membership of the House of Assembly) of any individual."

In addition to government-reserved time, the government has the right to require the licensee to broadcast any matter during times of emergency or "where it is determined that the matter is of such great national importance that it should receive full island-wide coverage".[14]

In Trinidad and Tobago also, concessionaires must grant free airtime (fourteen hours per calendar week) to the government to transmit any programme, announcement, information or other material that the government may require "as a matter of public interest" during the station's ordinary business hours.[15] The government may "reasonably declare any matter or event to be of public interest" and require the concessionaire to broadcast such matter or event.

The Guyana Broadcasting Act 2011 provides that licensees must comply with any ministerial notice to the National Broadcasting Authority to publish or refrain from publishing any matter specified by the minister responsible for broadcasting. An amendment specifies that "public broadcasting" programmes should be aired, up to sixty minutes each day, between the hours of 6 p.m. and 10 p.m. and include time allotted to presidential addresses and emergency notices or disaster warnings.

Although the aim of such clauses may be to secure broadcasters' cooperation in matters of national emergency, broadcasters complain that there is no definition of "public interest" or "national importance", and governments can too easily misuse this clause for cosmetic reasons and flagrant public relations. The Guyana amendment[16] seeks to fill the gap and defines "public service broadcasting" as the broadcast of a programme produced for the purpose of "informing and educating the public, and promoting policies and activities of the Government that benefit the public as a whole".

Another reason broadcasters frown at reserved airtime is that it conflicts with their high-advertising revenue programming periods. Indirectly, such conditions can hinder freedom of expression.

Faced with more regulation than the print media, broadcasters are often keen to discuss self-regulation, desirable for its own worth but also to stave off further government regulation.

The Trinidad and Tobago Publishers and Broadcasters Association has adopted a Code of Practice that the revived Media Complaints Council has ratified.[17] Trinidad and Tobago is the only English-speaking Caribbean country with a functioning media council.

CHAPTER 12

THE INVESTIGATIVE JOURNALIST

Freedom only to speak inoffensively is not worth having.

—Justice Stephen Sedley[1]

Gene Kelly, in the 1960 film *Inherit the Wind,* as an influential newspaper man covering a major trial, says to a prosecutor, "Mr Brady, it is the duty of a newspaper to comfort the afflicted and afflict the comfortable."[2]

That quote has been used humorously to sum up the spirit of investigative journalism. Investigation is at the heart of all good journalism but there is a deeper, broader approach that goes beyond the usual coverage of incidents and press conferences and seeks to expose malpractice and to right wrongs.

Sheila Coronel, a celebrated journalist from the Philippines, and a professor at Columbia School of Journalism, says investigative journalism is not daily beat reporting, leak journalism, single-source journalism or paparazzi journalism but it is watchdogging, exposing how law and regulations are violated and holding the powerful accountable.[3]

"The best investigative work", she writes, "exposes not just individuals, but also systemic failures. Investigative reports show how individual wrongs are part of a larger pattern of negligence or abuse and the systems that make these possible. They examine what went wrong and show who suffered from the mistakes. They probe not just what is criminal or illegal, but also what may be legal and overboard but nonetheless harmful."[4]

Investigative reporting is time-consuming, expensive, and its challenges criss-cross the fields of law and ethics. Journalists must daily confront such questions as whether they can use surreptitious methods to expose wrongdoing; whether they are entitled to withhold the truth or lie outright to discover important facts; and whether they can use telephoto lens to capture subjects in misconduct.

MEANS TO ENDS

Do the ends ever justify the means? Is it ever acceptable for a journalist to break the law to expose a bigger evil?

Such issues came into sharp focus during the *News of the World* phone-hacking scandal in the United Kingdom that led to the closure in 2011 of Britain's best-selling tabloid, a flurry of resignations, political strife and criminal charges against eleven individuals including four journalists, and the conviction of former editor Andy Coulson. Private investigators had intercepted thousands of communications of celebrities, politicians and crime victims, on the direction of news editors, in contravention of the Regulation of Investigatory Powers Act 2000.

Former UK director of public prosecutions Keir Starmer[5] said yes, journalists will be forgiven breaches of the law if there is sufficient public interest to do so, and he issued a list of guidelines as to how the public interest can be weighed.

Although journalists have no special status under the law, the public interest served by their actions is a relevant factor in deciding whether they should be prosecuted in an individual case.

So it is possible that a director of public prosecutions may decide not to prosecute a journalist who bought a small amount of marijuana to expose a drug-trafficking ring involving public officials. Or, bribing a public official might be forgiven if the bribe was for the purpose of exposing corruption.

At a 2012 parliamentary communications committee inquiry in the United Kingdom, Sky News reported that it purchased a firearm illegally to expose the person who was selling guns. The gun salesman was later convicted and the judge commended the journalists. Also, the *Sun* once sanctioned a reporter bribing an official in a magistrates' court because he was suspected of accepting bribes to remove driving offences from records. The official was later convicted of breaches of the Bribery Act.

According to the UK guidelines, criminal conduct by a journalist that may have a public interest defence could include:

- conduct capable of disclosing that a criminal offence has been committed, is being committed, or is likely to be committed;
- conduct capable of disclosing that a person has failed, is failing, or is likely to fail to comply with any legal obligation to which they are subject;

- conduct capable of disclosing that a miscarriage of justice has occurred, is occurring, or is likely to occur;
- conduct capable of raising or contributing to an important matter of public debate; and
- conduct capable of disclosing that anything falling within any one of the above is being, or is likely to be, deliberately concealed.

Looking at the seriousness of the criminality, prosecutors will assess:

- the impact on the victims of the conduct in question, including the consequences for the victims;
- whether the victim was under 18 or in a vulnerable position;
- the overall loss and damage caused by the conduct in question;
- whether the conduct was repeated or likely to continue;
- whether there was any element of corruption in the conduct in question;
- whether the conduct in question included the use of threats, harassment or intimidation;
- the impact on any course of justice (for example, whether a criminal investigation or proceedings may have been put in jeopardy);
- the motivation of the suspect insofar as it can be ascertained (examples might range from malice or financial gain at one extreme to a belief that the conduct would be in the public interest at the other); and/or
- whether the public interest in question could equally well have been served by some lawful means.

In the English-speaking Caribbean, directors of public prosecutions would observe similar considerations before initiating criminal prosecution. The guidelines are known as the "Full Code" test,[6] which requires consideration of the seriousness of the criminal behaviour, and whether there is a reasonable prospect of conviction. This test applies to all criminal matters, not just those involving journalists.

Journalists are not Gotham's caped crusaders. Do not dare think that it is okay to break the law willy-nilly because of some arrogant or misguided notion that you are saving the world.

Sir John Donaldson, in delivering the judgment of the English appellate court in a case of illegal wiretapping, remarked that yielding to a "moral imperative" does not excuse breaches of the law of the land, but such may be understandable and sometimes even praiseworthy. But such must be a rarity. He also warned that journalists are peculiarly vulnerable to confusing the public interest with their own interest: "Anyone who conceives himself to be morally obliged to break the law, should also ask himself whether such a course furthers his own interests. If it does, he would be well advised to re-examine his conscience."[7]

Before engaging in illegal or questionable conduct in the course of any investigation, journalists should have the approval of the editor and publisher. Clear guidelines should be prescribed with meticulous records maintained. Such would support a journalist's claim that the only reason the law was broken was to expose a greater wrong and no personal gain or sinister motive was involved.

EAVESDROPPING AND HACKING

Generally, legislation on interception of communication covers fixed and mobile telephone lines, emails, texts and pager messages. A person "intercepts" a communication by making some or all of the content of the communication available, while being transmitted, to a person other than the sender or intended recipient of the communication.

Only the police and security services are authorized to intercept communications, in the interest of national security, public health and safety, and to detect and prevent crime.

Belize, Jamaica, St Lucia, and Trinidad and Tobago have separate and comprehensive legislation on the interception of communication.[8] In the absence of such legislation, most countries rely on their Telecommunications Act, which generally prohibit unlawful access to any telecommunication or using the content of telecommunication having reason to believe it was obtained through unlawful interception or access.[9]

For example, Section 60 of the Grenada Telecommunications Act 31 of 2000 provides: "Any message transmitted over a public telecommunications network, shall be confidential and shall not be intercepted or interrupted without the consent of the sender, or without a court order made under this Act or any other enactment."

Antigua and Barbuda, Barbados, Cayman, Grenada, Jamaica, and Trinidad and Tobago also have legislation prohibiting unauthorized access to computer data, and altering, deleting or copying data.[10] Such conduct is punishable by imprisonment and a large fine. A more serious offence, attracting a longer custodial term (as heavy as twenty-five years in Jamaica) is "access to restricted systems" or "protected computers" concerning the director of public prosecutions, Central Bank, Customs, Elections and Boundaries, licensing authority, Lands and Survey, the forensic laboratory, defence force, police service, judiciary, Office of the Attorney General, national archives, inland revenue and educational examination material.

Remember, even if you do not conduct the hacking or interception yourself, you will still be liable in criminal law, if you pay, direct, encourage or assist someone else to do it for you. Even receiving computer data when you are not authorized to do so can give rise to a criminal charge. (See chapter 13, "Privacy and Confidence".)

But what about recording your own conversation with another party without that person's knowledge and consent? The definition of "intercept" in the Interception of Communications Act varies in the jurisdictions with such provisions. In Jamaica, it means "monitoring or modification of the network by means of which the communication is transmitted so as to make some or all of the contents available, while being transmitted to a person other than the sender of intended recipient of the communication".[11] So to record one's own telephone conversation for one's own use, let us say, for the purpose of double-checking one's notes, would not offend the legislation because there would be no intention to "make some or all of the contents available". The St Lucia and Belize legislation is in similar terms.[12]

Trinidad and Tobago's statute has a broader definition and does not refer to an intent to make the contents of any recording available to third parties. Section 5 defines "intercept" as "listening to, monitoring, viewing, reading or recording, by any means, such a communication in its passage over a telecommunications network without the knowledge of the person making or receiving the communication". During the parliamentary debates on the legislation, the primary concern was about limiting the ability of state agencies to intrude into the lives of citizens, except for good reason such as crime fighting. It was not raised whether journalists merely seeking to keep accurate records by recording their own conversations with a source or interviewee might be caught by the legislation.[13]

In the civil arena, covert recording of personal conversations can amount to breach of confidence or misuse of private information, where one seeks to publish or expose the contents. In the English case of D v. L,[14] a woman had secretly recorded her private conversations with her former domestic partner which concerned his sexual proclivities. An injunction was refused because there was no intent to publish; she had recorded the conversations for her own protection in the event of domestic violence proceedings. See chapter 11.

Apart from computer hacking and illegal interception of communication, journalists will be breaking the law by burgling premises to obtain documents or "evidence", forging identification to gain entry to premises, forging certificates to obtain employment to go undercover, impersonating a police officer and stealing mail.

COVERT OPERATIONS

On the other hand, it is not a criminal offence to fail to identify oneself as a journalist; to use a false name; or to pose as a patient to expose a negligent or corrupt medical service.[15]

One of the most celebrated cases of undercover reporting involve Nellie Bly, the alias of Elizabeth Cochran, a pioneering reporter at the *New York Record* who in the late nineteenth century feigned mental illness to gain admittance to the Women's Lunatic Asylum on Blackwell's Island to expose the horrific conditions. Campaigning and human rights groups such as Greenpeace and WITNESS have also used undercover techniques to expose such abuses as international human trafficking, exploited garment workers, the use of toxic chemicals and the illegal whale trade.

Such practices, however, are considered methods of last resort. As the Media Legal Defence Initiative, a non-governmental charity based in London that provides legal support to journalists, puts it: "Used in an ethical and focused fashion these are tools of last resort to expose the true practices of subjects of investigation, used to cast light on wrongdoing that cannot realistically be identified or proved by other means."[16]

So even when you have noble motives and you escape criminal or civil action, ethically, you may still be in a tangle. *Chicago Times* reporters in 1977 famously ran a bar undercover for six months to expose corruption and bribery among public officials that resulted in city and federal investigations and suspensions of city inspectors. They did not breach any law. Still, the paper did not win the Pulitzer, the most coveted award in the United States, for its "Mirage" (the name of the bar) series. The Pulitzer board considered there was a "mood of new moral stringency", and ethically ambiguous reporting methods had become less appealing. Ben Bradlee, the flinty and renowned managing editor of the *Washington Post,* put it tersely: "We instruct our reporters not to misrepresent themselves, period."[17]

PROTECTION OF SOURCES

A journalist's claim to be bound in honour not to reveal a source is of very long standing but there is no journalistic equivalent to the lawyer-client privilege. Journalists, like doctors and bankers who also claim confidentiality, can be compelled to attend court and give evidence under a subpoena or court order. To refuse to do so could constitute a contempt, and one could be fined or imprisoned. Where in a trial, a journalist seeks to claim protection of confidentiality, the issue should be raised in advance with the judge, in the absence of the jury, and a reasoned decision be made on the application.

Lord Donaldson commented, "In a parliamentary democracy, personal and professional honour surely equated with the acceptance of and obedience to the rule of law."[18] Disobedience to the law might be the honourable course if dictated by conscience and accompanied by a willingness to pay the penalty exacted by law.

In Bermuda in 1999, "Mr Marchant", an investigative journalist operating from Miami, Florida, appeared voluntarily for the claimants.[19] He was cross-examined by "Mr Potts", counsel for the defendants. The journalist was shown passages from *Inside Bermuda*, which he published, and Mr Potts asked him where he got his information. He refused to answer despite being directed by the judge on two occasions to do so. He also refused to write down the names of his sources. Mr Potts then applied for him to be committed for contempt.[20] The judge ruled that the journalist had a lawful excuse and dismissed the application for contempt, explaining that any restriction on journalistic confidentiality must be convincingly established before the court will punish the journalist.

In St Vincent and the Grenadines, in 1987, Attorney General Parnell Campbell, who was also minister of information, tried to smoke out the identity of "Quo Vadis", who had written a contentious article in the *Vincentian* newspaper that appeared to ridicule the judiciary. The writer was threatened with legal action and urged, via the government-controlled NBC radio station, to reveal himself to the attorney general who would keep his identity confidential. The public reacted with humour and fascination; stickers declaring "I am Quo Vadis" appeared everywhere.

Less amused was Justice Satrohan Singh who scolded both writer and attorney general. He had made no agreement with the writer, and he considered it an affront to judicial independence and integrity for the attorney general to attempt to do so. He then named the writer and publicly chastised him.[21]

In defamation actions, however, the so-called newspaper rule has developed through the common law. As early as the nineteenth century, the courts recognized a rule that in a defamation action, a defendant ought not to be forced to disclose who supplied the material for the offending publication. Only in exceptional circumstances should the rule be departed from.[22]

The rationale for the rule is discussed in *Hodder v. New Queensland Newspapers Property Ltd,*[23] where Davies J.A. and Byrne J in their joint judgment state: "There is a public interest in the free flow of information on matters of general concern. An apprehension that exposing confidential sources prejudices that interest by diminishing the media's capacity to report crimes, official misconduct or other public dangers and abuses largely accounts for the 'newspaper rule' of practice."

The rule is now reflected in civil proceedings rules. For example, Section 69 (7) of the Jamaican Supreme Court Civil Proceedings Rules states that in a defamation claim where the defendant is relying upon the defences of fair comment on a matter of public interest or privilege, the claimant may not make a request for "information as to the defendant's sources of information or grounds for belief".[24]

Within the newsroom, however, editors may have a policy that journalists disclose their sources to their editors. If so, the editor, too, is bound by the honour code not to reveal the identity of the source. The court can call upon the editor as well as the journalist to name names. Journalists can decline to accept information from sources unless they agree to be identified. Because once you have given your word, you should never break it. So if you think a jail cell is not for you, think carefully before you make promises you cannot be trusted to keep.

Also, beware of unintentionally exposing your source when using email, texts and digital documents that may have all kinds of electronic clues hidden in there.[25] The hiding place of fugitive computer programmer John McAfee who was named as a person of interest in a gunshot killing in Belize was accidentally disclosed by *Vice* magazine in 2012, when it braggingly posted a picture of McAfee, entitled "We Are with John McAfee Right Now, Suckers." The picture still contained the EXIF geolocation metadata. So the post revealed that it was captured with an iPhone 4S as well as the exact location in Guatemala where it was taken. He was eventually deported to the United States.

Granada Television got itself in a vice when it acquired from a source secret documents belonging to British Steel Corporation in breach of confidence and copyright.[26] British Steel obtained a court order that restrained further publication. Solicitors' letters were exchanged and Granada delivered up the documents but not before removing bits that, presumably, exposed the source to whom Granada had promised invisibility. Granada was ordered to reveal its source but appealed to the House of Lords.

The House of Lords held that the "media of information and the journalists who write for them" had no public interest immunity that shields them from the obligation to disclose their sources of information in a court of law, where the court in its discretion considers the disclosure necessary. The court held that the claimant was entitled to discovery because Granada had become involved in the wrongdoing of the source by mutilating the documents so as to prevent the claimant his remedy in taking legal action against the informer. The court said that by its reprehensible act of mutilation, Granada was disentitled to immunity.

In the end, the source "outed" himself to the *Sunday Times*[27] and British Steel dropped its claim and Granada dropped its appeal to the European Court of Human Rights.

THE *GOODWIN* CASE

In the United Kingdom, William Goodwin, a trainee journalist employed by the *Engineer,* put this notion of journalistic confidentiality to the test. In 1989, he had managed to obtain privileged information concerning a UK-based company called Tetra Ltd. He decided not to publish the information, however, but to seek comment from Tetra. Thus alerted, Tetra commenced legal proceedings against Goodwin and managed to obtain a publication ban as well as an order for Goodwin to reveal his source. The information Goodwin had managed to lay his hands on was contained in a corporate plan, of which only eight copies existed. Tetra argued that it needed to know who supplied Goodwin with the information to prevent any future leaks. Goodwin refused to reveal his source, and was cited for contempt of court. He was fined £5,000. The House of Lords upheld the citation, and Goodwin took his case to the European Court on Human Rights in Strasbourg.

The European Commission decided in Goodwin's favour.[28] It held the citation for contempt of court to be a violation of the freedom of the press as guaranteed in Article 10 of the European Convention on Human Rights. It was found that the protection of confidential sources was one of the essential means that enabled the press to perform its function of public

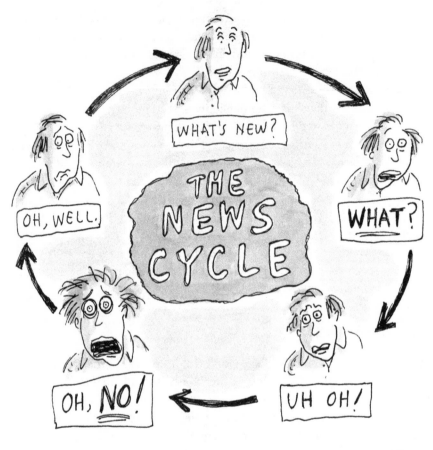

watchdog, and that disclosure of sources could be ordered only under exceptional circumstances. In the Goodwin case, the court found that no such circumstances existed.

The case was then heard before the full European Court on Human Rights. The court essentially maintained the commission's judgment, while adding that Tetra's main goal was to minimize harm to its company. This goal had already been reached by obtaining an injunction for the publication. The court was not convinced by the United Kingdom's arguments that Tetra's corporate interests outweighed the interests of free speech in this case, and consequently found that the UK courts had not properly balanced Goodwin's rights against the rights of Tetra.

The case is a landmark case, in that the problem of protecting journalists' sources had not been before the European Court of Human Rights yet. But the court was heavily divided on the issue – it was split eleven votes to seven.

WHISTLE-BLOWERS

Jamaica enacted the Protected Disclosures Act 2011 to protect employees from civil or criminal proceedings or any disciplinary proceedings who, in the public interest, make a protected disclosure to expose misconduct. Disclosures of a criminal offence, non-compliance with legal obligations, danger to health and safety of employees and damage to the environment are protected. Such disclosures are not to be regarded as inconsistent with the employee's obligations of confidentiality or secrecy. Such legislation is in keeping with international anti-corruption obligations.[29]

The legislation provides, however, that the disclosures are to be made in accordance with the internal procedure or where there is none, to "prescribed persons" such as the commissioner of police, director of public prosecutions, Bureau of Standards, attorney or ombudsman. You will notice that "journalist" is not included in the list of "prescribed persons". So the law does not shield employee leaks to the news media.

There is no protection if the employee commits an offence by making the disclosure – for example in breach of the Official Secrets Act 1911 and 1920.[30]

OFFICIAL SECRETS

The Official Secrets Act 1911, which was rushed through the English House of Commons in one day, when fears over German spying were escalating, was passed down to its colonies. In 1920, with similar haste, the act was amended to create additional powers, such as the right to exclude the public from a trial under the act on the basis that the publication of evidence would endanger national security. Also, Section 7 makes it a crime to attempt to commit an offence under the act or to incite someone else to do so.

The former British possessions that have never repealed the Official Secrets Act 1911 and 1920 include the Bahamas, Barbados, Jamaica, St Kitts, St Lucia, St Vincent, and Trinidad and Tobago.

Under the spy legislation, it is a crime for government employees to disclose any code word, password, document or information relating to security or intelligence, or any information employees obtained owing to their position or office. In particular, Section 2 provides that those receiving the information also commit an offence, if they had reasonable ground to believe it was obtained in contravention of the act.

There are no exceptions for intrepid journalists and no "public interest" defence. Also, the act is so broadly drafted, it means that a civil servant who discloses how many cups of tea are consumed in his office is guilty of an offence.

Viscount Burnham, during the passage of the Official Secrets Act 1920, raised concerns about the dangerously wide section and the vulnerability of the news media: "I do not know a single editor of a national paper who from time to time has not been in possession of official documents which have been brought into his office, very often not at his own request, and which it may be inconvenient to the Minister of the responsible Department should have gone out."[31]

One of the most controversial prosecutions was against Jonathan Aitken, a prospective parliamentary candidate, and the *Sunday Telegraph* in 1971 for publishing Foreign Office documents related to the Labour government's policy towards the Nigerian civil war. [32]Aitken said he had a duty to disclose the information in the interest of the state. He was acquitted of all charges. The trial judge also said that Section 2 should be "pensioned off" and replaced with a measure that provided greater clarity.

In 1984, Sarah Tisdall, a junior civil servant, was jailed for anonymously leaking two government documents to the *Guardian*. The documents concerned the arrival date of cruise missiles at Greenham Common and outlined defence minister Michael Heseltine's tactics for handling the announcement in Parliament and the press. The government also brought legal action against the newspaper, seeking an order requiring the newspaper to reveal its source. The *Guardian* complied with a court order to hand over the documents, which were identified as coming from a Foreign and Commonwealth Office photocopying machine.[33] The machine led to Tisdall, who pleaded guilty to a charge under Section 2 of the Official Secrets Act 1911. She was sentenced to six months in jail, but was released after four months.

But that sort of thing will not happen here in the Caribbean, right?

In 1976, during a state of emergency in Jamaica, a government minister and a permanent secretary were prosecuted under Section 2 of the act for conspiring (with people unknown) to communicate with other people a Cabinet document, which discussed the economic plight of Jamaica.

A copy of a Ministry of Finance "Cabinet submission" had fallen in the hands of the Leader of the Opposition Edward Seaga who, in a radio political broadcast, quoted from the document. The content of the confidential document was subsequently published verbatim in the *Daily Gleaner*.

Suspicion fell on the Ministry of Lands and Natural Resources as the source of the leak, and Allan Isaacs, the minister, and his permanent secretary, Horace Hardie-Henry, were put on trial. The Cabinet document was retrieved from the newspaper editor and used in evidence at the trial. Isaacs was acquitted while Hardie-Henry's conviction was overturned on appeal. The prosecution had failed to prove that the copy in the possession of the newspaper was a direct copy of the original stencilled Cabinet submission.[34]

Media associations, human rights organizations and politicians have repeatedly called for the removal of the Official Secrets Act, describing it as an oddity from days when government took place behind closed doors, in contrast to the new age of transparency. Such outdated legislation sits uncomfortably with freedom of information legislation and, in Jamaica, with the whistle-blower provisions.[35] Although prosecutions may be rare, until the legislation is repealed, it remains there in the shadows, like a poltergeist waiting to jump out and shout, "Boo!"

TRESPASSING

Trespassing is a civil matter.[36] There is no criminal charge of entering a front porch, for example, without invitation – otherwise the jails would be overflowing with every door-to-door salesperson, deliverer of junk mail and religious evangelist. Merely setting foot on someone's property even without invitation will not justify civil action. Trespass is an unjustifiable interference with land that is in the possession of another.[37]

Where there is an unlocked gate, journalists and other visitors are entitled to walk up the garden path and knock on anyone's door to enquire whether they may be admitted to conduct their lawful business. If asked to leave, then they must do so. Occasionally, an occupier of a household may grant a journalist or any visitor permission to enter the property, but the occupier may not be the person authorized to give such permission. Once the person entitled to give the permission withdraws it, the journalist must leave the property.[38]

It is risky for journalists to remain on property when they discover only minors are present and there is a likelihood the adult occupiers would not authorize or appreciate the visit. If, of course, the journalists are there to expose child abuse or neglect or some other matter of public interest, then one might be loath to think entry was unjustified.

Journalists are also entitled to stand on public property, which, by the way, their taxes support, and make observations and take photographs of people or of a private residence. They have no legal requirement that they must ask permission first. And if they can manage it, they are also able to fly overhead and take aerial photographs.[39]

Journalists may also attend public meetings, such as those held by local government councils. The United States provides an example of the almost comical extent some officials may go to in preventing a non-compliant journalist from reporting on their deeds, in *McBride v. Village of Michiana*.[40] Officials of a village council threatened to delay the start of the meeting until the reporter left; they threatened to bodily remove her; and they removed the press table. She also reported that on one occasion an official threw a chair at her. McBride stood her ground, and resorted to legal action against the officials.

The police are not entitled to seize film, cameras, notebooks or any property of journalists, unless they are making an arrest and such material is evidence in a criminal matter. To push, strike or point a weapon at a person, whether a journalist or a candlestick maker, is an assault. Words can also constitute an assault if they cause a person to be fearful. Be careful, though, not to obstruct the police in the lawful execution of their duty.

PHOTOGRAPHY

When on public property, such as streets and squares, you are entitled to take photographs of people, animals, buildings and objects. When on private property, if you are asked not to take photographs, please comply. Even public buildings may have private areas, such as patient wards. To disobey requests to leave or stop photographing would mean you are trespassing.

The right of photographers to click in public areas, or in the absence of trespass, in private areas, has been made clear by the 1918 English case of *Sports and General Press v. Our Dogs Publishing Co.*[41] The Ladies Kennel Club had purported to sell the exclusive rights to *Our Dogs*, a weekly journal, to photograph and publish its dog show. A freelance photographer who had bought a ticket captured the event, much to the embarrassment of the Ladies Kennel Club, which was unable to prevent the rival paper from using the photographs. Horridge J stated: "In my judgment, no one possesses a right of preventing another person photographing him any more than he has a right of preventing another person giving a description of him."

The Ladies Kennel Club, could have, had it wanted to, made it a condition of admission that no one take photographs, and it could have printed that condition on the tickets.

There is no law to prevent a photographer from taking pictures of police officers, soldiers and security officers as they go about their duties, so long as you do not behave unreasonably. However, if the police order you not to enter an area, you will be risking arrest and prosecution (for obstructing police in the course of their duty) by not complying, whether or not the property is private or public. Military installations, police stations and prisons will prohibit taking photographs in certain areas for security reasons.

Members of the public, witnesses in court matters, defendants and prisoners have no right to pictorial privacy. But juvenile defendants and juvenile witnesses are protected, and their photographs should not be published. No photos within the courts or lobby of the courthouses or halls of justice, please – without the express permission from the chief justice.

The Connecticut Appellate Court upheld the conviction of a newspaper photographer for interfering with a police officer's performance of a duty.[42] The journalist was videotaping from the centre of the westbound lane and the police officer repeatedly asked him to move to the shoulder of the roadway. The police had been securing the scene to preserve evidence while trying to maintain limited traffic flow. The photographer disregarded the instructions, saying he had a constitutional right to be there, and the police officer had no right to make him move. He was then arrested.

Irascible Trinidad and Tobago attorney-at-law Clyde Crevelle was convicted of assaulting *Guardian* photographer Brian Ng Fatt, by spitting on him on 10 August 1999, in the precincts of the Port of Spain Magistrates' Courts. Ng Fatt was on duty, along with other media photographers, covering a case involving Crevelle and senior public servant John Prince. Crevelle became annoyed with Ng Fatt who had been attempting to take his photograph.

On 21 August 2001, Magistrate Gail Gonzales ordered him to pay Ng Fatt TT$400 in compensation. The magistrate, however, reprimanded and discharged Crevelle under Section 71(b) of the Summary Offences Act, which meant that no conviction would be recorded against his name. The magistrate's decision was upheld on appeal but Hamel-Smith J commented that the media should observe a person's wishes not to have his photograph taken. [43]

Courtesy certainly goes a long way in defusing emotional issues but if journalists meekly awaited the permission of people in the public domain before taking their photographs, their jobs would become impossible.

Standing on public property but using long-lens cameras to capture private moments in private property, such as hotel bedrooms, is a controversial area. There is no tort of invasion of privacy, but "misuse of private information" is an actionable wrong (discussed in chapter 13), and media associations heavily frown upon such conduct. It could be forgiven if the objective is to expose corrupt or illegal practices in the public interest and no other means is likely to be successful.[44]

Section 10 of the Grenada Electronic Crimes Act 2013 creates the criminal offence of "violation of privacy", committed by capturing, transmitting or publishing, without lawful excuse or justification, images of the genitals, pubic area, buttocks or female breasts of a person (naked or in undergarments) in circumstances where the individual has a reasonable expectation of privacy. Section 8 of the Antigua Electronic Crimes Act is similarly worded, referring instead to capturing an image of the private area of a person "in a vulnerable position". St Vincent and the Grenadines Cybercrime Act 2016[45] refers to the "image of the private area" of another person without his consent where the other person has a reasonable expectation that "he could disrobe in privacy or his private area would not be visible to the public regardless of whether he is in a public or private place".

The practice of capturing private moments could also bear the quality of breach of confidence (which is discussed further in chapter 13). In *Hellewell v. Chief Constable of Derbyshire*,[46] Laws J said:

> If someone with a telephoto lens were to take from a distance and with no authority a picture of another engaged in some private act, his subsequent disclosure of the photograph would, in my judgment, as surely amount to a breach of confidence as if he had found or stolen a letter or diary in which the act was recounted and proceeded to publish it. In such a case, the law would protect what might reasonably be called a right of privacy, although the name accorded to the cause of action would be breach of confidence. It is, of course, elementary that, in all such cases, a defence based on the public interest would be available.

HARASSMENT

"Doorstep 'em!" That's the common tactic of journalists who encounter reluctant subjects. It means positioning yourself at a place where the subject is bound to cross your path. Outwitted, the subject can either duck and run or stand up and face a persistent journalist. So when journalists hear for the umpteenth time that the subject is "in a meeting", they may just take a seat in the waiting area, in the knowledge that the subject is bound to come up for air eventually – unless the subject clambers out the bathroom window.

When does persistence trespass into the dangerous area of stalking or harassment? *Thomas v. News Group*[47] decided that the persistent exercise of free speech could fall within the definition of "harassment". In that case, the *Sun*, the English tabloid, published a torrent of articles about a police clerk, who had complained against four police officers for their comments to a Somali refugee who had been robbed. Comments included "What is this country coming to? We let everyone in" and "They should be shot." The *Sun* published readers' letters attacking the whistle-blower clerk, and later admitted that the articles were inflammatory and aggressive. The paper also identified the station to which the clerk was assigned, and the angry readers sent a bundle of hate mail to her. In the first ruling of its kind, the Court of Appeal held that harassment can occur by repeated newspaper publication.

Some jurisdictions have enacted anti-stalking provisions, which prohibit intentionally alarming or causing a person distress by engaging in a "course of conduct" that involves following, taking photographs, stopping or accosting the person; watching, loitering or hindering access to or from the person's residence, workplace or place frequented by the person; making contact with the person whether by telephone, computer, post or gestures.[48] Behaving in such manner to people in familial or personal relationships with the subject is also prohibited.

In 2009, musician Amy Winehouse won a court ban on paparazzi at her home under the UK Protection from Harassment Act 1997.[49] The same year, singer Lily Allen obtained an injunction to restrict photographers who had been pursuing her for weeks, culminating in a car collision; even then the photographers continued to pursue her on foot after she got out of her vehicle.

It is a defence that the behaviour in all the circumstances was reasonable. This defence is the journalist's life jacket. The case of *Howlett v. Holding*[50] illustrates the point. A millionaire launched a campaign of harassment over a four-year period against Jennifer Howlett and said in libel proceedings that he intended to cause her "living hell" as retribution for publicly commenting, in her then capacity as a councillor of Castle Point, on a pending planning application by the millionaire's company. He trailed banners from his aircraft near the claimant's home, referring to her in abusive and derogatory terms; he dropped leaflets in the neighbourhood and he had her watched at various times.

The court held that the claimant was not seeking to restrain the millionaire's right to free speech, but that "Mrs Howlett's right to lead a peaceful life and to enjoy her privacy are also to be protected".[51] Injunctive relief was granted to Mrs Howlett.

The courts appreciate that minor irritations are bound to occur among people, and it is a question of reasonableness when considering whether someone has crossed the boundary from the regrettable to the unacceptable. In *Majrowski v. Guy's and St Thomas' NHS Trust*,[52] Lord Nicholls further explained:

> Courts will have in mind that irritations, annoyances, even a measure of upset, arise at times in everybody's day-to-day dealings with other people. Courts are well able to recognise the boundary between conduct which is unattractive, even unreasonable, and conduct which is oppressive and unacceptable. To cross the boundary from the regrettable to the unacceptable the gravity of the conduct must be of an order which would sustain criminal liability.

ANTI-CRIME SECRECY

Particularly in the area of financial regulation, it has become a criminal offence for employees and law enforcement officials to leak secret or confidential information.

Financial organizations have been forced to become increasingly vigilant about preventing and detecting money laundering, and financing terrorism and organized crime. Banks have to report suspicious activities, such as unusually large deposits, to financial intelligence units. It is a criminal offence for employees of banks, other financial institutions and the police who may be investigating the suspicious transactions to disclose material obtained in the course of their duties. Tipping off people who are under investigation for money laundering, in a manner likely to prejudice the investigation, is also an offence under Proceeds of Crime Act.[53]

For example, under Section 48 (2) of the Barbados Money Laundering and Financing of Terrorism (Prevention and Control) Act 2011, any person who receives reports or information under the act or who is involved in the administration or enforcement of the act shall regard as confidential and secret all documents, information or matters disclosed and received. To disclose is a criminal offence punishable by a fine of BDS$100,000 or imprisonment for five years or both. And by Section 48 (7), no person shall disclose any information that will

identify or tend to identify the person who made a report on a suspicious transaction or the person who handled the transaction that gave rise to the report.[54]

The Cayman Islands, which are known for their offshore financial centres,
put confidentiality on a statutory footing by virtue of the Confidential Relationships (Preservation) Law (2015 Revision). The law codified the banker-
client duty of confidentiality and extended it to other professional relationships
including financial businesses generally. It imposed criminal penalties on
anyone who divulged or threatened, offered or attempted to divulge or wilfully
obtained or attempted to obtain any confidential information. So it was an
offence even to try to get the information.

The law was criticized as too broad and unnecessarily draconian, and there
were calls to amend it, removing the criminal sanction.[55] It was soon repealed,
and the Confidential Information Disclosure Law 2016 was enacted; it is no
longer a criminal offence to disclose confidential information, and there is a
"whistle-blower" defence in some circumstances.

Therefore, anyone who, in good faith and in the reasonable belief that the
information is substantially true, discloses confidential information relating
to the commission of a criminal offence, failure to comply with a legal obligation, a miscarriage of justice or corruption, dishonesty or serious maladminis-
tration will now have a defence to any action against him or her.

The "whistle-blower" defence is also available for those disclosing confidential information where there is a serious threat to the life, health or safety
of a person or a serious threat to the environment. Without the criminal sanction, individuals and companies remain free to seek remedies in civil courts
for breach of the duty of confidence.

Journalists reporting on such subjects should thoroughly research the
relevant legislation and seek legal advice before ploughing in. Your source
could be prosecuted for leaking sensitive information or you yourself may
be committing an offence by publishing such material. You could also be liable
for breach of confidence and misuse of private information (discussed further
in chapter 13). Though such action is rare – financial organizations do not
want it publicized that they have sprung a leak, and legal action can also be
prolonged and costly – you should be careful where you tread.

Is the report truly in the public interest and not mere titillation? Can the
report be written or broadcast without making it known where the information came from? Have you done all you can to protect your source?

With the escalation of gangland warfare and the phenomenon of prosecution witnesses being killed, several states have introduced witness

protection programmes in which participants are relocated and their identities concealed. In the Bahamas, Jamaica, and Trinidad and Tobago, under the Justice Protection legislation, it is an offence punishable by a fine or imprisonment to disclose information about the identity or location of a participant in the witness protection programme or any information that compromises the safety and security of a participant or the integrity of the programme.

It is also an offence for participants (past or present) to disclose, without authorization, the fact of their participation, information about the way the programme operates or any details of any agreement the participant may have signed.[56]

SEARCH WARRANTS

Journalists' own good work can come back to haunt them. When journalists film riots and other violent confrontations, the police may want to use footage to identify suspects and as evidence at trial. A polite request may be sufficient. But occasionally, the police obtain search warrants to search the newsroom, journalists' desks and files, and to seize material relevant to their investigation.

In deciding whether a warrant to search media premises should be issued, the court will weigh a number of factors, including whether the search and seizure would inhibit the media's ability to carry out their functions as news gatherers and disseminators. The court has to strike a balance between the competing interests of the state in the investigation and prosecution of crimes and the right to privacy of media in the course of their news gathering and news dissemination.

The police would have to show they have exhausted alternative sources, such as their own closed-circuit television cameras, to obtain the information. If the material sought has already been broadcast or published in whole or part by the news media, the court is more likely to issue a warrant. And once a warrant is issued, if the search itself is conducted unreasonably, that may render the search invalid.

Issuing a warrant to search media premises is not a step to be taken lightly by courts because of the vital role the media play in a democratic society. In *Edmonton Journal v. R*, where the police were seeking documents and videos, Dixon J remarked: "The media have a vitally important role to play in a democratic society. It is the media that, by gathering and disseminating news, enable members of our society to make an informed assessment of the issues which may significantly affect their lives and well-being."[57]

In *Television New Zealand and Another v. the Police*,[58] at a national ceremony commemorating the signing of a treaty, the television companies each
shot about twelve hours' worth of film that included acts of disruption by
protesters, such as comments and conduct offensive to the prime minister and
governor general, spitting at the governor general and treading on the New
Zealand flag.

The police obtained a warrant to search the media premises for film of the
ceremony as evidence of offences, such as disorderly conduct and assault, and
offenders' identities.

Tapes were seized but the television stations obtained an order preventing
the police from using the tapes and sought a declaration that the search and
seizure had been invalid because the warrant was overbroad, there were insufficient grounds for issuing it and it infringed freedom of expression and the
right against unreasonable search and seizure guaranteed in the Bill of Rights.

Fisher J held that even if the search warrant was justified, media search
warrants were in a special category because they could have adverse consequences on the media, such as drying up confidential sources, promoting non-
cooperation with or violence to the media, requiring self-imposed censorship
and causing disruption to media outlets.

Such searches required special controls to protect confidentiality and minimize intrusion. Search warrants should be for "critically important" evidence
that cannot reasonably be obtained otherwise. They should be limited to
records of public events and should be refused for minor or non-serious
offences.

In that case, the judge held that although the warrants were overbroad,
the way the police conducted the search was not oppressive or unreasonable
and conformed with the Bill of Rights requirements that should have been
included in the terms of the warrant in the first place.

In such cases, the news outlet is viewed as an innocent third party. In other
situations, the police are investigating alleged offences by the news outlet itself.

In Trinidad and Tobago, police in 2011 searched the premises of CCN-TV6,
seizing a view of an apparent sexual assault on a minor that was aired on the
popular *Crime Watch* television show. The host of the show subsequently
pleaded guilty to breaches of the Sexual Offences Act.

In February the following year, the police also obtained warrants to search
the home of *Newsday* journalist Andre Bagoo and the *Newsday* premises for
what they described as unlawfully acquired information that was the basis of
an article on conflict within the Integrity Commission.

The police had sought disclosure of the source of the information reported in the newspaper following a complaint from Integrity Commission chairman Ken Gordon. The newspaper had refused to cooperate. Both searches and seizures were loudly condemned by the public, the Media Association of Trinidad and Tobago and the Association of Caribbean MediaWorkers. The Association of Caribbean MediaWorkers, in a release, reminded the government and the police that the right to keep sources confidential was a specific protection within the Inter-American Declaration of Principles on Freedom of Expression to which Trinidad and Tobago subscribes.

Principle 8 of the Declaration states: "Every social communicator has the right to keep his/her source of information, notes, personal and professional archives confidential."[59]

If police enter a news outlet or journalist's premises pursuant to a search warrant, resistance could result in criminal charges of obstruction and assault. There is the option of going to court, seeking an order that the warrant was invalid, that the items be returned, and that the police not use them in court.

CHAPTER 13

PRIVACY AND CONFIDENCE

I want to be forgotten even by God.

—poet Robert Browning[1]

Privacy is an elusive concept.

Although the right to privacy is guaranteed in our Commonwealth Caribbean constitutions, remedies against perceived constitutional breaches are available only against the state and public authorities, and not against private citizens, such as pesky journalists and photographers.

So if citizens feel aggrieved because someone revealed details of their private life, such as medical records or photographs captured in private moments, those citizens would not be able to seek redress by claiming a breach of the fundamental right to respect for their private life.

However, statute and common law developments have provided various ways to protect citizens from unfair or unjustified intrusion into their private lives. The Grenada Electronic Crimes Act 2013,[2] the Antigua Electronic Crimes Act 2013,[3] and the St Vincent and the Grenadines Cybercrime Act 2016[4] create the criminal offence of violation of privacy, committed by capturing, publishing or transmitting, without lawful excuse or justification, images of the private area (such as breasts, buttocks and genitals, whether naked or clad in undergarments) of people without their consent. The offence is committed under circumstances where the person has a reasonable expectation of privacy or is "in a vulnerable position". (See chapter 12, "The Investigative Journalist".) Data protection legislation prohibits unauthorized access to "personal information" and provokes much debate over balancing individual rights with privacy and freedom of expression.

In the civil arena, there is no freestanding tort of invasion of privacy. The Commonwealth Caribbean has no overarching right of privacy as in the

United States. English courts have repeatedly refused to create or recognize such a tort. Judges have stated that protection under a tort of invasion of privacy ought to be developed by Parliament and not the courts.

However, the equitable doctrine of breach of confidence and the tort of misuse of private information are being developed, massaged and expanded on a case-by-case basis in courts from Port of Spain to Strasbourg. Subject matters that give rise to court action range from photographing celebrities in private moments to "revenge porn" to the release of names of suspects in police investigations before they have been charged.

BREACH OF CONFIDENCE

In the 1981 movie *Absence of Malice,* newspaper reporter Sally Field defames businessman Paul Newman, linking him to murder and corruption. Wilford Brimley, as the crusty assistant US Attorney General James A. Wells, delivers in his tough-guy gravelly voice one of the most memorable quotes of the movie: "You had a leak? You call what's goin' on around here a leak? Boy, the last time there was a leak like this, Noah built hisself a boat."

"Leaks" are the stuff that great stories are made of. Famous gushers include the 1971 leaking of the Pentagon Papers (cablegrams, transcripts, policy papers and other classified documents on the Vietnam War) by military analyst Daniel Ellsberg to the *New York Times;* and the "Deep Throat" secret source who provided insider guidance to the *Washington Post* on the Watergate scandal, which led to the 1974 resignation of American President Richard Nixon. More recently, the 2015 leak of the Panama Papers, 11.5 million files from the database of the world's fourth largest offshore law firm Mossack Fonseca, was unprecedented. A German newspaper obtained records from an anonymous source and shared them with the International Consortium of Investigative Journalists.[5]

Journalists need reliable sources who are willing to reveal important information. But where the leak concerns confidential material, the aggrieved can bring an action for "breach of confidence" against the leaker and also against the journalist and media organization who published.

Although not commonly invoked, "breach of confidence" is an actionable wrong.[6] Apart from monetary damages, the claimant in a breach of confidence action will ask the court for injunctive relief – an order to prevent the newspaper or media house from publishing the material.

The seeds of the common law breach of confidence were sown in the nineteenth-century English case of *Prince Albert v. Strange.*[7] Queen Victoria and her husband, Prince Albert, enjoyed making etchings and drawings of domestic life, portraits of family members and their pet dogs, which they kept locked away, but when Prince Albert took a few to a shop for impressions to be made of them, a workman made copies that the defendant Sir John Strange published in a catalogue and sought to exhibit. The court injuncted (restrained) the catalogue as well as the exhibition on the basis that the defendant invaded the royal couple's privacy.

Traditionally, breach of confidence actions concerned trade secrets and spousal communication (a newspaper was restrained from publishing the Duke of Argyll's[8] account of his tumultuous marriage with the Duchess in the aftermath of a bitter divorce). But the categories are certainly not closed.

When film celebrities Michael Douglas and Catherine Zeta-Jones were married at the famed Plaza Hotel in New York City in 2000, they had sold to *OK!* magazine the exclusive right to photograph the wedding, and guests were forbidden from taking photographs. The couple put in place elaborate security measures, but a photographer infiltrated the wedding and sneaked unauthorized pictures, which the rival magazine *Hello!* published. The Court of Appeal held there was an unjustified intrusion into the private lives of individuals, but the couple's legal victory was not based on any allegations of breach of privacy – such a law did not exist – but rather under the law of confidentiality (personal and commercial).[9] The position of the *Hello!* defendants was akin to that of holders of trade secrets, and Lindsay J found that they had acted unconscionably.

WHEN AN OBLIGATION ARISES

Generally, an obligation of confidence arises in circumstances in which information of a confidential nature is used without the authorization of the confider. In *Attorney General v. Guardian Newspapers (No. 2)*,[10] Lord Goff summarized: "I start with the broad principle . . . that a duty of confidence arises when confidential information comes to the knowledge of a person (the confidant) in circumstances where he has notice, or is held to have agreed, that the information is confidential, with the effect that it would be just in all the circumstances that he should be precluded from disclosing the information to others."

In St Lucia, the *Crusader* newspaper had to pay damages after the judge found it had broken an obligation of confidence by publishing a story about the death of a baby girl who had starred in a dental care advertisement.[11] The paper reported that the child had died of HIV/AIDS and the mother had also died of the illness. The father and common law husband successfully brought suit for breach of confidence (as well as defamation, the innuendo being that he too was infected). The judge held that although the mother and child were dead, the information was the property of the father by association, and he had given no consent to its release.

Information cannot be plugged simply because there is a confidential stamp on it. There must be some enforceable duty to keep the secret. To divulge the exact recipe for Angostura bitters, for example, would amount to breach of confidence. Businesses that conduct research and develop patents are often advised to ensure visitors to their premises sign confidentiality or non-disclosure agreements relating to confidential information they might acquire about the business before they enter the premises.[12]

Some employment and consultancy contracts have secrecy clauses. Bank employees usually have to sign confidentiality agreements. Senior civil servants, such as the chief personnel officer and commissioner of inland revenue, and their secretaries, have to take oaths of secrecy. Financial and banking organizations have legislation that forbids their auditors and employees from disclosing confidential information. Even without specific secrecy clauses, the courts will imply such an undertaking or obligation upon employees not to reveal secret or confidential material that may harm or disadvantage their employers, except where the disclosure is in the public interest, such as the exposure of a criminal offence.[13]

"In the public interest" does not include disclosure to the news media, although the courts would be loath to deny employees protection because they made a disclosure of serious wrongdoing to the "wrong" person. In *Initial Services v. Putterill,*[14] a sales manager who left his job handed over confidential documents belonging to his employer to the *Daily Mail,* alleging that UK laundry firms were artificially keeping prices up. His former employer contended he could not avail himself of the public interest defence because he blabbed to the press and not to the proper authority. The Court of Appeal refused to strike out the defence.

Lord Denning stated, "The disclosure must, I should think, be to one who has a proper interest to receive the information. Thus it would be proper to disclose a crime to the police; or a breach of the Restrictive Trade Practices Act to the registrar. There may be cases where the misdeed is of such a character that the public interest may demand, or at least excuse, publication on a broader field, even to the press."[15]

Confidentiality agreements do not cover trivial water-cooler gossip and the peccadilloes of colleagues. In *Coco v. A. N. Clark (Engineers) Ltd*,[16] Megarry J defined the nature of confidential material that the courts will protect: "First, the information must be of a confidential nature. . . . The second requirement is that the information must have been communicated in circumstances importing an obligation in confidence. . . . Thirdly, there must have been an unauthorised use of the information to the detriment of the person communicating it."

Therefore, information that is already common knowledge cannot provide proceedings for breach of confidence. However confidential the information, there is no binding obligation, if the information is blurted out in public or in other circumstances that negative a duty of holding it confidential. The Privy Council decision in *Paymaster (Jamaica) Ltd and another v. Grace Kennedy Remittance Services Ltd and another*[17] is a reminder that information will not qualify as confidential information, for example, if it is not particularly different from information that can be pieced together from the public domain. Describing a document as confidential will not make the contents confidential. However, if an organization would like to maximize the chances of protecting information that could be considered as confidential, it should obviously restrict access to that information and ensure that any disclosure is subject to a confidentiality agreement.

Circumstances that give rise to obligations of confidence are not always easily defined, but Megarry J provides a guiding principle: "If the circumstances are such that any reasonable man standing in the shoes of the recipient of the information would have realised that upon reasonable grounds the information was being given to him in confidence, then this should suffice to impose upon him the equitable obligation of confidence."[18]

It is a matter of some debate whether the claimant must show detriment to be successful, and even Megarry J said it was best to keep open that question on whether detriment was really required. The House of Lords in the *Spycatcher* case said that it would not always be necessary to demonstrate detriment. And what constitutes detriment is also an open question. It may be detrimental to some people that disclosure of the information exposes them to public criticism and comment.[19]

Where journalists know a source has obtained information by breaching a confidence, they could be liable. If the journalists aided and abetted and acted in an underhand way, the court may be more likely to find against the journalists too. Much will depend on the circumstances of the case.[20]

Even where journalists or news organizations came by the information second- or third-hand, and were not party to the initial confider-confidant relationship, they may still be bound by an obligation not to use or publish the information. In the *Spycatcher* case, Lord Keith said that it is a "general rule of law that a third party who comes into possession of confidential information which he knows to be such, may come under a duty not to pass it on to anyone else".[21]

In *British Steel Corporation v. Granada Television*,[22] the television station conceded it had received and used confidential papers in violation of the rights of the steel corporation. The papers had been volunteered by a source who showed up without appointment and who neither sought nor received any payment or benefit for them. Entitled "The Steel Papers", the programme quoted extensively from the documents and the camera captured the word *Secret* stamped in large letters thereon. The editors certainly knew what they had in their hands. The day after the programme aired, British Steel immediately sent a telex to Granada Television that the documents were confidential and publication was breach of confidence as well as breach of copyright. The court granted an ex parte injunction prohibiting further publication or reproduction of the papers. Granada also conceded that had British Steel acted in time, it could well have prevented the publication in the first place.

So even where confidential material appears anonymously in the journalists' mailboxes, once journalists become aware of the confidential nature of the information, they are bound by a duty of confidence. "Turning a blind eye" to obvious clues would offer no protection. The UK Supreme Court, in *Vestergaard Frandsen v. Bestnet Europe*,[23] referred to "blind-eye knowledge" and stated that a duty of confidence arises where knowledge is acquired. In that case, the appellant was successful because she did not herself acquire the trade secrets nor did she know the material was being used by the company she had helped set up.

Lord Goff in *Spycatcher* popped balloons in newsrooms when he saw a duty of confidence arising even in circumstances where an "obviously confidential document is wafted by an electric fan out a window into a crowded street, or where an obviously confidential document such as a private diary is dropped in a public place and is then picked up by a passer-by".[24] The key factor is not whether the stranger is acting illegally but rather whether the stranger knows the information is private or confidential. For example, in *Shelley Films v. Rex Features*,[25] a stranger took photographs of the set of the film *Frankenstein* without permission, and the court found that signs at the entrance to the film studio that said "Absolutely no Photography" would have fixed the photographer with knowledge that the claimant regarded the information as confidential. Similarly, a duty of confidence was imposed on a freelance photographer who took, on behalf of the *Sun*, unauthorized photographs of the band Oasis preparing for an elaborate shoot (a Rolls Royce was lowered into a half-drained swimming pool) for their album cover. Because of the security arrangements to prevent photographs of the posed set, the photographer ought to have realized the event was meant to be confidential and unpublished, even though not utterly secret.[26] On that basis, the judge granted an injunction restraining further publication of the photographs.

IN THE PUBLIC INTEREST

Journalists can rely on the public interest defence, arguing that the confidential material should be published because of its public importance.[27] Since the nineteenth century the courts have recognized the principle that there is no confidence in iniquity.[28] So, in essence, someone who confides in another criminal activity or reprehensible behaviour cannot expect to sew up the confidant's lips on the secret which he or she has been so bold to disclose.

The editors and publishers of the *Daily Express* in England successfully relied on the public interest defence when the paper revealed that equipment being used by a company to test alcohol levels in drivers was defective. The newspaper had obtained confidential material from ex-employees of the company. The claimant sought to restrain the newspaper from further publication and also sought damages for breach of confidence. But the appeal court held that the newspaper was free to publish, leaving the claimant to his remedy in damages, because it was unquestionably in the public interest that information should be made public that showed the instrument was unreliable.[29]

Stephenson LJ stated: "There may be circumstances in which the public has a right to receive, and the media have a right or even a duty to publish, confidential information, even if the information has been unlawfully obtained in flagrant breach of confidence and irrespective of the motive of the informer."[30]

In another English case,[31] the writer of a book on Scientology described some of its practices and courses on the basis of material obtained in confidence. But the Court of Appeal refused to grant an injunction, on the ground that the courses contained such dangerous material that it was in the public interest that it should be made known.

The court must balance freedom of expression and the right to confidentiality. Lord Woolf CJ in *A v. B plc and Anor*[32] formulated guidelines to assist in addressing the balance between freedom of expression and the right to confidentiality:

> The fact that if the injunction is granted it will interfere with the freedom of expression of others and in particular the freedom of the press is a matter of particular importance. . . . Any interference with the press has to be justified because it inevitably has some effect on the ability of the press to perform its role in society. This is the position irrespective of whether a particular publication is desirable in the public interest. The existence of a free press is in itself desirable and so any interference with it has to be justified. Here we would endorse the approach of Hoffmann LJ in *R v. Central Independent Television plc*[33] where he said: "Publication may cause needless pain, distress and damage to individuals or harm to other aspects of the public interest. But a freedom which is restricted to what judges think to be responsible or in the public interest is no freedom. Freedom means the right to publish things which government and judges, however well motivated, think should not be published. It means the right to say things which "right-thinking people" regard as dangerous or irresponsible. This freedom is subject only to clearly defined exceptions laid down by common law or statute. . . . The principle that the press is free from both government and judicial control is more important than the particular case."

In Bermuda in 2007, the commissioner of police and attorney general brought an action against several media houses after a television station broadcast on its evening news programme a report that implied it had documents from a police investigation into the Bermuda Housing Corporation.[34] The police had not authorized the release of the material and so began an investigation into the "theft of confidential police documents". In the meantime, other media houses carried articles relating to the documents. The police obtained and executed search warrants on the premises of ZBM and Mid-Ocean News. They found nothing. The deputy police commissioner stated that the "theft" of the records attacked the integrity of the police investigation, and she feared that further confidential and possibly unsubstantiated information would find its way into the public domain. The material that had been published until then represented only a fraction of the contents of the "stolen" documents.

The documents contained allegations that the premier of Bermuda and other prominent figures were engaged in corruption at the Bermuda Housing Corporation. The newspaper report included the advice of the director of public prosecutions that no criminal offence had been disclosed and suggested the Bermuda Housing Corporation retain advice on whether any civil action was indicated.

The chief justice refused to grant the injunction, stating that a weighty and powerful consideration was the media's right to inform the public of serious allegations concerning public figures:[35]

> The allegations are not gratuitous, in that there is some evidence to support them, as set out in the material so far reported. Nor do the allegations concern the private personal life of those concerned. They touch upon their conduct in office. In those circumstances I think that the public interest is genuinely engaged, and this is not a case of the public being officiously interested in matters which do not concern them. I think, therefore, that the balance comes down firmly against restraining the media's freedom expression.

The matter trudged all the way to the Privy Council, and the chief justice's decision was upheld. It was a good day for freedom of expression. The police used the sledgehammer approach but the public interest won over their own sensitivity.

However, even where there is good reason to reveal private or sensitive information, not every gory detail deserves to be published. Ultimately, it is a question of proportionality.

In *Theakston v. MGN Ltd*[36] the claimant, who was the host of the popular *Top of the Pops* television programme aimed at teenagers and youngsters, had visited a brothel, and a prostitute sold her story to the *Sunday People*. She had surreptitiously taken photographs and tried to blackmail him. The judge granted an injunction restraining the use of all photographs – but not against the article. He considered that the publication of such photographs was "outweighed by the peculiar degree of intrusion into the integrity of the claimant's personality" that their publication would entail.

In another kiss-and-tell case,[37] the claimant was a Premier League footballer who had extramarital affairs with two women who sold their stories to a national newspaper, describing him as a liar and predator who concealed the fact he was married. To prevent his wife from finding out about the affairs, the claimant sought to obtain an injunction restraining the newspaper from publishing.

The Court of Appeal set aside the injunction, stating:

> A public figure was entitled to have his privacy respected in appropriate circumstances, but should recognise that because of his public position he had to expect

and accept that his or her actions would be more closely scrutinised by the media. Conduct which, in the case of a private individual, would not be the appropriate subject of comment, could be the proper subject of comment in the case of a public figure. Such a person might be a legitimate subject of public attention whether or not he had courted publicity. In balancing the respective interests of the parties, the court should not act as censors or arbiters of taste.

Or as the editor of the newspaper sneered, in true tabloid language, the court's rulings should not operate as a "love-rat's charter".[38]

CHILDREN

Where children are concerned, journalists have to be especially careful. Even where the parents are public figures, that is not sufficient justification for focusing on the children. In *Murray v. Big Pictures UK Ltd*,[39] the famous writer of the Harry Potter books J.K. Rowling and her husband were out in public with their infant son on an Edinburgh street. A commercial picture agency took covert photographs, using long-range lenses, and the *Sunday Express* published one image. The parents had not courted media exposure of the child but rather had taken steps to secure his privacy.

The child, through his parents, claimed damages against the newspaper and the photographic agency alleging a breach of his right to respect for his privacy under Article 8 of the Convention for the Protection of Human Rights and Fundamental Freedoms in that without his parents' knowledge or consent, the agency had taken, retained and supplied, and the newspaper publisher had published private and confidential information contained in a photograph in respect of which he had a reasonable and legitimate expectation of privacy.

The published photograph showed the nineteen-month-old boy being pushed by his father in a pushchair on a public street, with his mother walking alongside, on their way to a café, and showed the infant's face in profile, the clothes he was wearing, his size, the style and colour of his hair and the colour of his skin. There was no suggestion that the child had suffered distress or harassment as a result of the taking or publication of the photograph.

The newspaper publisher settled the proceedings against it. On an application by the photographic agency, and on the assumption that the pleaded facts were true, the judge struck out the claim and gave summary judgment for the photographic agency, holding that innocuous conduct in a public place or routine activities such as a simple walk down the street or a visit to the shops, as distinct from engagement in family and sporting activities, did not attract any reasonable expectation of privacy. The Court of Appeal disagreed, holding that on a trial of a complaint of wrongful publication of private information, the test to be applied in determining whether the claimant had a reasonable expectation of privacy so as to engage his Article 8 rights was what a reasonable person of "ordinary sensibilities" would feel if placed in the same position as the claimant and faced with the same publicity.

The Court of Appeal stated that whether a claimant had a reasonable expectation of privacy was a broad question of fact that took account of all circumstances of the case including attributes of the claimant; the nature of the activity in which the claimant was engaged; the place at which it was happening; the nature and purpose of the intrusion; the absence of consent and whether it was known or could be inferred; the effect on the claimant and circumstances in which and the purposes for which information had come into the hands of the publisher.

Noting that children have their own right to respect for their privacy distinct from that of their parents, the Court of Appeal affirmed the right of a child not to suffer intrusive media attention when photographs were taken without consent, and the photographer knew or ought to know that such would be objected to on behalf of the child.

MISUSE OF PRIVATE INFORMATION

The equitable doctrine of breach of confidence is being expanded into a new tort (or wrong) called the misuse of private information, which may cover circumstances that do not bear the nature of confidentiality. So it concerns purloined information, acquired surreptitiously or unlawfully, that recipients know or should know they are not free to use.

This new variant was identified in *Campbell v. Mirror Group Newspapers Ltd*,[40] in which supermodel Naomi Campbell obtained damages when a newspaper published articles and photographs about her drug treatment. The shape of the "misuse of private information" tort is being influenced by the European Court of Human Rights and the Strasbourg Jurisprudence. Lord Nicholls said in *Campbell* that the effect of the development of human rights law is a shift in the centre of gravity of the action for breach of confidence when it is used as a remedy for unjustified use of private information by private citizens: "Instead of the cause of action being based upon the duty of good faith applicable to confidential personal information and trade secrets alike, it focuses upon the protection of human autonomy and dignity – the right to control the dissemination of information about one's private life and the right to the esteem and respect of other people."[41]

The Caribbean has little history of jurisprudence in this growing area, and it is left to be seen just how the courts will interpret and apply the European learning to domestic cases. In a landmark case from Trinidad and Tobago, concerning "revenge porn" and social media, Justice Frank Seepersad confirmed there was no tort of invasion of privacy, but remarked that the time had come for statute to step in:[42] "Given the rapid pace with which the face and fabric of society has changed, and cognizant of the infinite reach of social media, it cannot be denied that the privacy of the person is under attack and there is dire need for the enactment of statute to afford protection for citizens' personal privacy."

So the courts, even in the absence of statute, must consider whether it is necessary and proportionate to limit an individual's right to privacy in the interest of freedom of expression of others.

When a claim is made, the first step is deciding whether the claimant holds a "reasonable expectation of privacy" over the subject matter. If the answer is yes, the second stage involves the "ultimate balancing test" of whether the privacy or freedom of expression interests should prevail.

A lot depends on the specific facts of each case, and there is no "bright line which can be drawn between what is private and what is not".[43] Information usually understood to be private includes an individual's mental and physical health, personal relationships, family relationships, emotional distress and bereavement, financial status, religious affiliations, and to some extent political beliefs, opinions and affiliations.[44] Information that is generally not considered private includes corporate information, identity of an author, current criminal behaviour – information that is already in the public domain and trivial or anodyne information.

In *Campbell*, although the claimant was a public figure, the private nature of drug treatment therapy was a relevant factor. The anonymous nature of the meetings is essential to encourage those with addictions to come forward and get help. The judges found that details of the supermodel's attendance at Narcotics Anonymous meetings were "obviously private". However, the mere fact of her addiction was not a violation, because she had gone out of her way to establish herself as drug-free and as one of the few models who remained so. Where public figures make untrue statements, the media are generally entitled to set the record straight.

The European Court of Human Rights has held that protected information includes an individual's HIV status.[45] Exposing an individual's bereavement or distress has also been protected, as in *Peck v. United Kingdom*,[46] in which the applicant had been captured on CCTV in the aftermath of a suicide attempt. Two television stations aired the footage, and in some cases his identity was not masked. The European Court concluded that the disclosure constituted a serious interference with the applicant's right to respect for his private life.

In *Holden v. Express Newspapers*,[47] in England, Eady J granted an injunction to restrain publication of topless photographs of an actress who was standing in the garden of a hotel. In *Venables v. News Group*,[48] mere details of claimants' residences were protected. Dame Elizabeth Butler-Sloss imposed an injunction on the basis of breach of confidence and privacy that restrained the publication of any information likely to expose the whereabouts of the two teenage boys who had murdered toddler James Bulger. The aim was to protect them from the "real possibility of serious physical harm and possible death from vengeful members of the public or the Bulger family".

In performing the ultimate balancing test, the courts respect journalistic professionalism and the freedom of journalists to choose how best to present a particular story. Judges must make allowance for the colour and punch of storytelling. Lord Steyn has explained that when journalists are unable to colour their stories with reference to personalities, stories can become disembodied and just plain dull. Readers will become less interested, writers will be discouraged and, in the long run, informed debate would suffer.[49]

In a controversial case involving a hugely popular public figure, the tension between privacy and freedom of expression attracted international attention. In 2018, famous rock and roller Sir Cliff Richard was awarded substantial damages against the British Broadcasting Corporation[50] when the court found that the news organization had violated his privacy by reporting that police were investigating him in relation to allegations of sexual abuse against a teenage boy twenty-five years earlier. The court held that the police had breached confidence by leaking or at least confirming to a BBC reporter that the police intended to search the Sunningdale, Berkshire apartment of the rock star. Sir Cliff was never arrested and never charged. It took two years after the search before the police announced that they would not lay any charges.

Although the report was accurate, it ran afoul of the subject's privacy rights, in the view of the court. The BBC put a lot of emphasis on the fact that Sir Cliff was a public figure but the court remarked that a public figure is not necessarily deprived of legitimate expectations of privacy. In determining whether Sir Cliff's privacy rights, under Article 8 of the European Convention on Human Rights, trumped the BBC's freedom of expression, under Article 10, the judge considered three main factors: the information disclosed by the BBC (the name and the alleged crime), the manner in which it was disclosed (the "sensationalist" element) and the effect on Sir Cliff.

The court then considered whether despite the breach, the BBC was justified in broadcasting the story in the public interest. Justice Mann held that although the police investigation of historic sexual abuse allegations, particularly by those who may have abused their celebrity status, was of legitimate public interest and concern, it did not follow that the identity of the subject of the investigation in the particular case was of legitimate public interest:[51]

> Knowing that Sir Cliff was under investigation might be of interest to the gossip-mongers, but it does not contribute materially to the genuine public interest in the existence of police investigations in this area. It was known that investigations were made and prosecutions brought. I do not think that knowledge of the identity of the subject of the investigation was a material legitimate addition to the stock of public knowledge for these purposes.

The court awarded damages. The police apologized and settled out of court. The BBC released a statement admitting it had made some mistakes, expressing regret over the distress caused to Sir Cliff and conceding defeat. To appeal would be to go down an "expensive legal cul de sac", it said, and prolong Sir Cliff's distress. But the BBC called upon Parliament as lawmakers to consider a review of the law to "protect the right to properly and fairly report criminal investigations, and to name the person under investigation".[52]

The outcome of these proceedings was much debated and controversial, with lawyers and journalists commenting that to give suspects anonymity would hamper police investigations.[53] One argument was that publishing the names of suspects could enable other potential victims to come forward.[54]

However, withholding the names of suspects who have not been charged has long been standard journalism practice, even though such may not be specifically incorporated in codes of ethics. The primary reason for not publishing names of mere suspects has been to avoid libel actions if the suspect is not charged. Now, journalists (and their police sources) need to be more aware of privacy and ethical considerations.[55]

The Sir Cliff Richard case is a reminder that public figures are not fair game for any sort of coverage, and although reporting on police investigations is difficult and even frustrating for serious journalists, the law is not likely to be sympathetic when reporting the news veers into sensationalism.

DATA PROTECTION

Trinidad and Tobago and the Bahamas have passed Data Protection Act,[56] which prohibits obtaining, keeping, processing and disclosing personal information or data. The Cayman Islands Data Protection Law was passed by the Legislative Assembly in March 2017, and will be enacted on a date set by Cabinet order.[57] Breaches may be punished by imprisonment or fine.

Governments consider this type of legislation vital or at least desirable for the financial services industry, which is keen to access European markets that have been operating with data protection laws since the 1990s.

The main difficulty with the legislation in Trinidad and Tobago and the Bahamas is that it contains no exemptions for journalists legitimately going about their business of news gathering and investigating matters in the public interest.

The knowledge and consent of individuals are required for the collection, use or disclosure of personal information about them. Even someone's marital status, age and address are deemed protected information that cannot be disclosed. This applies to public bodies as well as the private sector, which includes media houses. St Vincent also passed a Privacy Act 2013, which has similar provisions, except that it is limited to public bodies.

"Personal information" covers everything and the kitchen sink. For example, Section 2 of the Trinidad and Tobago Act bulges at the seams with this list:

a.   information relating to the race, nationality or ethnic origin, religion, age or marital status of the individual;

b.   information relating to the education or the medical, criminal or employment history of the individual or information relating to the financial transactions in which the individual has been involved or which refers to the individual;

c.   any identifying number, symbol or other particular designed to identify the individual;

d.   the address and telephone contact number of the individual;

e.   the name of the individual where it appears with other personal information relating to the individual or where the disclosure of the name itself would reveal information about the individual;

f.   correspondence sent to an establishment by the individual that is explic-
     itly or implicitly of a private or confidential nature, and any replies to
     such correspondence which would reveal the contents of the original
     correspondence;
g.   the views and opinions of any other person about the individual; or
h.   the fingerprints, deoxyribonucleic acid, blood type or the biometric char-
     acteristics of the individual.

The definitions of "data"[58] and "processing" are so broad that it would
be impossible, in the absence of further provision, to deal with almost any
information about individuals (whether automated or traditionally handled)
without their consent.

Researching and publishing a newspaper article, for example, will inevitably involve many acts that amount to processing data that go into the story.
Furthermore, in many situations, it would be unreasonable, undesirable and
even foolhardy to have to notify people about data held on them or to allow
them to access it.

The Bahamian and Trinidadian legislation makes no acknowledgement of a public interest exemption, which would protect journalists from
"prior restraint" interim injunctions preventing them from proceeding with
processing information with a view to publication and also from claims for
compensation once publication had taken place.

The legislation in this way differs markedly from similar legislation in the
United Kingdom and Canada.[59] For example, the UK Data Protection Act 1998
provides that personal data processed for the purposes of journalism, literature
and art are exempt, provided the "data controller" reasonably believes that, having
regard in particular to the special importance of the public interest in freedom of
expression, publication would be in the public interest, and the data controller
reasonably believes that, in all the circumstances, compliance with that provision
is incompatible with the special purposes. For example, in the *Douglas v. Hello!*
case, Lindsay J found no credible evidence the publishers believed there was any
public interest in the celebrity wedding photographs published.[60]

The Bahamian legislation was modelled after the Irish Data Protection Act
1988, which was amended in 2003,[61] to include a journalism exemption, but
that was after the Bahamian act was passed into law. The Bahamian legislation
remains to be tested in the courts, but it is left to be seen how it is interpreted
in the context of Article 23 of the constitution, which guarantees freedom of
expression.

After a flood of criticism, the Trinidad and Tobago legislation only partially came into force via Legal Notice 2 of 2012, the offending sections remaining in limbo. Government promised to review it.

CYBERCRIME

Cybercrime legislation, which targets cyberbullying, online identity theft and child pornography, has claws in other areas and has been of serious concern to journalists, with governments grappling with ensuring protection of freedom of expression.

In the British Virgin Islands, in 2014, lawmakers added a public interest exemption to the Computer Misuse and Cybercrimes Act, which mandates a prison term of up to fifteen years for unlawfully obtaining information from a protected computer. The original provision provoked international outcry from press freedom, tax justice and anti-corruption advocates.

The provision was first proposed following a series of reports the International Consortium of Investigative Journalists published using leaked information that revealed that the British Virgin Islands had become a favourite destination for elite and powerful Chinese offshore clients. The reports published the identities of dozens of owners of anonymous British Virgin Island companies.[62] St Vincent and the Grenadines Cybercrime Act 2016 also includes a "public interest" defence to the offence of obtaining computer data not meant for oneself or that is protected against unauthorized access.[63]

Prime Minister Ralph Gonsalves, himself an attorney-at-law, gave this interpretation: "So that if someone gets some information that a public official, a politician or whatsoever is corrupt, they get data on it, you obtain it, this information, when you publish it, they can't come at you because you will have what is called a public interest defence, which did not exist before when the Bill was originally drafted."[64]

In Jamaica, Section 9 of the Cybercrimes Act 2015[65] creates the offence of "malicious communication", punishable by imprisonment of four years and a fine. The new law created headlines and heated discussion.[66]

In March 2017, police in Jamaica charged Latoya Nugent, the co-founder of a rights movement, under the Cybercrimes Act for naming on social media members of a church as sexual predators and rapists. An attorney wrote to her, asking her to delete the post. She responded in vituperative terms.[67]

By May the same year, the prosecution had offered no evidence and the charge was discontinued. Director of public prosecutions Paula Llewellyn,

QC, published an advisory statement, explaining that words which are defamatory do not mature into a criminal offence because they are sent via computer.[68] Llewellyn found that although the post was offensive, it did not reach the criminal threshold.

The Press Association of Jamaica had warned that the section could be misused to introduce criminal defamation through the cyberspace back door. Similar complaint may be made of Section 4 of the Antigua Electronic Crimes Act 2013, which prohibits sending by electronic means or devices "information that is offensive or threatening; or information which is false, causing annoyance, inconvenience, danger, obstruction, insult, injury, intimidation, enmity, hatred or ill will persistently".

The Barbados Computer Misuse Act 2004 also creates the criminal offence of malicious communication,[69] and at least two people have been charged under it, one after he allegedly made comments on social media in response to a statement uttered on a political platform.[70]

St Vincent and the Grenadines – unlike Jamaica, Grenada, Antigua and Barbuda, and Trinidad and Tobago – has not abolished criminal defamation and buttresses its position by creating an additional offence of "libel by electronic communication" punishable by two years imprisonment in its Cybercrime Act 2016. Criminal defamation is already an offence under its criminal code. Although criminal libel has fallen into disuse, the fear is that the cyber-libel provision will give it new life. Combined with the new offences of cyber-bullying and cyber-harassment, the act has the potential to create an overall "chilling effect" on journalism, according to media associations and press freedom groups.[71]

The Vincentian Cybercrime Act defines cyberbullying (Section 17) as repeatedly transmitting any information, statement or image that causes another person to feel frightened, distressed or intimidated. "Harassment by electronic communication" (Section 18) is committed by using a computer system to send another person any information, image or statement that is (a) obscene, menacing or constitutes a threat; and (b) thereby causes another person to feel intimidated, harassed or threatened.

Unlike the Barbadian and Antiguan and legislation, the Vincentian Cybercrime Act offers a salve, in Subsection 3: "For the avoidance of doubt nothing in [either section] shall be construed as restricting the right of freedom of expression under the law on any subject."

Nevertheless, the complaint is that in the hands of the overzealous, corrupt or just plain foolish, the cyberbullying and cyber-harassment provisions could be broadly interpreted in a manner to suppress legitimate investigation and ventilation of matters of public interest. This is especially so as journalism is now firmly part of the digital age and relies more and more on cyber-publishing.

This is where an independent judiciary comes in. Each case will have to be decided on its own facts. The courts will have to balance the need to protect people from unwanted intrusion into their personal affairs with the upholding of freedom of expression.

The Association of Caribbean Media Workers told the Vincentian lawmakers that they were setting a bad example to their neighbours. The following year, one of those neighbours, Trinidad and Tobago, passed the Cybercrime Act 2017, amid more outcry.

The Trinidad and Tobago statute creates the offence of causing harm by communication using a computer system.[72] Factors to be taken into consideration include whether the communication is anonymous, whether it is repeated, the extremity of language used and whether it is true or false.

A main cause of friction in the Trinidad and Tobago statute is the provision that creates the offence of receiving computer data knowing it to have been stolen. A person who "intentionally and without lawful excuse or justification receives or gains access to computer data knowing the same to have been stolen or obtained [through unauthorized access] commits an offence" and is liable on summary conviction to a fine of TT$100,000 and imprisonment for two years, or on conviction on indictment to a fine of TT$500,000 and imprisonment for three years.

The protection for journalists may lie in the phrase "intentionally and without lawful excuse or justification". Though it remains to be tested in the courts of law, this means that a journalist who receives information anonymously, in the mailbox, for example, not knowing from whence it came, would have a defence. Also, one could argue that the exposure of criminal wrongdoing and threats to public health and the environment would be protected notwithstanding how the data were obtained.

In contrast, Section 12 of the Barbados Computer Misuse Act 2004 seems to be harsher and more restrictive. There is no defence of "lawful excuse or justification". It is a criminal offence for an "unauthorised person" to receive computer data "whether or not the person from whom the programme or data was received or through whom access was attained was authorised to make it available to him".

More than ever, journalists operate in a world of information leaks, and obtaining and using purloined or stolen documents, whether old-fashioned "hard copy" or digital, are fraught with legal and ethical issues. The aggrieved can mix and match their legal complaints and allege breach of data protection, computer misuse, breach of confidence, threatening national security, invasion of privacy and defamation, as well as theft – all over a single exposure or leak. Sources can lose their jobs, their reputations, their freedom, their sanity.

You should be prepared for any eventuality (legal and ethical) before you publish. Go brave, not reckless. Peter Preston, who edited the *Guardian* in the United Kingdom from 1975 to 1995,[73] had this to say about handling secret, confidential or leaked material: "It is the job of editors to publish, not keep secrets."[74]

CHAPTER 14

FREEDOM OF INFORMATION

Secrecy, being an instrument of conspiracy, ought never to be the system of regular government.

—Jeremy Bentham[1]

Freedom of information is an extension of the constitutional right to freedom of expression, which includes the "right to receive and impart information without interference", as guaranteed in the various regional constitutions.[2]

Freedom of information legislation is sometimes called "right to know" law. It allows full or partial disclosure of unreleased material controlled by the government. This type of legislation emerged in Scandinavia, with Sweden's *His Majesty's Gracious Ordinance Relating to Freedom of Writing and of the Press* in 1766 being the oldest.[3] Now over one hundred countries worldwide have some form of freedom of information legislation.

Belize passed freedom of information (FOI) legislation in 1994, followed by Trinidad and Tobago in 1999, with the act coming into effect in 2001. Jamaica, St Vincent, Antigua and Barbuda, Cayman Islands, Bermuda, Guyana, and the Bahamas also have freedom of information legislation.[4] Barbados, Grenada and St Kitts have drafted bills.

The freedom of information legislation is meant to support greater transparency in the conduct of public affairs and the accountability of public authorities. For example, Section 2 of the Jamaica Access to Information Act 2007 describes the objectives of the legislation:

to reinforce and give further effect to certain fundamental principles underlying the system of constitutional democracy, namely –

a.   Government accountability
b.   Transparency
c.   Public participation in national decision-making.

All members of the public have the right to seek access to information about or in the possession of public authorities. Public authorities must publish information about their structure and operation, policies, rules, practices and documents in their possession. Public authorities include government ministries and departments, local government, Parliament, law courts, public hospitals, police and prison services, and companies owned or controlled by the state.[5]

However, the statutes create many exemptions, and public authorities generally have up to thirty days to respond to requests – and even then you are not sure to get what you are looking for.[6] To journalists, time is of the essence and inordinate delay could effectively stifle an investigation.

Exempt documents (which can be released if in the public interest to do so) include:

- cabinet documents
- defence and security documents
- international relations documents
- internal working documents
- law enforcement documents
- documents affecting legal proceedings or subject to legal professional privilege
- documents affecting personal privacy
- documents relating to trade secrets
- documents containing material obtained in confidence
- documents affecting the economy and commercial affairs
- certain documents concerning the operations of public authorities
- documents to which secrecy provisions apply.

Exempt documents can be made available if reasonable evidence that any of the following has or is likely to have occurred:

- significant abuse of authority or neglect in the performance of official duty; or
- injustice to an individual; or

- danger to the health or safety of an individual or of the public; or
- unauthorized use of public funds.

The authority is also required to give access to exempt documents if it has been determined to be in the public interest to do so, having assessed the benefit or damage that might result. Proper reasons must be given for any refusal to provide the requested documents, and the authority has a mandate to determine whether documents, though exempt, should be released.

TO MAKE A REQUEST

Read the statements published by public authorities in the newspapers. Fill out and submit the freedom of information request form if you would like to see an official document held by a public authority. You can copy the form from the last page of the act, ask for one from any public authority or download a copy from the website. If there is no such form, write a letter, which may be sent via email.[7] You may only apply for access to documents that are not already in the public domain (readily available to members of the public).

Decide exactly what information you need and then determine which public authority is most likely to have this information. The legislation requires that public authorities help applicants to fill out the form to ensure their requests comply with the requirements of the act.[8] You may request all records of a particular description or all records relating to a particular subject. But try to limit your request to what you really want. Don't give the agency an excuse to delay its response, or you risk needlessly running up search and copying costs. If you know that your request involves a great volume of records, try to state both what your request includes and what it does not include.

The request form may be submitted in person or mailed into the authority. The authority will probably receive the form more quickly if it is hand-delivered. You should record the mode of delivery. If the request form is delivered by hand, you should record the date and time of delivery and the name of the person receiving the request document on behalf of the authority. For third-party, mail or courier deliveries, you should record the date and time, and mailing location.

Be sure to keep a copy of all correspondence to and from the agency. You may need it if you write an appeal or go to court later. Take notes during all phone conversations – the date, what was said, who you spoke to and so on.

Follow up phone conversations with a letter addressed to the official you spoke with.

Confirming phone conversations in writing will help ensure there are no misunderstandings, and it is also useful if your request needs to be forwarded to another office or agency. Written notes can also clear up any misunderstandings that might arise. In general, it can be useful to establish a regular contact in the agency's Freedom of Information Act office who you can ask for by name, if this is possible.

The time limit in which an authority is required to issue a response is calculated from the date on which the form is received (mail registry stamped) by the authority. It does not include periods of consultation between an applicant and the designated officer. Accordingly, if an authority consults with an applicant over two days, for example, time is suspended (for the purposes of the request) during the consultation period. The calculation of processing time resumes at the end of the two-day consultation. You should receive a written response from the authority within the prescribed period. The authority must advise of its decision to grant, defer or refuse access to all or part of the document you have requested. It must also explain its reasons for the decision taken.

If your request is granted, you may make arrangements to examine the document collated or you may request a copy of the document. Fees may be charged for the search, retrieval, editing and copying of documents requested. Any fees being charged by the authority must be paid before access will be given. The designated officer will advise of any fees payable.

REFUSAL

If the authority has refused access to one or more of the documents requested, you may formally challenge this decision. You have the right to apply to the ombudsman or High Court for judicial review of the public authority's decision.[9] In Jamaica, the aggrieved may apply for an internal review and, if unsuccessful, lodge an appeal with a tribunal.[10] In Cayman, a disappointed applicant may request an internal review and appeal that decision to an information commissioner. If dissatisfied with the commissioner's decision, the applicant may appeal to the Grand Court by way of judicial review.[11] Complaint to the ombudsman or information commissioner usually must be made within twenty-one days of receiving the decision of the public authority.

The Trinidad and Tobago case of *Caribbean Information Access Ltd v. the Hon. Minister of National Security*[12] illustrates the test of reasonableness that must be applied when deciding whether to release documents.

In that case, twelve requests were made to the commissioner of police pertaining to the status of police investigations into the death of Chaguanas resident Harnarine Ramjattan, whose body was found in March 2001 in Wallerfield, Arima. The request included names and addresses of people interviewed; the number of unsolved murders for the past fifteen years; bank accounts in the name of the deceased; insurance policies in the name of the deceased; names of police officers assigned to the investigation; and the police theory of the investigation.

The request was made in June 2002, and no response was received until October, which was long overdue. The Ministry of National Security lethargically responded that the investigation was ongoing and the release of most of the material would prejudice the investigation and endanger the lives of the police. The documents fell into the exempt category of "law enforcement" documents. The applicant sought judicial review and the judge upheld the respondent's refusal to disclose the material (with one exception). The Court of Appeal disagreed with the judge's orders.

Justice of Appeal Weekes stated:[13]

> A delicate balancing of competing policy interests must be engaged. Thus, in my opinion the appropriate test, as I have indicated, is one of reasonableness: Is it reasonable, balancing the competing interests and in light of the explanations given (and where necessary, the evidence supplied), to uphold the exemptions claimed? This is an objective test and the public authority must satisfy the court on the civil standard of likelihood.

The Court of Appeal said it was insufficient for the authority to merely reply that investigations were ongoing, or that disclosure of police officers' names would place them in danger, without some "asserted factual context" to support that. The disclosure of personal information must be unreasonable and the authority must state specifically why such disclosure is unreasonable.

The Court of Appeal remitted most of the requests to the ministry for reconsideration in light of the public interest override.[14] But the ministry was ordered to grant access to the names of the police officers involved in the investigations as well as the list of unsolved murders for the last fifteen years, including the names, addresses and dates of death of the victims. The applicant was required to clarify other requests.

Despite the long-winded procedure involved in obtaining information, journalists have been able to obtain important documents to support worthwhile investigations. One of the earliest regional freedom of information requests came from Camini Marajh, award-winning *Express* investigative journalist in Trinidad and Tobago. In 2001, she obtained valuable material that confirmed her leads and expanded information already unearthed during her probe into the granting of a special multimedia telecommunication licence to a company. The company was operated by relatives of the then minister with responsibility for telecommunications. The series of articles led to resistance from the permanent secretary and later revocation of the licence.

In Jamaica, the *Gleaner* newspaper used the access to information provisions to publish information on overseas travel by government ministers in 2013. Although only the Office of the Prime Minister and seven of the sixteen ministries responded, providing a breakdown of fares, accommodation and per diem, readers were informed on a matter of public interest; seven ministers had spent more than J$25 million in overseas travel expenses in the first six months of 2013.

In Cayman, since the enactment of the legislation, many public boards and authorities have taken to publishing meeting minutes on their websites.[15] In Belize, in 2017 and 2016 there were no applications to the ombudsman for review of the decisions by public authorities.[16]

Generally, poor record keeping, inadequate resources, misunderstanding by public officials of their role in achieving freedom of information, and reluctance to change from a culture of secrecy to transparency are obstacles to the effective implementation of freedom of information legislation. In 2019, Guyana's Chief Justice Roxane George ordered the government to provide furniture and staff to the Office of the Information Commissioner to ensure proper execution of his duties.[17]

In Cayman, it took about four years for reports concerning an anticorruption investigation named Operation Tempura to be released. The Tempura investigation began in September 2007 and ended in October 2009; it cost millions of dollars and many reputations.

The investigation was prompted by a request from the Cayman police commissioner Stuart Kernohan to the then commissioner of the Metropolitan Police Service (Scotland Yard) in England for assistance in investigating allegations that a senior policeman was passing sensitive police information to Desmond Seales, editor in chief of the *Cayman Net News,* one of two Cayman newspapers. The investigation also concerned allegations that a High Court judge had orchestrated a search of the offices of *Cayman Net News* to find out who was the author of five letters that had been published in the newspaper and that were critical of the judiciary and administration of justice.[18]

UK journalist John Evans,[19] who admitted to spying on his boss by searching Seales's office to find a non-existent box file that supposedly contained evidence of Seales's collusion with the police, requested from the police a copy of the report or complaint by Martin Bridger, the Tempura investigator.

The police said no, and the information commissioner agreed that the documents were exempt but urged the police to consider release in due course so the public could be enlightened.[20] In 2016, information commissioner Jennifer Dilbert ruled that the majority of the documents should be released. Governor Helen Kilpatrick agreed to do so, stating that she still believed it was not in the public interest to release a complaint consisting almost entirely of false allegations but recognized her obligation under the Freedom of Information Law 2007. The (redacted) documents are now available on the governor's website.[21]

CHAPTER 15

COPYRIGHT

Do you see a man skilful in his work? He will stand before kings; he will not stand before obscure men.

—Proverbs 22:29

You make it, you own it. That's the essence of copyright, which secures for the creator of a creative effort the exclusive right to control who can make copies, make works derived from the original work or perform and broadcast the work. If you create something, and it fits the definition of a creative work, you get to control who can reproduce it and how they do so.

So, essentially, copyright is a legal term referring to the rights creators have over their literary and artistic efforts.

These rights may be divided into two broad areas: economic and moral. Economic rights protect the economic value of a work that the copyright holder exploits by holding a monopoly on the reproduction or use of a work. Moral rights are personal in character, and include the right to be named as the author or creator of a work and the right to prevent derogatory treatment of the work, such as poor-quality reproduction of a book with chapters missing or rife with errors.

Modern copyright laws have been largely standardized through the international treaty known as the Berne Convention for the Protection of Literary and Artistic Works, which was first established in 1886 and revised over the decades.[1] The convention requires member states to provide strong minimum standards of protection for "every production in the literary, scientific and artistic domain, whatever the mode or form of its expression".[2]

Member states[3] are required to ensure that certain core rights are protected, such as the right to translate, to make adaptations and arrangements of the work, to broadcast and to recite and perform in public dramatic and musical works. The convention permits exceptions, such as the free use of protected material for

"Hey, that's my song. That's copyright infringement."

CartoonStock.com

teaching purposes and the reporting of current events. These core provisions are reflected in the copyright legislation in the Commonwealth Caribbean.

OWNER, AUTHOR, CREATOR

The first owner of the copyright in any of the original works will be the author[4] or creator, except in the case of an employee who is employed to produce such works, in which case the copyright's first owner will be the employer. Example:

Grenada Copyright Act 2011, Section 28 (5) states: "In respect of a work created by an author employed by a natural person or legal entity in the course of his employment, the original owner of copyright shall be, unless provided otherwise by agreement, the employer."

The 2015 amendment to the Jamaica Copyright Act takes a different approach, providing that the author/employee retains the copyright in the absence of agreement to the contrary.[5]

A freelance journalist owns the copyright in an article (or radio or television production), which he submits to a media house for publication. Freelancers should specify in written agreements whether they are allowing their work to be used for print as well as electronic versions of a newspaper (for example, on a website or on CD-ROM).

In the Canadian case of *Robertson v. Thomson Corporation*,[6] a freelance author wrote two articles that were published in the *Globe* newspaper. One, a book excerpt, was the subject of a written agreement between the newspaper and the publisher of her book; the other, a book review, was written under oral agreement with the author. Copyright was not addressed in either case. The author objected to the presence of her articles in three databases: Info Globe Online, CPI.Q and the CD-ROMs. Info Globe Online was a commercial database that provided subscribers with access to stories from the *Globe* for a fee. It also allowed subscribers to find articles in many other newspapers, news wire services, magazines and reference databases. CPI.Q was the electronic version of the Canadian Periodical Index, which indexed selected newspaper articles from various newspapers and allowed subscribers to search the electronic archives of indexed periodicals by keyword and to retrieve articles electronically.

The articles in the databases contained references to the newspaper they were published in, the date they were published and the page number where the article appeared. The CD-ROMs contained the *Globe* and several other Canadian newspapers from a calendar year: users could navigate using search engines and retrieve and print articles. The content of the CD-ROM was fixed and finite, and users were able to view a paper as a single day's edition.

The Supreme Court held that newspaper publishers were not entitled as a matter of law to republish in electronic databases freelance articles they had acquired for publication in their newspapers, without compensation to the authors and without their consent. Their copyright over the newspapers they published gave them "no right to reproduce, otherwise than as part of those collective works (their newspapers), the freelance articles that appeared therein".[7]

DURATION

Every creative work is copyrighted the moment it is created. No notice or registration is necessary. You can place the copyright symbol, the date and your name on your original documents, but such is not necessary to gain the protection of the law. Generally, the copyright lasts during the life of the author and until fifty years after the author dies. In St Vincent and the Grenadines, the period is seventy-five years[8] and in Jamaica, it is ninety-five years.[9] At the expiration of the period, the work is in the public domain and anyone can make use of it. Duration of copyright in films and recordings, cable programmes, broadcasts and typographical arrangements may be for differing periods and varies among states.

REMEDIES

The injured party can take civil action for infringement of copyright, seeking an injunction to prohibit further copying as well as damages. The approach to awarding damages is the same as with other torts: the court will seek to put claimants in the position they would have enjoyed had there been no wrong committed.[10] A claimant can also ask for an account of profits and "delivery up" of the infringing copies. This is an equitable remedy that deprives defendant of any profits flowing from the infringement.

Copyright infringement is also a criminal offence. For example, a person who commits an infringement of a right protected under the Trinidad and Tobago Copyright Act 1997 for "profit-making purposes, knowing or having reason to believe that he is committing an infringement, commits an offence and is liable on summary conviction to a fine of one hundred thousand dollars and to imprisonment for ten years".[11]

CREATIVE EFFORT

Just about anything you write, photograph, sculpt, draw or record is going to be a creative work. To be protected by copyright, the work must satisfy the test of originality. Skill, creativity, effort or time must have been put into it. Titles, headlines and trivial sayings or slogans are usually not protected because they consist of only a few words and lack the necessary originality.[12]

Copyright covers speeches, pamphlets, maps, illustrations, photographs, recipes, articles and cartoons but does not extend to any official text or translation of a legislative, administrative or legal nature, and political speeches and speeches delivered in the course of legal proceedings.

The law protects literary and artistic works that are original intellectual creations.[13] A literary work is not confined to literature but means any work, other than a dramatic or musical work, which is written, spoken or sung and includes a computer program. You can also do creative editing or collecting work. So although facts cannot be copyrighted, clever organization of the facts can be. Such collections become original by reason of the selection, coordination or arrangement of their contents. A musical work consists of music, exclusive of any words or actions intended to be sung, spoken or performed with the music. An artistic work could be graphic work, photograph, sculpture, collage or architecture, being a building or model for a building or any work of artistic craftsmanship. A sound recording includes film, compact discs and audiocassettes. Material that is available on the Internet does not cease to be protected just because it is in a different medium, so copyright applies to digital books and MP3s too.

INFRINGEMENT

This takes place when the work is copied, performed, shown to the public, broadcast or adapted without permission or authorization. This interferes with the economic rights of the copyright holders who are entitled to enjoy the fruits of their labour.

Permission is usually granted for one use only, not perpetually. So, a photograph cannot be used repeatedly unless you bought the copyright too.

The copying need not be conscious or deliberate. An infringement will arise if a substantial part of the original or earlier work is taken. Mere similarity in form and general idea would not be an infringement. Competent workers in a field are expected to be familiar with outstanding work in their field and inevitably would be influenced by such at some level. That is not infringement.

It is not infringement to copy someone's style of writing or filmmaking. For example, the irreverent Trinidadian writer B.C. Pires in his "Thank God, It's Friday" weekly column in the *Daily Express* once copied the (until-then inimitable) style of the newspaper's celebrated editor-at-large Keith Smith, who uniquely wrote in the vernacular, and spoke uncomfortable truths through humour and wavy, run-on sentences that could dingolay across the page like a king of the bands commanding the whole Savannah stage without a damn-care for the judges' score card, only caring to make the people bawl and beg for more, holding their belly low as if they just get news that a car lick down their only child on the highway. (You get the idea.)

However, it is sometimes difficult to distinguish between inspiration or drawing on a common stock of work and making improper use of other people's work.

In *Bauman v. Fussell and Others*,[14] a photographer of high repute took photographs of a cockfight in Cuba for the *Picture Post* magazine. Fussell, a painter, saw Bauman's photo in the *Picture Post*, cut it out, pinned it to his studio wall and from it painted a picture of two fighting cocks in the same position and attitude as the birds in the photograph.

The photographer claimed damages for breach of his copyright in the photograph. The judge heard evidence from experts on both sides; he had the two images before him and studied the position of the birds, the claws, the colours, the use of shadow and many details.

The Court of Appeal considered the "feeling and artistic character" of the respective works and upheld the trial judge's finding that the painter used the photograph as inspiration but had not copied it; rather he made a new work of art of his own.

When buying material, photographs in particular, from individuals, news organizations should ensure that the person actually owns the copyright and is not peddling someone else's work. Some news organizations ask such people to sign a form, declaring that they own all copyright in the work. Ignorance is no excuse but may limit damages.

For example, the Jamaica Copyright Act, Section 32 (3) provides: "Where in an action for infringement of copyright it is shown that at the time of the infringement the defendant did not know and had no reason to believe that copyright subsisted in the work to which the action relates, then, the plaintiff is not entitled to damages against him, but without prejudice to any other remedy."[15]

However, one is not entitled to overlook suspicious circumstances. The *Daily Mail* in 1978 bought photographs of Princess Margaret (one of her in wig and dress to resemble bawdy American actress Mae West) and new playboy companion Roddy Llewellyn from someone who admitted that he did not take the photographs himself but owned copyright in two. He said nothing of the others. The paper made no further inquiries. The paper could not claim innocent use because it flagrantly disregarded the obvious suspicious circumstances.[16]

And, the *Sun*, in England, published a photograph of a hospital patient who had been convicted of two murders to accompany an article about him being taken on a rehabilitation visit to a local town. The photograph was used without the consent of the hospital or patient, and there was no dispute the hospital owned the copyright. The reporter said an anonymous source had provided him with the photograph. The judge, in awarding additional damages, considered that the photograph was "obviously stolen", the flagrancy of the infringement, as well as the degree of upset caused to the hospital.[17]

LICENCES

Broadcast media houses often negotiate exclusive licences (by payment of a fee to the copyright holder) to broadcast important events, such the Olympics, World Cup and international beauty pageants. The media house, as the exclusive licensee, can bring an action for breach of its licence as if it is the copyright holder, and there is no need to join the copyright holder as a claimant.

In 2015, Television Jamaica Ltd obtained the exclusive licence to broadcast the International Association of Athletics Federations World Athletics Championships in Beijing.[18] CVM Television came up with the clever idea for a counter-programme, titled *Return to the Nest,* to cover the same event the rights holder was broadcasting. CVM could have entered into a sub-licensing arrangement with Television Jamaica but instead sought to evade the copyright issue by using material from the IAAF live stream.[19] CVM seemed to think that once it did not take material directly from Television Jamaica's broadcast, there would be no breach. Television Jamaica wrote to CVM about the breach but CVM persisted. Athletics Management and Services, the company that had issued the exclusive licence to Television Jamaica, also wrote to CVM, pointing out the breach.

The Court of Appeal described CVM's actions as an "audacious taking and using of exclusive licence-protected material" and "deliberate, calculated risk-taking". Damages of more than US$125,000, plus costs, were awarded to Television Jamaica.

EMBARGOES

The manuscript from which a speaker reads is protected. The owner of embargoed material has the right to enforce terms for its use. To breach an embargo and publish a speech prematurely is an infringement of copyright. In 1992 the *Sun* published Queen Elizabeth II's famous *annus horribilis* Christmas message two days before the broadcast under the headline "OUR DIFFICULT

DAYS by the Queen". The queen pursued her rights, and the newspaper paid damages to a charity for breach of copyright.

INCIDENTAL USE

The law allows for incidental use of copyrighted material and fair dealing. Copyright use will not be infringed if you are using the material by the way or as background material. For example, if you are interviewing a family at home and the photograph captures an original artwork in the background, you will not be infringing copyright. But if you are writing about a new library complex and wish to use an artist's impression of the building and landscape, get permission first. Such use will not be merely incidental.

FAIR DEALING

Journalists may legitimately include in their articles material from other newspapers, magazines or broadcasts for the purpose of reporting current events. Such use constitutes fair dealing, fair use or fair practice and is accompanied by an acknowledgement of the original work and its author. This does not apply to photographs. You cannot lift a photograph from another newspaper or magazine, whether published locally or overseas, and use it to accompany a news item. Clever cropping or computer embellishments may not disguise it from the owner and will not provide a defence.

Do not reproduce more material than is necessary to make the point in producing current affairs or critical reviews. In *PCR Ltd v. Dow Jones Telerate Ltd*,[20] for example, a reporter could not rely successfully on fair dealing because she used more quotes than necessary from another journalist's report.

Domestic legislation lists factors the court will consider in determining whether a "borrow" constitutes fair dealing.

For example, Section 55 of the St Kitts and Nevis Copyright Act 2002[21] provides:

> For the purpose of determining whether an act done in relation to a work constitutes fair dealing, the court determining the question shall take into account all factors which appear to it to be relevant, including
>
> a.   the nature of the work in question;
> b.   the extent and substantiality of that part of the work affected by the act in relation to the whole of the work;

c.   the purpose and character of the use; and

d.   the effect of the act upon the potential market for, or the commercial value of, the work.

The English Court of Appeal in *Hyde Park Residence Ltd v. Yelland*[22] identified, in the context of news reporting, three principles that should be considered central in establishing whether the dealing is fair:

1.   the motive of the infringer;
2.   the extent and purpose of the use;
3.   whether the extent of use was necessary to report the current event in question.

In that case, an employee responsible for security at Villa Windsor in Paris, misappropriated stills from a security camera and gave them to a reporter for the *Sun,* which published them as part of an article headlined "Video That Shames Fayed".

Hyde Park was a company controlled by Mohammed al Fayed, the father of Dodi al Fayed, and was the owner of the copyright in the film from which the stills were printed. The *Sun*'s defence was that the stills were necessary to expose the falsity of Mr al Fayed's claims that his son and Princess Diana were about to get married and had spent two hours at Villa Windsor in preparation for their new life together. The stills showed Diana spent twenty-eight minutes there.

But the Court of Appeal observed that "misappropriation and the use of other people's property is not likely to be regarded as fair dealing".

The Court of Appeal further stated that the court must judge the fairness by the objective standard of whether a "fair-minded and honest person" would have dealt with the copyright work, in the manner that the *Sun* did, for the purpose of reporting the relevant current events. The Court of Appeal concluded that a "fair-minded and honest person would not have paid for the dishonestly taken driveway stills and publish them in a newspaper".

The law does not specify how many words of an article or seconds of a broadcast you can safely use. It is a question of degree.[23] Lord Denning in *Hubbard v. Vosper*[24] stated:

It is impossible to define what is fair dealing. It must be a question of degree. You must consider first the number and extent of the quotations and extracts. Are they altogether too many and too long to be fair? Then you must consider the use made of them. If they are used as a basis for comment, criticism or review, that may be a fair dealing. If they are used to convey the same information as the author, for a rival purpose, that may be unfair. Next, you must consider the proportions. To take long extracts and attach short comments may be unfair. But short extracts and long comments may be fair.

The BBC brought action against British Satellite Broadcasting in 1988 over its news broadcasts of the World Cup finals, which included footage from the BBC broadcasts. The BBC had paid £900,000 for the right to transmit live coverage of the World Cup. British Satellite Broadcasting used excerpts from the live broadcasts to show highlights of the matches on its sports channel. The excerpts lasted between fourteen and thirty-seven seconds each and were shown up to four times in the period of twenty-four hours that followed each match. The judge held that the showing of the excerpts was fair dealing.[25]

CRITICISM AND REVIEW

The fair dealing doctrine lets critics include a clip from a film or a passage from a novel in their reviews to illustrate a point. Because negative critics would never get permission to do this, the fair use exemption exists to stop copyright law from being used to stifle criticism. This means that if you are commenting on a copyrighted work, making fun of it, teaching about it or researching it, you can make some limited use of the work without permission. For example, you can quote excerpts to show how poor the writing quality is. You can teach a course about Derek Walcott and quote lines from his poems to the class to do so.

As underscored in *ProSieben AG v. Carlton UK Television Ltd*,[26] the terms "criticism or review" and "reporting current events" are often broad, and their precise boundaries cannot be precisely defined. In that case, German television company ProSieben recorded and broadcasted in Germany an exclusive interview with a woman who was intent on carrying to term eight embryos despite medical advice. Carlton, a British television company, made and broadcasted a programme on the subject of "chequebook journalism", in which it incorporated a thirty-second extract of ProSieben's programme. Subsequently, ProSieben complained of copyright infringement by Carlton using the extract from its programme. In deciding the case, the court had to determine whether Carlton was protected under the "fair dealing" provisions.

The court had to raise the issues of whether Carlton used the programme for the purpose of criticism or review and/or for reporting currents events and whether it was used fairly. It also had to consider whether the programme incorporating the infringing material was a genuine piece of criticism or review, or was it "something else, such as an attempt to dress up the infringement of another's copyright in the guise of criticism" (at page 618).

The Court of Appeal held that the programme was made for the purpose of criticism of works of chequebook journalism, especially because the extract shown was very short and was not audible with the original English soundtrack, and that the usage did not lead to an unfair competition or exploitation of ProSieben's right.

The extent of criticism was further defined in *Time Warner Entertainment v. Channel Four Television Corporation*[27] in which the defendant used twelve clips, amounting to 12.5 minutes from the film *A Clockwork Orange* to criticize the copyright owner's decision to withhold it from circulation. The court explained that "criticism of a work need not be limited to criticism of style. It may also extend to the ideas to be found in a work and its social or moral implications".

On the other hand, the *Sunday Telegraph* was unsuccessful in its fair dealing defence when it published verbatim extracts from a lengthy confidential minute prepared by Paddy Ashdown, a former member of Parliament and former leader of the Liberal Democratic Party. The extracts contradicted denials emanating from Downing Street of stories in other newspapers concerning the extent of planned cooperation between New Labour and the Liberal Democrats.

The court[28] found that the Telegraph Group did not make use of the minute for the purposes of criticism or review; they rather criticized the actions of the minister, and so the newspaper did not need to copy the minute at all.

Three factors were considered on the assessment of fair dealing:[29] "(1) whether the alleged fair dealing was in commercial competition with the owner's own exploitation of the work, (2) whether the work had already been published or otherwise exposed to the public and (3) the amount and importance of the work which had been taken".

The Court of Appeal held that the *Sunday Telegraph*'s publication was in conflict with Ashdown's own intention to publish his memoirs, that the minute had not been previously published and that finally a substantial part was copied.

This might be a bitter pill; journalists, to demonstrate the accuracy and reliability of their reports, would instinctively wish to display the supporting documents. Perhaps, in similar circumstances, it would be sufficient to report that the journalists had a copy of the minute and to use smaller extracts just to prove so.

CARNIVAL COVERAGE

Distinctively, Trinidad and Tobago's copyright law protects "works of mas" and Grenada's law refers to "works of carnival"[30] but the definition is the same. News coverage and taking photographs of mas bands for current events will not be an infringement of copyright. However, a souvenir *Carnival* magazine or television documentary would be. Media houses and photographers usually negotiate the payment of fees with the National Carnival Broadcasting Association and the National Carnival Development Foundation in Trinidad and Tobago and the Spicemas Corporation in Grenada.

MORAL RIGHTS

The creators or authors of copyright work also enjoy moral rights that are independent of their economic rights.[31] They have the right to be identified, not to have their work subjected to derogatory treatment and not to have work falsely attributed to them. Infringement of moral rights is prohibited by statute and is also actionable at common law. Thus, Lord Byron succeeded in an action for a false representation that a book was his work.[32] Derogatory treatment means mutilation, deletion, distortion or other modification that would be prejudicial to their honour or reputations.

For example, Grenada Copyright Act 2011, Section 20 (1),[33] provides:

> Independent of his economic rights, and even where he is no longer the owner of the economic rights, the author of a work shall have the right—
> (a) to have his name indicated prominently on the copies and in connection with any public use of his work; (b) to not have his name indicated on the copies and in connection with any public use of his work; (c) to use a pseudonym; (d) to object to any distortion, mutilation or other modification of, or other derogatory action in relation to his work which would be prejudicial to his honour or reputation.

An illustration of what amounts to distortion is found in *Delves-Broughton v. The House of Harlot*.[34] An original photograph of a model was cropped, the image reversed and the forest background deleted. The court held that such treatment was a distortion because considerable time and effort went into the composition of the original photograph and it was important to the photographer that the forest appear for artistic reasons. However, *Gatley on Libel and Slander* (twelfth edition) casts doubt on this interpretation of the law and prefers the view in *Pasterfield v. Denham,*[35] in which the court stated that the claimant must also establish damage to professional reputation or honour as a result of the "distortion".

These rights do not apply to fair dealing with any work made for the purpose of reporting current events or any copyright work created for publication in a newspaper, magazine, periodical, encyclopedia or to any work made available for such publication with consent of the author.

"False attribution" is an infringement of moral rights. If someone grants an interview and the newspaper publishes an article that purports to have been written by the interviewee, without the interviewee's consent, he or she may have an action for false attribution.

In *Moore v. News of the World,*[36] in England, Dorothy Squires, a professional singer, was interviewed by a reporter who took notes of the interview and wrote them up into an article the same night. The singer was not shown the article and knew nothing of its contents until she saw it in the paper. The lengthy article described her relationship with her divorced husband. The article stated that it was written "by" the singer followed by the words, in smaller print, "talking to" the reporter. The article was written in the first person as if Ms Squires had been herself talking. She had not, however, used the words in the article, and she claimed that much of the article was fiction. She was able to obtain damages for false attribution (as well as libel because the article portrayed her as an embittered and unprincipled woman).

Parodying someone's work is permissible but a parody could take on the quality of false attribution.

In the unusual case of *Clark v. Associated Newspapers,*[37] a member of Parliament who was well known for his diaries that documented his public and private life, succeeded in a passing off claim when a London evening paper with over a million readers published a series of articles parodying his diaries together with a photograph of the plaintiff.

Underneath the headline was an introductory paragraph containing in capital letters the name of the real author and words to the effect that the author was imagining how the plaintiff would record the day's events.

Although the articles referred to current events as strands of reality on which the imagined entries were based, much of the contents of the articles were obvious fantasy and wild exaggeration.

The writer intended that the contents of the introductory paragraph, with the prominent reference to the author's real name, the use of the word *secret* in the title and the obviously exaggerated text would indicate to readers that the articles were parodies and not in fact written by the plaintiff. The claimant brought an action against the defendant claiming it had infringed his right not to have a literary work falsely attributed to him as author and that, in so doing, the defendant had unlawfully appropriated and diluted his goodwill and reputation as an author.

The court granted an injunction restraining the continued publication of the articles, holding that the prominent display of the name and photograph of the plaintiff constituted a distinct and unequivocal representation that he was the author and that representation was not sufficiently neutralized by the counter-indications in the articles to prevent a substantial number of readers being deceived.

PRIVACY OF PHOTOGRAPHS

Moral rights also include the right to privacy in photographs, film and audio-visual work. Even when someone does not own the copyright, he or she can complain about the use. People have the right not to have copies of their private photographs or videos issued to the public.

The Antigua and Barbuda Copyright Act, Section 17, is typical:[38]

[A person] who for private and domestic purposes commissions the taking of a photograph or the making of a film has, where the resulting work is a protected work, the right not to have –

a.   copies of the work issued to the public;
b.   the work exhibited or shown in public; or
c.   the work broadcast or included in a cable programme service".

For example, if a bride commissions[39] a photographer to record her wedding, the copyright will belong to the photographer, unless there was an agreement to the contrary.[40] Some time later, the bride becomes newsworthy and a media house obtains photographs of the bride on her wedding day. The media house that publishes the images may have infringed the rights of the bride as well as the commercial rights of the photographer.

LETTERS AND MANUSCRIPTS

When someone submits a letter to the editor or an article, it is presumed it is for publication. The editor has the right to alter it, even substantially, unless the terms of an agreement expressly say otherwise.[41]

NOM DE PLUME

Where journalists write under pen names or pseudonyms, the property of the pseudonym belongs to the journalists as part of their stock in trade, but that rule can be displaced by an agreement express of implied that provides it belongs to the journalist's employers.[42]

NEWS STORIES

There is no copyright in news itself. Being the first one to break a story does not invest you with ownership of the information. However, there is copyright in the mode of expression or form in which the information is conveyed, and that includes the skill, labour and judgment employed by the journalist in creating the article. This means that you cannot stop rivals from repeating facts of public importance, but no one has the right to take a substantial portion of your research, argument, illustrations or authorities for the purpose of making or improving a rival publication.

On payment of syndication fees, the news media can use or publish articles and photographs from wire services, such as Caribbean Media Corporation and Associated Press,[43] without fear of violating copyright. In 2008, Associated Press accused competitor All Headline News of copying material without permission and without paying a fee. They eventually settled the dispute. But in 2005 a photographer sued Associated Press for distributing without her permission a picture she took in 2001 of the mushroom cloud caused by the crash of United Flight 93 in a field near her house.[44] The parties settled.

In *Walter v. Lane*,[45] a *Times* reporter was entitled to damages when his version of a politician's public speech was copied word for word by a rival newspaper. Rudyard Kipling's news dispatches, printed in the *Times*, were regularly and substantially reproduced without that newspaper's consent in the *St James Evening Gazette*. Justice North held that their copyright had been infringed.

Merely rewriting someone else's work to save oneself the trouble of conducting one's own inquiries will be a sham and of no protection. Although there is no copyright in facts, news or information, persistent "lifting" of facts from another media house may still be an infringement because of the skill, labour and time invested in researching and verifying those bulletins and stories.

Radio stations have been known to nakedly copy stories from the print media without even an attempt at rewriting. And print journalists are not above listening to a public figure being interviewed on television or radio and reproducing substantial chunks in their own publications.

Copyright also attaches to such supporting material as illustrations and maps, and before use, journalists must seek permission from the copyright owner. For example, in 1997, a group of Trinidadians flew to St Vincent and the Grenadines to watch a cricket match. The plane disappeared and the Trinidad *Express* wished to use a chart of the area to illustrate an article on the tragedy. It had to seek permission from the copyright owners to publish the chart for the E.T. Joshua Airport, St Vincent, which was granted for the specific occasion.

IMAGE RIGHTS

Although editorial use of someone's image for the purpose of reporting or commenting on current events is permissible, unauthorized exploitation of someone's name and image for commercial gain is not.

Such actions would constitute the common law tort of passing off.

Irvine v. Talksport Ltd[46] involved an action for passing off on the grounds of false endorsement. Talksport radio published, in a promotional brochure, a doctored photograph of former racing driver Eddie Irvine listening to a Talksport radio, creating the false impression that he had endorsed Talksport.

Irvine had to establish that he had a significant reputation as a racing driver and that the actions of Talksport were a misrepresentation that damaged his goodwill.[47] A more recent case of passing off involved Barbadian pop star Rihanna who argued successfully that Topshop used her image without permission on a T-shirt.[48]

Journalists, too, can become celebrities and are entitled to protect the use of their names and reputation. In India, well-known television journalist and author Barkha Dutt[49] filed a complaint with the WIPO Arbitration and Mediation Center against Easy Ticket and Vas Kapavarapu,[50] who had registered the barkhadutt.com domain in 2007. WIPO held that the complainant had acquired fame by her work of journalism and the respondent's use of the registered domain name was in bad faith. WIPO thus ordered the respondent to transfer the domain name to the complainant.

However, in most Commonwealth jurisdictions, neither celebrities nor lesser mortals can complain of merely being photographed. There must be something more to bring about legal action, such as passing off, copyright infringement, breach of confidence, breach of contract or harassment.[51]

Jamaica took a bold step to creating a tort of wrongful misappropriation of personality in *Robert Marley Foundation v. Dino Michelle Foundation*.[52] The case concerned the defendant's use of the image of the late reggae legend Bob Marley on T-shirts. Clarke J held that, "Although no West Indian or English decisions recognize property in personality per se", dicta in other earlier cases[53] support the concept of "property interest as distinct from a privacy interest attached to personality". The judge held that Bob Marley, a "celebrity of renown at home and abroad", had a right to the exclusive use of his name and likeness or image. The right entitled him to exploit it commercially. The commercial use of Bob Marley's name and likeness or image by the defendant without the consent of the Robert Marley Foundation "constitutes an invasion or impairment of the plaintiff's exclusive right . . . resulting in damage to the plaintiff. Such conduct on the defendant's part constitutes the tort of appropriation of personality, separate and distinct from the tort of passing off".

The case has not been affirmed in the appellate court, and UK cases continue to resist this new or extended tort.

CHAPTER 16

DAMAGES

Reputations are not bought and sold on the open market and there is no standard therefore to adjudge the extent of the damaged reputation.

—Justice Vasheist Kokaram[1]

History scholars say the first fully reported case of libel being tried in an English court occurred during the reign of James I (1567–1625) who had outlawed duelling. From that time, less violent remedies were sought to deal with insults.

Damages for defamation are usually large in the case of media organizations because the courts think that they can pay more for their mistakes than individuals can. Money is a poor remedy for the damage to someone's good reputation.[2] The taint can have devastating consequences; people lose jobs and friends; they endure humiliation, and some really do suffer emotional agony. A Jamaican banking employee who was libelled by a newspaper, said when the defamatory article was published, his mother called from abroad and, despite what he told her, said, "I never know I bring up a t'ief."[3]

Justice Kokaram in the Trinidad and Tobago case of *Faaiq Mohammed v. Jack Warner* summed it up like this:

> A good reputation is a precious commodity. It can be built over years to symbolize the reputation established by a family over generations. A name and a reputation carries meaning in small-knit communities as it does on the national arena. It has value and worth. It is an inviolable asset in a community of beings. It is part of the dignity of one's existence and instils a sense of self confidence, honour and pride. But just as it is difficult to establish a good name it conversely is easy for it be damaged by unjustified stigmas, unprovoked baseless attacks and ill informed, unwarranted assaults on character that unfortunately occur in the daily exchanges of expression between members in society.[4]

The court[5] will consider such factors as the gravity of the allegation, its prominence, its social context, the mode, extent and duration of circulation of the medium in which it was published, its enduring nature and its repetition. So defaming someone on page one in a daily with national circulation will attract more damages than a snippet in a box tucked away near an item about a charity barbecue. Also, the Internet has a huge circulation and is a "world of infinite memories".[6]

The *Express* newspaper in Trinidad and Tobago had a traumatic experience in 2009 when it appealed a judgment against it in favour of Conrad Aleong, former chairman of the national airline BWIA, only to have the Court of Appeal increase the award of general damages from TT$450,000 to TT$650,000.[7] The prominence of the articles was a key factor. The series had been published over a five-week period, Sunday after Sunday, "adding to the respondent's distress, hurt and humiliation", which the appeal court considered to be an aggravating feature.

The court will also weigh the position, reputation, standing and credibility of a claimant, as well as the stature of the defendant and the extent to which his statements will be given prominence and belief. Public figures and political heavyweights may receive greater sums than Joe Bloggs. For example, in Trinidad and Tobago, awards between TT$250,000 and TT$800,000 have been awarded to politicians and prominent business people. Keith Rowley, as leader of the opposition, was awarded TT$475,000 to reflect the gravity of the "corruption bogey" and impact on his career as a politician.[8]

In Jamaica, in *Gleaner Co. Ltd v. Abrahams*,[9] the Privy Council affirmed the Jamaican Court of Appeal's award of J$35million (then equivalent to £533,000) to a former Minister of Tourism who was accused of taking bribes.

In Guyana, one of the highest sums awarded in a libel matter was G$4.5 million,[10] to a highly qualified specialist in neurosurgery who was libelled in several articles published by the *Kaieteur News* in 2002, which suggested he was of unsound mind, incompetent and a self-important dictator who was executing a stranglehold on the medical association. The Court of Appeal elevated the award to G$15 million[11] but the Caribbean Court of Justice, in 2016, reinstated the original award.[12]

The Caribbean Court of Justice held that the trial judge had properly considered all relevant factors, including the damage to the claimant's professional and personal life; the lack of apology by the newspaper; the limited reach of the *Kaieteur News*, which was not a daily and not available online – as well as the potential of high awards to inhibit responsible journalism and even economically ruin a publisher.

Subjective features include the effect on the claimant's feelings, importance of reputation for working life, the importance of reputation in the eyes of those who heard or read the defamatory remarks and the difficulty of remedying the libel.

Damages can be reduced if the defendant retracts the statements and publishes an apology. Evidence of the bad reputation of the claimant may also be a mitigating factor, as in the case of Mr Jones who denied he was a pimp and had links with the KGB but agreed he was a heavy drinker, teller of obscene stories and a womanizer who allowed his flat to be used for prostitution.[13]

As in any civil court case, the judge may also award costs against you if you lose, or will simply say that each side should pay their own costs of the case.

One complaint about the higher damages courts have been willing to award is the "chilling effect" on journalism. The concern is that media houses would prefer to abort their unborn stories, or settle out of court, rather than risk huge damages. Tour de France cyclist Lance Armstrong retained a heavyweight firm of lawyers and sued the *Sunday Times* in England in 2004, after it published allegations of his doping. After protracted legal wrangling, the newspaper settled for £300,000 in 2006. After Armstrong was exposed as a liar and doper in 2012, the *Times* sued Armstrong for the return of the payment plus £720,000 in interest and costs.[14]

There are several kinds of damages – general, aggravated, special and exemplary, and they all hurt when you have to pay them.

General damages compensate the person's loss of reputation, shame or hurt feelings. Under common law, once the court has found that a claimant has been defamed, the person does not have to prove that actual harm has been done.[15] General damages do not have to be large sums of money. If a judge or jury finds that a claimant has been defamed but that no real harm has been done, the claimant may be awarded nominal damages of a few dollars. Nominal damages may also be awarded if the court feels that an accused person has been only slightly at fault or that the claimant was in some way responsible for the defamation in the first place. In *Dering v. Uris*,[16] a doctor who had been forced by the Nazis at Auschwitz concentration camp to perform experimental surgery on other prisoners sued the defendant Leon Uris over a reference to him in his book, *Exodus*. But the jury, as an expression of their contempt for the doctor, awarded Dering damages in the sum of halfpenny, the lowest coin of the realm.

Special damages compensate for any loss of business or earnings the claimant may have suffered as a result of the defamation. These could also include any money the claimant has spent as a result of the defamation, for example, in placing advertisements or sending letters to clients denying allegations. With corporate claimants, the focus will be on their business or trading reputation. Any falling off of custom, loss of specific contracts, particular employment and hospitality can also be allowed, once pleaded and proved.[17]

Aggravated damages can be awarded if the court thinks that the defamation was deliberate, possibly out of ill will or any other improper motive or malice. For example, if you knew you were publishing something false and defamatory, but went ahead with the story to stir up a scandal and boost readership or listener numbers, the court would probably award aggravated damages against you. They may also award aggravated damages if the defamation was said in a particularly nasty way.

The irrepressible Jack Warner, former FIFA vice president, created the Independent Labour Party after being fired from the government led by Prime Minister Kamla Persad-Bissessar. He commanded huge media attention every time he publicly opened his well-known mouth.

The local government elections in 2013 had resulted in a deadlock in the Chaguanas Borough Corporation among three political parties – the Independent Labour Party, the United National Congress and the People's National Movement. Warner accused a young Muslim[18] Independent Labour Party councillor of receiving a TT$2.5 million bribe from the United National Congress to cast a vote for one of its candidates. He ranted at two media conferences, vented on a morning television programme and repeated the accusations via a loudspeaker on the roof of a vehicle driven through Chaguanas area and the Charlieville community of the young councillor.

The defamation was aggravated by the unabated and vicious attacks. Warner contemptuously declared he would throw the pre-action protocol letter in the dustbin – behaviour that the claimant described as "hooliganism". The court declared the attack entirely unfounded and unsubstantiated and awarded the sum of TT$200,000, which included aggravated damages (plus TT$50,000 for exemplary damages).[19]

Exemplary damages can be awarded where the defamation is so severe that compensatory and aggravated damages are an inadequate remedy. The defamation will bear the quality of "outrageousness" with an element of flagrancy, cynicism or oppression.[20] In *Keith Mitchell v. Steve Fassihi, George Worme, Grenada Today and Express Newspapers Ltd*,[21] the prime minister of Grenada was defamed in the *Grenada Today* newspaper. The article was a reprint of a petition that Fassihi had sent to the queen in which he accused the prime minister of using his office to harbour criminals, assist in money laundering, using public funds to set up private family businesses, financing his election campaign with money from criminals, appointing known criminals as ambassadors and so on.

Worme was editor and proprietor of the newspaper that was printed by Express Newspapers Ltd. None of the defendants ever filed a defence. Neither was there ever an apology or retraction. Damages were awarded in the sum of EC$100,000 but the judicial officer or master[22] did not award exemplary damages. The Court of Appeal, however, found the master was at fault, and awarded Mitchell EC$50,000 in exemplary damages.

Gordon JA stated:[23]

> The lack of any defence, or even an affidavit on the issue of damages, leads ineluctably not only to the conclusion that the Respondents had not a scintilla of proof, nor even a whiff of suspicion, of the truth of their statements, but also to the conclusion that they were contemptuous of the right and entitlement of every citizen to enjoy his reputation for rectitude, absent proof to the contrary.

And if that were not enough, the newspaper repeated the libel in a subsequent issue. The Court of Appeal viewed such behaviour as a clear and proper inference that the paper was contemptuous of any sanction the law might provide. Compensatory damages even with aggravated damages were an inadequate remedy in those circumstances.

APPENDIX

Revised Association of Caribbean MediaWorkers Code of Ethics[1]

4 October 2015

Members of affiliated organizations of the ACM and individual members commit to the belief that ethical journalism provides a foundation for ensuring the free exchange of accurate, fair and thorough information.

We subscribe to the principles that require journalists to seek truth and report it, minimise harm, act independently and be accountable and transparent.

Ethical journalism should be accurate and fair and journalists should be honest and courageous in gathering, reporting and interpreting information. Journalists should, at all times, fight the tendency towards subjectivity, and be professionally fair in all aspects of their work.

Journalists should:

1. Verify information before releasing it and use original sources whenever possible;
2. Refrain from engaging in self-censorship to suppress information that the public has the right to know;
3. Identify sources clearly but, when anonymous sources are cited, explain why anonymity is necessary in that instance and maintain the integrity of secret sources of information;
4. Resist and refuse bribery of any kind;
5. Diligently seek subjects of news coverage to allow them to respond to criticism or allegations of wrongdoing;
6. Seek to ensure that the public's business is conducted in the open, and that public records are open to all;
7. Avoid stereotyping;

8. Never deliberately distort facts or context, including visual information;
9. Balance the public's right to know against the need to minimise harm;
10. Consider those who may be affected by news coverage, particularly when children, victims of sex crimes and other vulnerable groups are involved;
11. Avoid pandering to lurid curiosity and salacious detail;
12. Resist favoured treatment of organizations or individuals including politicians, business interests or advocacy groups to influence coverage;
13. Respond quickly to questions about accuracy, clarity and fairness and acknowledge mistakes and correct them promptly and appropriately;
14. Be transparent in their work and expect to be held to the same standard as others, and oppose unethical conduct within the fraternity;
15. Not plagiarise.

GLOSSARY

acquittal. Jury verdict that a criminal defendant is not guilty, or the finding of a judge that the evidence is insufficient to support a conviction.

admissible. Term used to describe evidence that may be considered by a jury or judge in civil and criminal cases.

advocate. Person who speaks on behalf of another in court, usually a lawyer with rights of audience in the courts.

affidavit. Written or printed statement made under oath.

affirmed. In the practice of the Court of Appeal, it means that the Court of Appeal has concluded that the lower court decision is correct and will stand as rendered by the lower court.

alternate juror. A juror selected in the same manner as a regular juror who hears all the evidence but does not help decide the case unless called on to replace a regular juror.

alternative dispute resolution (ADR). A procedure for settling a dispute outside the courtroom. Most forms of alternative dispute resolution are not binding, and involve referral of the case to a neutral party such as an arbitrator or mediator.

amicus curiae. Latin for "friend of the court". It is advice formally offered to the court in a brief filed by an entity interested in, but not a party to, the case.

appeal. Request made after a trial by a party that has lost on one or more issues that a higher court review the decision to determine if it was correct. To make such a request is "to appeal" or "to take an appeal". One who appeals is called the "appellant"; the other party is the "respondent".

arraignment. A proceeding in which a criminal defendant is brought into court, told of the charges in an indictment or information and asked to plead guilty or not guilty.

arrestable offence. A serious offence, one for which the maximum punishment is at least five years in prison.

assizes. High Court sittings. Assizes used to be periodic criminal courts held by visiting judges in towns in England until 1972, when replaced by the permanent Crown Court.

attorney general. Principal law officer for the state or the crown.

bachelor of law. Degree in law from a law school, abbreviated to LLB.

bail. Release, prior to trial, of a person accused of a crime, under specified conditions designed to assure that person's appearance in court when required. Also can refer to the amount of bond money posted as a financial condition of pretrial release.

balance of probabilities. Standard of proof in civil matters. One party meets the standard by showing that his or her version of events is more probable than not.

Bar. Collectively, all attorneys.

bench trial. Trial without a jury, in which the judge serves as the fact-finder.

beyond reasonable doubt. The standard of proof required in a criminal trial. The prosecution must prove to the magistrate or jury that there is no reasonable doubt that the defendant committed the offence for which he is charged.

bona fide. Latin for "good faith", it signifies honesty, the "real thing".

brief. A written statement submitted in a trial or appellate proceeding that explains one side's legal and factual arguments.

burden of proof. The duty to prove disputed facts. In civil cases, claimants or plaintiffs generally have the burden of proving their case. In criminal cases, the prosecution has the burden of proving the defendant's guilt. (See *Standard of proof*.)

capital offence. A crime punishable by death.

case law. The law as established in previous court decisions. A synonym for legal precedent. Akin to common law, which springs from tradition and judicial decisions.

caseload. The number of cases handled by a judge or a court.

cause of action. A legal claim.

chambers. The offices of a judge and his or her staff. Also law offices.

claimant. Person bringing a claim against another. Another term for plaintiff.

collateral. Property that is promised as security for the satisfaction of a debt.

common law. The legal system that originated in England and is now in use in many Commonwealth countries, as well as the United States, which relies on the articulation of legal principles in a historical succession of judicial decisions. Common law principles can be changed by legislation. The legal system is distinct from the Continental system of law known as civil law.

community service. A special condition the court imposes that requires an individual to work, without pay for a civic or nonprofit organization.

complaint. A written statement that begins a criminal process, in which the person making the report details the allegations against the defendant. The person making the report or complaint is called the complainant. Sometimes, the police officer who lays the charge is called the complainant and the aggrieved party is the virtual complainant.

concurrent sentence. Prison terms for two or more offences to be served at the same time, rather than one after the other. Example: Two five-year sentences and one three-year sentence, if served concurrently, result in a maximum of five years behind bars.

contempt. Criminal offence relating to interference with the proper administration of justice.

copyright. A property right that exists in original literary, dramatic, musical or artistic works; sound recordings, films, broadcasts or cable programmes, and the typographical arrangement of published editions.

damages. Money that a defendant pays a claimant or plaintiff in a civil case if the claimant or plaintiff has won. Damages may be compensatory (for loss or injury) or punitive (to punish and deter future misconduct).

de facto. Latin, meaning "in fact" or "actually". Something that exists in fact but not as a matter of law.

defamation. Cause of action that may be slander or libel and concerns a person's reputation.

default judgment. A judgment awarding a claimant or plaintiff the relief sought in the complaint because the defendant has failed to appear in court or otherwise respond to the complaint.

defendant. In a civil case, the person or organization against whom the claimant or plaintiff brings suit; in a criminal case, the person accused of the crime.

de novo. Latin, meaning "anew". A trial de novo is a completely new trial. Appellate review de novo implies no deference to the trial judge's ruling.

deposition. An oral statement made before a magistrate in committal proceedings.

director of public prosecutions. Legal officer of the state who brings prosecutions; the head of the prosecution service.

discharge. Release of a defendant.

disclosure. Statements and other material that one side (usually the prosecution) gives or discloses to the other side in criminal matters.

docket. List of cases for trial.

due process. In criminal law, the constitutional guarantee that a defendant will receive a fair and impartial trial. In civil law, the legal rights of someone who confronts an adverse action threatening liberty or property.

equitable. Pertaining to civil suits in "equity" rather than in "law". In English legal history, the courts of "law" could order the payment of damages and could afford no other remedy. A separate court of "equity" could order someone to do something or to cease to do something, by granting an injunction, for example.

equity. A branch of law based on a judicial assessment of fairness as opposed to the strict and rigid rule of common law. Also, the value of a debtor's interest in property that remains after liens and other creditors' interests are considered.

evidence. Information presented in testimony or in documents that is used to persuade the fact-finder (judge or jury) to decide the case in favour of one side or the other.

exclusionary rule. Doctrine that says evidence obtained in violation of a criminal defendant's constitutional or statutory rights is not admissible at trial.

exculpatory evidence. Evidence indicating that a defendant did not commit the crime.

ex parte. A proceeding brought before a court by one party only, without notice to or challenge by the other side.

fair comment. Defence to an action for defamation based on a comment, fairly made, on a matter of public interest.

file. To place a paper in the official custody of the clerk of court to enter into the files or records of a case.

guardian/guardian ad litem. A person given legal authority by law or court order to have custody of another person or their property or both, because they are not able to manage their own affairs.

habeas corpus. Latin, meaning "you have the body". A writ of habeas corpus generally is a judicial order forcing law enforcement authorities to produce a prisoner they are holding, and to justify the prisoner's continued confinement.

hearsay. Evidence presented by a witness who did not see or hear the incident in question but heard about it from someone else. With some exceptions, hearsay generally is not admissible as evidence at trial.

House of Lords. Upper House of the Parliament in the United Kingdom; the apex court or court of last resort in the United Kingdom. In 2009, the Supreme Court of the United Kingdom assumed role of the new court of final appeal in United Kingdom.

in camera. Latin, meaning "in a room". Often means outside the presence of a jury and the public. In private.

inculpatory evidence. Evidence indicating that a defendant did commit the crime.

indictment. Written accusation or the formal charge issued by prosecution that is read to the jury at start of a trial.

information. A formal accusation by the prosecution that the defendant committed a misdemeanour. See also indictment.

injunction. A court order preventing one or more named parties from taking some action. A preliminary injunction often is issued to allow fact-finding, so a judge can determine whether a permanent injunction is justified.

judgment. The official decision of a court finally resolving the dispute between the parties to the case.

judicial review. Application to the High Court pertaining to the legality of the action of a certain body, such as an inferior court or other private or public body.

jurisdiction. The legal authority of a court to hear and decide a certain type of case. It also is used as a synonym for venue, meaning the geographic area over which the court has territorial jurisdiction to decide cases.

jurisprudence. The study of law and the structure of the legal system.

jury. The group of people selected to hear the evidence in a trial and render a verdict on matters of fact.

jury instructions. A judge's directions to the jury before it begins deliberations regarding the factual questions it must answer and the legal rules that it must apply.

justification. Defence to action in defamation based on the truth or factual accuracy of the words published by the defendant.

lawsuit. A legal action started by a claimant or plaintiff against a defendant based on a complaint that the defendant failed to perform a legal duty that resulted in harm to the plaintiff.

libel. Defamatory publication in a permanent form.

lien. A charge on specific property that is designed to secure payment of a debt or performance of an obligation. A debtor may still be responsible for a lien after a discharge.

limitation. The time within which a lawsuit must be filed or a criminal prosecution begun. The deadline can vary, depending on the type of civil case or the crime charged.

liquidation. The sale of a debtor's property with the proceeds to be used for the benefit of creditors.

litigation. A case, controversy, or lawsuit. Participants (claimants or plaintiffs and defendants) in lawsuits are called litigants.

magistrate. A judicial officer of the lower court who conducts summary criminal and petty civil matters and initial proceedings in criminal cases.

mistrial. An invalid trial, caused by fundamental error. When a mistrial is declared, the trial must start again with the selection of a new jury.

mitigation. Address to the court by defendant or advocate at sentencing with a view to reduce the sentence.

moot. Not subject to a court ruling because the controversy has not actually arisen, or has ended.

motion. A request by a litigant to a judge for a decision on an issue relating to the case.

motion in limine. A pretrial motion requesting the court to prohibit the other side from presenting, or even referring to, evidence on matters said to be so highly prejudicial that no steps taken by the judge can prevent the jury from being unduly influenced.

natural justice. Legal doctrine that refers to the rule against bias (no man must be a judge in his own cause) and the right to a fair hearing (the right to be heard).

next friend. Person (often a relative) who voluntarily helps a minor.

nolle prosequi. (Pronounced *no-lay pro-say-kwee*) Latin for "we shall no longer prosecute".

objection. Attorneys may object to evidence being adduced by the other side or to particular questions being asked.

opinion. A judge's explanation of the decision of the court. Because three or more judges may hear a case in the Court of Appeal, the opinion in appellate decisions can take several forms. If all the judges completely agree on the result, one judge will write the opinion for all. If all the judges do not agree, the formal decision will be based upon the view of the majority, and one member of the majority will write the opinion. The judges who did not agree with the majority may write separately in dissenting or concurring opinions to present their views. A dissenting opinion disagrees with the majority opinion because of the reasoning and/or the principles of law the majority used to decide the case. A concurring opinion agrees with the decision of the majority opinion, but offers further comment or clarification or even an entirely different reason for reaching the same result. Only the majority opinion can serve as binding precedent in future cases. See also *Precedent*.

per curiam. Latin, meaning "for the court". In appellate courts, often refers to an unsigned opinion. Per incuriam means "through lack of care". A judgment may be overturned because it was given per incuriam, without consideration of a relevant statute or case.

peremptory challenge. The right to exclude a certain number of prospective jurors without cause or giving a reason.

plaintiff. A person or business that files a formal complaint with the court. Under new Civil Procedure Rules, the term *claimant* is used.

plea. In a criminal case, the defendant's statement pleading "guilty" or "not guilty" in answer to the charges.

pleadings. Written statements filed with the court that describe a party's legal or factual assertions about the case.

precedent. Court decision in an earlier case with facts and legal issues similar to a dispute currently before a court. Judges will generally "follow precedent", meaning that they use the principles established in earlier cases to decide new cases that have similar facts and raise similar legal issues. A judge will disregard precedent if a party can show that the earlier case was wrongly decided, or that it differed in some significant way from the current case.

pretrial conference. A meeting of the judge and lawyers to plan the trial, to discuss which matters should be presented to the jury, to review proposed evidence and witnesses, and to set a trial schedule. Typically, the judge and the parties also discuss the possibility of settlement of the case.

prima facie. Latin, "on the face of it".

puisne. Judge inferior in rank to appellate court judges.

remand. Send back.

res gestae. Latin for "things done", an exception to the hearsay rule in criminal cases.

res ipsa loquitur. Latin for "the thing speaks for itself".

res judicata. Latin for "the thing has been judged".

sanction. Penalty or other type of enforcement used to bring about compliance with the law or with rules and regulations.

sequester. To separate. Sometimes juries are sequestered from outside influences during their deliberations.

standard of proof. Degree of proof required. In criminal cases, prosecutors must prove a defendant's guilt "beyond a reasonable doubt". In civil cases, the standard is "on the balance of probabilities", which is lower than criminal standard.

standby. Right of prosecution in some jurisdictions to exclude a juror without giving reasons. This is separate from peremptory challenge.

statute. Law passed by a legislature.

sub judice. Latin, "under the judge". A case is under judicial consideration and public discussion elsewhere is prohibited.

subpoena. Command, issued under a court's authority, to a witness to appear and give testimony.

subpoena duces tecum. Command to a witness to appear and produce documents.

tort. A civil, not criminal, wrong. A negligent or intentional injury against a person or property, with the exception of breach of contract.

transcript. Written, word-for-word record of what was said, either in a proceeding such as a trial, or during some other formal conversation, such as a hearing or oral deposition.

uphold. The appellate court agrees with the lower court decision and allows it to stand. See affirmed.

verdict. Decision of a trial jury or a judge that determines the guilt or innocence of a criminal defendant, or that determines the final outcome of a civil case.

voir dire. Trial within a trial held in absence of jury.

warrant. Court authorization, most often for law enforcement officers, to conduct a search or make an arrest.

NOTES

FOREWORD

1   (2019) 3 WLR 18, at para 1.
2.   (2019) UKPC 38, at para 3.
3.   Ian Benjamin is an attorney with more than thirty years' experience in practising and teaching law in Trinidad and Tobago, the United Kingdom, and Australia. He is head of Bethany Chambers in Trinidad and Tobago and was appointed senior counsel in 2018.

CHAPTER 1

1.   Inter-American Court of Human Rights, 2 July 2004. Ulloa was a journalist who was jailed after publishing articles about a state diplomat. The court found Costa Rica had violated the freedom of thought and expression (Article 13) of the American Convention on Human Rights.
2.   On 5 April 2016, ruling on the constitutionality of market caps for cable TV providers.
3.   Audio Visual Communications Law, Judgment No. 79 of 5 April 2016.
4.   E. Lanza, *National Case Law on Freedom of Expression* (Office of the Special Rapporteur for Freedom of Expression on Inter-American Commission on Human Rights, 2016), para 26.
5.   *Handyside v. UK* (1976) EHRR 737.
6.   *Redmond-Bate v. DPP* (1997) 7 BHRC 375.
7.   Trinidad and Tobago modelled its short and general Bill of Rights on the 1960 Canadian Bill of Rights. See T. Robinson, A. Bulkan and A. Saunders, *Fundamentals of Caribbean Constitutional Law* (London: Thomson Reuters, 2015).
8.   Antigua (Section 12), Bahamas (Section 23), Barbados (Section 20), Belize (Section 12), Dominica (Section 10), Grenada (Section 10), Guyana (Article 2),

Jamaica (Section 22), St Kitts and Nevis (Section 12), St Lucia (Section 10), St Vincent (Section 10), Trinidad and Tobago (Section 12).

9.   3 AER 400 HL.

10. *Frank Hope Competent Authority and the Attorney General v. New Guyana Co. Ltd and Vincent Teekah* (1979) 26 WIR 233.

11. *Attorney General and Others and Antigua Times Ltd* (on appeal from the Court of Appeal of West Indies Associated States Supreme Court, Antigua) (1976) AC 16.

12. *Cable and Wireless Dominica Ltd v. Marpin* (2000) 57 WIR 141, at 151. See also Robinson, Bulkan and Saunders, *Fundamentals of Caribbean Constitutional Law*.

13. *T&T Newspaper Publishing Group Ltd v. Central Bank and Attorney General of Trinidad and Tobago* (1989) HC 24.

14. The court conducted a comparative study and found that the constitutions of Barbados, Dominica, Jamaica, St Lucia and Guyana do not specifically refer to freedom of the press.

15. *Courtenay v. Belize Broadcasting Co. Ltd* (1990) 38 WIR 79.

16. *Rambachan v. Trinidad and Tobago Television Ltd* (No. 1789 of 1981) (17 January 1985).

17. *Benjamin v. Minister of Broadcasting and Information* (2001) UKPC.

18. Para 49.

19. (1966) 2 AER 459.

20. (2001) UKPC 11.

21. *Hector v. AG of Antigua and Barbuda* (1990) 37 WIR 216, at 219.

22. Of course, the private sector also engages in advertising boycotts or threats to boycott when journalists offend, but this chapter focuses on the exercise of government power within the constitutional framework for freedom of expression and freedom of the press. Among private citizens, ostracism has long been used as a form of peaceful advocacy, as during civil rights protests in the United States. *NAACP v. Claiborne Hardware Co.* (1982) 458 US 886.

23. This was drafted by former democratic presidents, Nobel Prize winners, journalists and leaders and approved at the Inter American Press Association hemispheric conference on freedom of expression in Mexico City in 1994.

CHAPTER 2

1.   The doctrine of *stare decisis*, which means "to stand by things decided".

2.   Further reading: Rose-Marie Antoine, *Commonwealth Caribbean Law and Legal Systems* (London: Routledge-Cavendish, 2008).

3. The Judicature (Resident Magistrates) (Amendment and Change of Name) Act 2015 amended existing legislation so that magistrates became parish judges and part of the judiciary; previously magistrates were treated as civil servants. A chief parish judge was also appointed.

4. Guyana has abolished appeals to the Privy Council since 1970.

5. Examples: Barbados Magistrates Courts Act, 1996–27, Section 238; Bahamas Magistrates Act, Ch 42, Section 8; Dominica Magistrates Code of Procedure, Ch 4.20, Section 141; Guyana Summary Jurisdiction (Appeals) Act, Ch 3:04, Sections 2–3; Jamaica Justices of the Peace (Appeals) Act, Section 3 and Judicature (Resident Magistrates) Act, as amended by Act No. 6 of 2016, Section 293; Trinidad and Tobago Summary Courts Act, Ch 4:20, Section 128.

6. In *Barry Francis and Roger Hinds v. the State* (Crim App Nos. 5 and 6 of 2010), which considered the constitutionality of a mandatory minimum sentence of twenty-five years for drug trafficking, five judges of the Trinidad and Tobago appellate bench heard the appeal.

7. Anguilla, Antigua, British Virgin Islands, Dominica, Grenada, Montserrat, St Kitts and Nevis, St Lucia, and St Vincent and the Grenadines.

8. Parties request documents through their attorneys before the trial commences. This information-gathering process helps attorneys prepare for trial.

9. Jury Act, Section 242.

10. *Allman v. Hardcastle* (1903) JP 440.

11. For example, murder, kidnapping, robbery, rape and most other sexual offences, serious assaults.

12. A matter that can be tried only on indictment before a judge and jury or judge alone.

13. Antigua Magistrates Code of Procedure Amendment Act, No. 13 of 2004; Barbados Magistrates Court Act 15 of 2016; Jamaica Committal Proceedings Act 2013; St Lucia Act 11 of 2008.

14. Dominica Act, No. 14 of 1995, the Criminal Procedure (Preliminary Enquiries) Act 1995, Section 2 amended by Act, No. 1 of 2004; Grenada Act, No. 35 of 1978, Criminal Procedure (Preliminary Enquiries) Act 1978, Section 2; Guyana Sexual Offences Act, Ch 803, First Schedule Trinidad and Tobago Act, No. 23 of 2005, Section 10, creating new Section 23A to Ch 12:01.

15. Cayman Islands made the change in 1995. Trinidad and Tobago introduced the Miscellaneous Provisions (Trial by Judge Alone) Act, 10 of 2017, in 2019 whereby a defendant can elect to be tried by a judge alone. The Turks and Caicos published its Trial without Jury Ordinance in 2010 and the Constitution Order 2011/1681 came into force in 2012 with the right to jury trial omitted. Belize had its first

judge-only trial in 2012, after passing legislation in 2011 making no-jury trials mandatory for murder, attempted murder and conspiracy to murder. Since 1974, Jamaica introduced its Gun Courts, initially with magistrates, but from 1976, a justice of the Supreme Court must try such matters.

16. *Nankissoon Boodram v. the State* (1997) 53 WIR 353.

17. Further reading on criminal system: Dana Seetahal, *Commonwealth Caribbean Criminal Practice and Procedure,* 5th ed. (London: Routledge, 2019).

18. *Mary Neptune (administratrix of estate of Anisha Neptune) v. the Attorney General of Trinidad and Tobago and Nicholas Leith PC,* Civ 2008-00481.

19. Example: In 1970, during Black Power unrest in Trinidad and Tobago, army lieutenants Rex Lasalle and Raffique Shah led a mutiny and, in 1971, were famously court-martialled and found guilty of mutiny and other military and civil offences, but successfully appealed and were released in 1972. Shah became a union leader and newspaper columnist while Lasalle emigrated and became an alternative medicine practitioner. See *R v. Lasalle and Others* (1972) 20 WIR 425.

20. Ch 88:01.

21. Ch 4:50.

22. Ch 94.

CHAPTER 3

1. *Sports Illustrated,* 7 February 1994. Barkley became known for compulsive gambling. Harding's ex-husband orchestrated an attack on figure skater Nancy Kerrigan before the 1994 Olympics. Harding was banned for life.

2. *Othello,* Act 3, Scene 3.

3. 13 DLR 3d 484.

4. Defamation law in region is governed by statute and common law. Statute, generally, is silent on the definition of defamation.

5. *Eden Shand v. Caribbean Communications Network,* HCA 1782 of 1994.

6. *Melodrum v. Australia Broadcasting Corporation* (1932) VLR 425.

7. (2017) Cv 2008/00225.

8. The judge distinguished this from a TV documentary copies of which were distributed, as in *Eden Shand.*

9. Cv 2014/03990.

10. Ch 6:03.

11. Barbados Defamation Act 1996, Ch 199, Section 3 (1); Jamaica Defamation Act 2013, Section 6; Antigua and Barbuda Defamation Act 2015, Section 6. "The distinction at law between libel and slander is abolished."

12. "Chicken v. Ham: The Lawyer's Dream", 71 *The Uncommon Law* 73 (1955).
13. *Abraham Mansoor v. Grenville Radio Ltd et al.,* ANUHCV 2004/0408.
14. *Howlett v. Holding and Another* (2003) EWHC 286 (QB) (25 February 2003, QBD).
15. *Loutchansky v. Times Newspapers Ltd* (No. 2) (2001) EMLR 36, at 13.
16. See chapter 4, "Cyberlibel".
17. *Duke of Brunswick v. Hamer,* QBD 2 Nov 1849.
18. *Anderson v. Southeastern Fidelity Insurance Co.* (1983) 307 SE2d 499, at 500, as per Weltner J. Case had to do with interpretation of an insurance clause.
19. (1835) 2 Cr M and R 156. Injurious allegations against a man on trial were reported but the palliative was that the report included the fact he was found not guilty by the jury.
20. (1937) 2 AER 204.
21. *Clive Hubert Lloyd v. David Syme and Co. Ltd* (1986) 2 WLR 69.
22. *Panday v. Gordon* (2005) UKPC 36.
23. *Kenneth Gordon v. Daniel Chookolingo (as executor of the will of Patrick Choo-kolingo) and Others* (1988) UKPC 19.
24. *Robin Montano v. Harry Harnarine and Hindu Credit Union Communications,* CV No. 2007-02612.
25. *Rajnie Ramlakhan v. TNT News Centre,* HCA S-634 of 1999.
26. *Forde v. Shah and TnT News Publishing Group* (1990) 1 TTLR 73.
27. *Gleaner Co. v. Abrahams* (2003) UKPC 55.
28. Ch 11:16. Also, Belize Libel and Defamation Act, Ch 169, Section 6; BVI Ch 42, Section 10; Dominica Libel and Slander Act 7:04, Section 10; Grenada Libel and Defamation Act, Ch 171, Section 6; St Kitts and Nevis, Ch 4.18, Section 10; St Vincent and the Grenadines, Ch 128, Section 14.
29. Ch 6:03.
30. (1967) 19 Trin LR (Pt II) 117.
31. (1931) AER 131.
32. (1940) 3 AER 31.
33. *Baturina v. Times Newspaper* (2011) AER (D) 268 Mar.
34. *HRH Prince Alwaleed Bin Talal Bin Abdulaziz Al Saud and Another v. Forbes LLC and Others* (2014) EWHC 3823. (QB).
35. V. MacCullum, "Pain and Libel", *Law Society Gazette,* 9 August 2001, at 24. Jeffrey Howard Archer, Baron Archer of Weston-super-Mare, was a member of Parliament, then a best-selling novelist who became deputy chairman of the Conservative Party before he resigned amid allegations that he paid a prostitute for sex. He won record damages of £500,000 and £5700,000 in costs from the *Star* newspaper.

He was convicted in 2001 on two charges of perjury and two for perverting the course of justice and sentenced to four years in prison.

36. Charleston v. News Group Newspapers", *The Times,* 31 March 1995.

37. Supreme Court of Georgia, SE 2d 534 (Ga 1984).

38. (1902) 4 F 645.

39. "Madd Chicken Song".

40. ECSC 2010/2009.

41. *Le Roux v. Dey* (2011) 4 LRC 688.

42. *Elton John v. Guardian News and Media* (2008) All ER (D) 134 (Dec).

43. (1964) AC 234, at 258.

44. But despite accuracy of report, one may still incur actions for breach of confidence and misuse of private information. See chapter 13.

45. (1981) 31 WIR 107.

46. Page 112.

47. (1981) 3 All ER 450. See also *P. C. Ramdhan and Others v. Assang, Grant, and Trinidad Express Newspaper,* Civil Appeal 54 of 2004, in particular para 14. See also *Panday v. Gordon,* Civil Appeal 175 of 2000 per Hamel Smith J.A., at paras 17–20, 25, 57.

48. Barbados Defamation Act, Ch 199, Section 26 (1).

49. *Flynn v. Higham* (1983) 149 Cal.App.3d 677, 197 Cal.Rptr. 145, citing *Saucer v. Giroux* (1921) 54 Cal.App. 732, 733 (202 P. 887).

50. *Gairy v. Bullen* (No. 1) (1972) 2 OECSLR 115 (Court of Appeal, Eastern Caribbean States).

51. *Jordan v. The Advocate Co. Ltd* (1998), HC, 727 of 1996, unreported.

52. *Newstead v. London Express Newspaper Ltd* (1940) 1 KB 377.

53. Unintentional defamation is discussed in chapter 5 on defences.

54. As per Lord Atkin in *Knuppfer v. London Express Newspapers* (1944) 1 AER 495, at 498.

55. (1952) 107 F Supp 96.

56. *Bodden v. Bush* (1986) CILR 100 (Grand Court, Cayman Islands).

57. (1944) 1 AER 495.

58. *Grappelli v. Derek Block Holdings Ltd* (1981) 1 WLR 822; *Hayward v. Thompson* (1982) QB 47. Lord Denning who heard both English cases arrived at opposing conclusions. His reasoning for distinguishing the two has been rejected.

59. UKPC (2019) 38.

60. At para 3: "It is a feature of the common law of defamation that neat conceptual solutions do not always provide satisfactory answers to the endlessly varied fact-sets with which judges and (in some jurisdictions) juries have to wrestle, for

the purposes of achieving an outcome which properly accords with justice and common sense."

61. Barbados Defamation Act, Ch 199, Section 26.
62. *Hardline Marketing v. Republic Bank Limited,* CV No. 2014/429.
63. (1964) AC 234.
64. HCA, 1071 of 1995, Trinidad and Tobago.
65. (1993) AC 534, [1993] 1 All ER 1011.
66. (2013) EWHC 196 (QB).
67. But see chapter 5 on defence of "innocent dissemination".
68. Antigua and Barbuda, Grenada, Jamaica, and Trinidad and Tobago have abolished their provisions.
69. The judge stopped the case on account of insufficient evidence that she had written the letters.
70. *Worme and Anor v. Commissioner of Police* (Grenada) (2004) UKPC 8.
71. Antigua Seditious and Undesirable Publications Act, Ch 396; Dominica Seditious and Undesirable Publications Act, Ch 10:03; Grenada Criminal Code, Article 327; St Lucia Criminal Code, Section 329; Trinidad and Tobago Sedition Act, Ch 11:04.
72. Section 6 (1).
73. *Commissioner of Police v. Ordan Graham,* Mag Appeal 56 of 2006.
74. Sedition is overt conduct, such as speech and organization that tends towards insurrection. When it is in a written or other permanent form, it is called seditious libel.
75. The charge was under Section 53 (1) (b) of the Criminal Code.
76. Abu Bakr, as leader of the Jamaat-al-Muslimeen, led an insurrection against the government in 1990.
77. When necessary to report potentially seditious material as a news item, journalists must be careful not to adopt the statements as their own.
78. *Joyce v. Sengupta* (1993) 1 AER 897. The claimant chose an action for malicious falsehood rather than defamation because legal aid was available for the former.

CHAPTER 4

1. (2009) HV 000/70, at para 58. The judge, delivering judgment in a libel case, was making the point that newspapers have no special dispensation. Freedom of expression belongs to all, and newspapers and news media have no greater protection under the constitution than anyone else.
2. The International Telecommunication Union, an agency of the United Nations, estimated that at end of 2018, the number of world Internet users was 3.9 billion;

www.itu.int, accessed 14 March 2019. As of 30 June 2018, the number of world Internet users was estimated at 4,208,571,287 by Internet World Stats, www .internetworldstats.com, accessed 14 March 2019.

3. HCA 56 (10 December 2002).

4. This chapter focuses on the tort of defamation in cyberspace. But Internet users, whether professional journalists or Joe and Jane Bloke, should be aware that laws governing malicious falsehood, breach of confidence, misuse of private information, data protection, copyright and contempt of court also apply to online as well as offline publications. These areas are discussed elsewhere in this book.

5. Vol. 32 (2012), at para 566.

6. *Godfrey v. Demon* (2001) QB 201.

7. *Al Amoudi v. Brissard and Another* (2006) AER (D) 21.

8. DomHCV2011/17, at paras 55–64. The judgment was overturned by Privy Council on a different point, pertaining to the defence of *Reynolds* privilege.

9. *Crookes and Another v. Newton* (2012) 1 LRC 237.

10. *Barrick Gold Corp supra.*

11. (2002) HCA 56.

12. The High Court of Australia is the supreme court and the final court of appeal in Australia.

13. Two years after the decision, Dow Jones settled the case out of court.

14. (2004) EWCA Civ 75.

15. Newspapers and electronic media will also be liable for imprudent comments posted by readers and audiences that give rise to contempt of court.

16. (2001) EWCA Civ 1805, (2002) QB 783, (2002) 1 All ER 652.

17. The common law "multiple publication" rule is that each publication is a fresh libel; this rule is particularly oppressive where online statements are concerned because every time the material is accessed, the limitation period begins afresh. The "single publication" rule is also called the "first publication" rule and means that the limitation period runs from the date of the first publication and not the last. The wording of the Jamaican and Antiguan legislation suggests the intention of the provisions was to set the clock ticking from the date the material is "first published" but there is some uncertainty. The Hansard record of the debate in the Jamaican Parliament does not reveal any such consideration. A model "single publication" provision is Section 8 of the UK Defamation Act 2013, which provides in Subsection 3 that for purposes of the time limitation of defamation actions, "any cause of action against the person for defamation in respect of the subsequent publication is to be treated as having accrued on the date of the first publication".

18. *Lord McAlpine of West Green v. Bercow* (2013) EWHC 1342 (QB).

19. J. Best, "Comedian Alan Davies Pays Lord McAlpine £15,000 Damages over 'Distressing' Retweet", www.mirror.co.uk.
20. 26 October 1998, unreported.
21. (2004) 71 OR (3d) 416 (CA)
22. Paras 32–34.
23. CV No. 2016/02974.
24. Where media houses are publishing online, it is easy enough to identify the defendant. With individuals, who often use fake profiles, it can be challenging to identify the author of a post. Evidence from service providers and IT professionals may be necessary. One can also rely on circumstantial evidence, including the pattern of communication, photographs, details of activities and social events. The court will hold, on a balance of probabilities, whether the account in issue is controlled by the purported owner.
25. *Tamiz v. Google* (2013) EWCA Civ 68.
26. (1995) WL 323710 (NY Sup Ct.)
27. There is no reason such an approach would not be followed in our jurisdictions.
28. Section 22 (5) f and g.
29. Section 23 (2) f and g.
30. TNLR 128, *The Times*, 15 March 2001.
31. This type of order is known as a *Norwich Pharmacal* order after the landmark decision in *Norwich Pharmacal Co. v. Customs and Excuse Commissioners* (1974) 1 AC 133, in which innocent defendants had information on the identity of wrongdoers.
32. "Collaborative journalism" is another term sometimes used synonymously with "citizen journalism".
33. "Freedom, Facts and Fake News: Straddling Media Communications in the 21st Century", hosted by University of the Southern Caribbean, 5 and 6 February 2019, at Radisson Hotel, Port of Spain, Trinidad.
34. And who brought down the futuristic, corrupt and genocidal government of Vivienne Rook (Emma Thompson) in the edge-of-the-seat 2019 television series *Years and Years*? Citizen journalists with their cell phones, recording and exposing the death camps!
35. A second pathologist found that Tomlinson had died of internal bleeding from blunt force trauma.

CHAPTER 5

1. HCA 1490 of 1984 (unreported, Trinidad and Tobago).
2. 1971, unreported.

3. See Section 3, Libel and Defamation Act 1846, Trinidad and Tobago.

4. See Cayman Defamation Law 27 of 1966 (1995 revision), Section 6; Jamaica Defamation Act 2013, Section 20; Guyana Defamation Act, Cap 6:03, Section 7; Grenada Libel and Slander Act, Cap 171, Section 12; Section 7 (2) Barbados Defamation Act 1997, Cap 199, Section 7 (2), which provides that a defence of truth or justification shall not fail by reason only that the truth of every charge is not proved if the words not proved to be true do not "materially injure" the claimant's reputation.

5. *Lewis v. Daily Telegraph* (1964) 2 WLR 736.

6. (1982) 39 OR 2nd 100.

7. *France v. Simmonds* ECSC Civ App 2 of 1985, unreported; (1990) 38 WIR 72.

8. *Guerra v. Trinidad Guardian,* CV No. 2007-02612.

9. (2002) QB 735, at para 25.

10. (2010) UKSC 53, at 22.

11. 2001 EMLR.

12. This defence usually arises in commentaries and reviews, rather than in news reporting where one expects journalists to be balanced and neutral.

13. Civ 2004/2353.

14. *Newsday,* 7 June 2004, at 13.

15. *Clapham v. Daily Chronicle* (1944) LRBG 71, Supreme Court, British Guiana.

16. *Tse Wai Chun Paul v. Albert Cheng* (2001) EMLR.

17. *Vander Zalm v. Times Publishing* (1980) 18 BCLR 210 (BCCA).

18. 1987 High Court, Barbados 317 of 1986 (unreported) Carilaw BB 1987 HC 41.

19. (1909) 2KB 444.

20. Guyana Defamation Act, Ch 6:03, Section 12; Trinidad and Tobago Libel and Defamation Act, Ch 11:16, Section 5; Belize Libel and Defamation, Ch 169, Section 4; Dominica Libel and Defamation Act, Ch 7:94, Section 3; BVI Libel and Defamation Act, Ch 42, Section 3; St Kitts/Nevis Libel and Defamation Act, Ch 4:18, Section 3; St Vincent and the Grenadines Libel and Defamation Act, Cap 128, Section 15; Antigua Defamation Act 2015, Section 11 refers to offer to make amends and correction; similarly, Barbados Defamation Act, Ch 199, Section 16.

21. Sometimes, the term *conditional privilege* is used.

22. Apart from common law protection, legislation protects fair and accurate reports of public proceedings of the legislature "anywhere in the world" (e.g., Antigua Defamation Act 2015, Section 1; Jamaica Defamation Act 2013, Section 10 (a) Part II) or in "any Commonwealth country" (e.g., Barbados Defamation Act 1997, Ch 199, Section 1).

23. *Express,* 3 July 2004, at 3.

24. Examples: Trinidad and Tobago Libel and Defamation Act 1846, Section 13; Jamaica Defamation Act 2013, Section 23; Antigua Defamation Act 2015, Section 25, which omits "contemporaneous"; Belize Libel and Defamation Act, Cap 169, revised edition 2000, Section 8; Barbados Defamation Act 1997, Ch 199, Section 9 (1).

25. (1893) 1 QB 65, at 68.

26. *PCs Ramdhan, Morales, Matas and Williams v. Trinidad Express Newspapers Ltd and Others*, Civ App 54 of 2004.

27. (1996) 3 AER 385.

28. Page 20.

29. *Brewster v. Bridgemohan and Trinidad Publishing Co. Ltd,* 1222 of 1999, unreported.

30. (1993) Bda LR 13, CA.

31. (1980) Sup. Ct. Civ. Jur. No. 56.

32. *Mitchell v. Victoria Daily Times* (1944) 1 WWR 400.

33. *Cook v. Alexander* (1971) C 8698.

34. Para 13.37, 12th ed.

35. HC 2488/97.

36. (1868) LR 4 QB 74.

37. *Gatley on Libel and Slander*, para 15.37, 12th ed.

38. *Curistan v. Times Newspapers Ltd* (2008) EWCA Civ 432; *Buchanan v. Jennings* (2004), *The Times*, 19 July.

39. *Keith Rowley v. Michael Annisette* (2010) Cv 04909, Trinidad and Tobago.

40. Also, Antigua and Barbuda Defamation Act 2015, Section 25 (2).

41. Section 10 (1).

42. Ch 199, Schedule, Part I, Section 12 (2).

43. Defamation Act 2013, Section 11, Part II.

44. *Turkington and Others v. Times Newspapers* (2000) All ER (D) 1652.

45. Part II, Section 11.

46. See also Section 14 (1) First Schedule, Jamaica Defamation Act 2013.

47. (1892) 2 QB 56.

48. *Dwyer v. Esmonde* (1878) 2 LR Ir. 243, at 254.

49. *Watts v. Times Newspapers Ltd* (1997) QB 650.

50. *Turner v. MGM Pictures* (1950) 1 All ER 449, at 470–471.

51. *Joseph v. Partap, Mills, Daily News Ltd* (2005) HC 437.

52. (1999) 4 All ER.

53. Para 6.19, 12th ed.

54. Jamaica Defamation Act 2013, Section 22. Antigua Defamation Act 2015, Section 23.

55. Barbados Defamation Act 1996, Ch 199, Section 15.

56. (2013) HC, 780 of 2010, unreported.

57. "It is not a defence to a claim in defamation that the circumstances of the publication of the matter complained of were such that the person defamed was not likely to suffer harm to his reputation."

58. Antigua and Barbuda Defamation Act 2015, Section 33; Jamaica Defamation Act 2013, Section 28.

59. Antigua and Barbuda Defamation Act 2015, Section 11; Barbados Defamation Act, Ch 199, Section 16; Belize Libel and Defamation Act, Section 3; Guyana Defamation Act, Ch 6:03, Section 9; Jamaica Defamation Act 2013, Section 14; St Kitts/Nevis Libel and Slander Act, Ch 4:18, Section 2; Trinidad and Tobago Libel and Defamation Act, Ch 11:16, Section 4.

60. See *TV3 Network Ltd v. Eveready New Zealand Ltd* (1993) 3 NZLR 435 and *Moore v. Canadian Newspapers Co. Ltd* (1989) 69 OR (2d) 262 (Divisional Court).

61. Civ App 2015/01184.

62. Bahamas, six years, Limitation Act, Ch 83, Section 5; Barbados, three years, Defamation Act, Ch 199, Section 29; Belize, six years, Limitation Act 2000 (revised), Section 4; Cayman, three years, Limitation Law 1996, Section 4; Grenada, four years, Limitation of Actions Act, Ch 173, Section 40; Guyana, one year, Limitation Act, Ch 7:02, Section 9; Jamaica, two years, which may be extended to four, Defamation Act 2013, Section 33; Trinidad and Tobago, four years, Limitation of Certain Actions Act, Ch 7:09, Section 3.

CHAPTER 6

1. *Reynolds v. Times Newspapers Ltd* (1999) 4 All ER.

2. Section 22.

3. England has since abolished the *Reynolds* defence by virtue of the Defamation Act 2013. Instead, there is now a "public interest" defence and the test is reasonableness.

4. Page 627.

5. Page 627.

6. (2006) UKHL 44.

7. Pages 20–21.

8. *Grobbelaar v. News Group Ltd* (2002) 1 WLR 3024.

9. Lord Bingham remarked, at page 3036, "The tort of defamation protects those whose reputations have been unlawfully injured. It affords little or no protection to those who have, or deserve to have, no reputation deserving of legal protection."

10. Page 658.

11. (2001) EWCA Civ 536.

12. ANUHCV 2004/0408.
13. (2012) 2 AC 273.
14. Para 113.
15. UKPC 64 of 2014.
16. The panel of judges on the Judicial Committee of the Privy Council is called the board.
17. *Augustine Logie v. National Broadcasting Network Ltd and Ruskin Mark*, HCA Civ 556 of 001.
18. (2002) UKPC 31.
19. *Loutchansky v. Times Newspapers Ltd and Others* (No. 2) (2001) EWCA Civ 536.
20. Page 654.
21. Personal communication.
22. (2001) EWCA Civ 1634.
23. (2006) All ER (D) 182 (May).
24. In *Al-Fagih* the newspaper happened to be in support of the government and was not in political sympathy with either of the protagonists, yet it was able to avail itself of the reportage defence.
25. Para 15.
26. (2008) 1 All ER 750.
27. Page 766.
28. Much of the book also portrayed the trial of the informant and so was also protected by statutory privilege.
29. 12th ed. (London: Sweet and Maxwell), para 15.17, page 666.
30. Para 28.
31. (2008) 1 All ER 965.
32. (2014) JMSC Civ 167.
33. Slang for mix-up or mess.
34. 54/2004.
35. 118/2008.
36. Para 115.
37. *Conrad Aleong v. Trinidad Express Newspapers and Others*, CV 2006-02092.
38. Civ 2007/00348.
39. Para 107.
40. *National Media Ltd v. Bogoshi* (1998) (4) SA 1196, which held "reasonable conduct" could be a defence for media and false defamatory allegations would not be unlawful.
41. *Raja Gopal v. State of Tamile Nady* (AIR 1995) SC 264: magazine had right to publish purported autobiography of a prisoner, in which he describes corrupt

practices, even without his permission and could not be restrained by the state or its officials.

42. *Majid Nazami v. Muhammad Rashid* (PLD 1996) Lahore 410: reasonableness is a restriction on freedom to highlight matters of public importance.

43. *Lange v. Australian Broadcasting Corporation* (1997) 189 CLR 520.

44. PC Appeal No. 71 of 1998.

45. (2017) 3 LRC 573.

CHAPTER 7

1. *Scott v. Scott* (1913) AC 417.

2. (1987) 1 QB 582, 591H.

3. Similarly, Section 29 (1), Antigua and Barbuda Sexual Offences Act 1995; Section 138, St Lucia Criminal Code No. 9 of 2004.

4. Section 28 (3) Jamaica Sexual Offences Act; Section 29 (1) (a) Antigua and Barbuda Sexual Offences Act 1995; 138 (1) (a) St Lucia Criminal Code No. 9 of 2004.

5. 1993 Ch 154.

6. See Trinidad and Tobago, Section 41, Preliminary Enquiry (Indictable Offences) Act, Ch 12:01.

7. See Antigua Magistrates' Code of Procedure (Amendment) Act No. 13 of 2004; Barbados Magistrates Court Act 15 of 2016; Jamaica Committal Proceedings Act 2013; St Lucia Act No. 11 of 2008.

8. (1985) 150 JP 71.

9. Media law experts Geoffrey Robertson, QC, and Andrew Nicol, QC, hold the view that *Peacock* was wrongly decided and say that media comment on inquests need not be suppressed. *Media Law,* 4th ed. (London: Penguin, 2002), 495–96.

10. *Assistant Deputy Coroner v. Channel 4 Television Corporation* (2007) EWHC 2513 (QB).

11. Disparaging words about God, Jesus, the Bible. It applies only to the Christian religion. Muslims failed to have Salman Rushdie prosecuted for blasphemy on account of his book *Satanic Verses,* first published in 1988.

12. Similarly, Section 8, Libel and Defamation Act, Ch 169, Belize; Section 11 (3), Barbados Defamation Act.

13. Further reading: Seetahal, *Commonwealth Caribbean Criminal Practice,* chapter 19.

14. Children Act 12 of 2012; Family and Children Division Act 6 of 2016.

15. Sections 8–10 Youth Court Act 2005.

16. Sections 50–51, Juvenile Justice Act 2012 (Grenada); Section 6, Youth Court Act 2005, BVI; Section 21, Juveniles Act (Montserrat); Section 13 and Section 153, Children and Young Person Act (Dominica); Section 3 (1), Juvenile Courts Act (Anguilla); Section 4, Juvenile Act (Antigua); Section 147(1), Child Protection Act (Bahamas); Section 97, Juvenile Offenders Act (Barbados); Section 32, Juveniles Act (St Vincent); Section 87 (4) and (5) and Section 97, Children Act (Trinidad and Tobago).

17. (1998) 2 AER 673.

18. Anguilla Adoption of Children Act, Ch A35, Rules, Section 6; Antigua Adoption of Children Act, Ch 9, Rules, Section 7; Dominica Adoption of Infants Act, Ch 37:03, Rules, Section 8; Jamaica Children (Adoption of) Act, Rules, Section 6; Montserrat Adoption of Children Act, Ch 5:04, Rules, Section 7; St Kitts and Nevis Adoption of Children Act, Ch 12:01, Rules, Section 7; St Lucia Adoption Act, Ch 4:07, Rules, Section 11 (secrecy of applicants); St Vincent and the Grenadines Adoption of Children Act, Ch 225, Rules, Section 6; Trinidad and Tobago Adoption of Children Act, Ch 46:03, Rules, Section 6; Virgin Islands Adoption of Children Act, Ch 269, Rules, Section 7.

19. Section 153.

20. Section 147.

21. Section 11 (1). It is a criminal offence to publish in contravention of this section.

22. *Parens patriae* is Latin for "parent of the nation". In law, it refers to the public policy power of the state to act as the parent of any child or individual who is in need of protection.

23. Bakr rose to infamy when he led an insurrection in 1990. The sedition prosecution arose out of his Eid-ul-Fitr sermon at a mosque in November 2005, in which he spoke of the Islamic principle of paying a percentage of one's wealth to charity. The trial ended in a hung jury and a retrial was ordered.

24. Ch 11:16.

25. Ch 45:51.

26. In St Vincent and the Grenadines, in relation to any application under the Maintenance Act, Ch 234, which deals with financial provision for spouses and children, it is a criminal offence to publish more than names and addresses of parties, concise statement of the application and legal submissions, as provided in Section 24.

27. Ch 4:20.

28. Section 209 (2).

29. Further reading: Seetahal, *Commonwealth Caribbean Criminal Practice*.

30. Examples: Rule 28.16 Barbados Supreme Court Civil Procedure Rules; 2008; Rule 28.16 Belize Supreme Court Civil Procedure Rules 2005; Chapter 53 Bahamas

Supreme Court Rules of the Supreme Court; Rule 3.14 of Eastern Caribbean Supreme Court Civil Procedure Rules; Rule 28.17 Jamaica Supreme Court Civil Procedure Rules; Rules 28.16 and 28.17 of Trinidad and Tobago Civil Procedure Rules.

31. *Bermuda Press Holdings v. Registrar of the Supreme Court* 307 of 2015.

32. Pursuant to Section 3 (1) c of the Supreme Court Records Act 1955, which provides "subject to any Rules of the Court made under this Act, the Registrar, upon the application of any person and upon payment of the appropriate fee . . . shall cause to be prepared and furnished to that person a certified copy of any of the records of the Supreme Court".

33. The cherry on top for the *Royal Gazette* is that the chief justice quoted from a commentary written by John Barritt in the newspaper to explain why the media were entitled to receive copies of the documents on the court file used in a high-profile case in public hearing: "The cat's out of the bag and the public will want to know exactly what went down. This is their Government that is being talked about and called into question."

34. Prior to the case, the chief justice had drafted proposals for broadening access and draft amendments to the Rules of the Supreme Court, approved by the Bar Council, had been forwarded to the attorney general in late 2014.

35. 2015. Revised May 2016.

36. www.cps.gov.uk/publications.

CHAPTER 8

1. *AG v. BBC* (1981) 303, at 342.

2. Contempt of Court Act 1981.

3. Breaching an anonymity order may also be a criminal offence, as in St Vincent and the Grenadines, Section 11 (5) Witness (Special Measures) Act 2013. It is punishable by imprisonment of two years.

4. *Attorney General v. BBC* (1980) 3 AER 161 HL, where a local valuation court was not protected from contempt.

5. (1960) 2 QB 188, at 198.

6. (1962) NI 15.

7. (1963) 109 CLR 593.

8. (1992) 1 AER 503.

9. *Independent,* 6 July 1994.

10. *Her Majesty's Attorney-General v. Associated Newspapers Ltd and News Group Newspapers Ltd* (2011) EWHC 418 (Admin).

11. *Secretary for Justice v. Li Pang Kay* (2016) HKEC 766.

12. Just as it is no defence for the publisher of a libel to plead that he did not know that the matter was defamatory and had no intention to defame. *R v. Odhams Press Ltd* (1956) 3 WLR 796, at 801.

13. 2 Atk 469.

14. *R v. Odhams Press Ltd* (1956) 3 WLR 796.

15. (1980) 1 NSWLR 362, at 386.

16. (1991) 1 WLR 1194.

17. See *Re Central Television plc* (1991) 1 AER 347.

18. He later was hanged in Trinidad and Tobago in 1972 for the murder of barber Joe Skerritt. He was never tried for the murder of English model and socialite Gail Ann Benson, daughter of Conservative member of Parliament Leonard Plugge.

19. *AG v. Associated Newspapers Ltd,* 31 October 1997.

20. *Harding and Others v. Judy Diptee and Lennox Grant,* HC 4986/1992.

21. (1973) 3 AER 54, at 294.

22. Cr 06/08. In the matter of an application by the director of public prosecutions for an order of committal against Khamal Georges, Rosemary Sant and Guardian Media Ltd, *The State v. Barry Alphonso.*

23. In the matter of Power 102FM, 27 April 2010.

24. *Boodram v. AG of Trinidad and Tobago* (1996) 47 WIR 459 PC.

25. His conviction was overturned and he was found not guilty at a second trial in 1966. But he was a ruined man who never regained his skill as a surgeon. He drank heavily and died at age forty-six.

26. P. Davies, "Papers Cleared of Contempt in Knights Case", *Independent,* 1 August 1996.

27. *R v. Taylor* (1994) 98 Cr App R 361.

28. *BBC News,* 17 December 2003.

29. *A-G v. New Statesman and Nation Publishing Co. Ltd* (1980) 1 All ER 644.

30. Page 7.

31. *Solicitor General v. Radio New Zealand Ltd* (1994) 1 NZLR 48.

32. *The Bahamas Case,* 18 March 1883.

33. *Law Times Reports* (1900) Vol. 82: 534; *R v. Gray* (1900) 2 QB 36.

34. "Cet Animal est Mechant: One Judge's View of the Media", 1992. Holdsworth club 1, at 19.

35. *Spycatcher* is the autobiography of Peter Wright, former assistant director of Britain's counterintelligence agency. The government of Prime Minister Margaret Thatcher engaged in a twenty-three-month battle to ban the book and any reports about it in Britain and the Commonwealth. That helped fuel interest, and the book became a runaway bestseller that was widely available in America, and

was smuggled into the United Kingdom. It also sparked a showdown between a defiant Fleet Street and a stubborn prime minister over Britain's press and secrecy laws. Major newspapers violated the ban.

36. (1985) AC 339, HL.

37. *McLeod v. St Aubyn* (1899) AC 549, 68 LJPC 137.

38. *Attorney General v. Lingle* (1995) 1 SLR 696, as quoted in *Arlidge, Eady and Smith on Contempt* 1999, second edition, at 358.

39. *Attorney General for Trinidad and Tobago* (1981) 1 AER 244 PC.

40. *Re Peacock, Nora*, 202 of 1987, HC.

41. See chapter 12, "The Investigative Journalist".

42. *Wong Yeung Ng v. Secretary of State for Justice* (1999) 3 HCK 143 (CA).

43. Notwithstanding offensive reference at page 709 to "small colonies, consisting principally of coloured populations" by way of pointing out that courts will pay attention to "local conditions".

44. *Ambard v. Attorney General for Trinidad and Tobago* (1936) AC 322, at 335.

45. *R v. Metropolitan Police Commissioner, ex parte Blackburn* (No. 2) (1968) 2 All ER 319.

46. D. Seetahal, "Curious Judgments in Contempt Case", *Guardian*, 13 June 2004. See also *Independent Publishing Co. Ltd v. A-G and DPP of Trinidad and Tobago* PC 5 of 2003 and *TT News Centre and Others v. A-G and DPP of Trinidad and Tobago* PC No. 7 of 2003.

47. On the campaign trail, he had said, "Every man must build his castle. Every man must build him his big house."

48. Founder and principal of *18 Degrees North* investigative television show.

49. HCV (2016) 02296. *Between the Most Honourable Andrew Holness and Radio Jamaica Ltd, Television Jamaica Ltd, Zahra Burton and Global Reporters for the Caribbean LLC.*

50. *New York Times v. United States* (1971) 403 (US) 713.

51. Justice Stewart, with whom joins Justice White.

52. *Bonnard v. Perryman* (1891) 2 Ch 269; *Greene v. Associated Newspapers Ltd* (2005) QB 972.

53. *Southern Medical Clinic v. Cherry Ann Rajkumar* (2019) CA S-062; 00617. A former patient was injuncted from further displaying placards and posting on Facebook injurious allegations about her treatment at the clinic.

54. As per Jones J, at 10.

55. As per Rajkumar J, at 71.

56. *Hindu Credit Union Cooperative Society v. TnT News Centre Ltd and Others*, 2511/2004.

57. In Guyana, the chancellor is the head of the judiciary while the chief justice is the senior judge of the High Court.
58. *R v. D (Vincent)* (2004) EWCA Crim 1271.
59. (1989) 89 Cr App R 243.
60. Pan Am flight 103 was destroyed in 1988 by bombing over Lockerbie, Scotland. All passengers and crew were killed.
61. *In the matter of Paul Griffin* (1996) EWCA Crim 1262. The court spared him because counsel had been so unguarded that it was open to Griffin to think he was permitted to borrow the photographs, but held that the invasion of the privacy of counsel's papers could amount, in appropriate circumstances, to contempt.

CHAPTER 9

1. Antigua Constitution Section 58 (1); Belize, Section 54; Dominica, Section 43; Guyana, Article 72 (2); Jamaica, Section 49 (3); St Kitts and Nevis, Section 45; St Lucia, Section 42; St Vincent and the Grenadines, Section 45 (1); Trinidad and Tobago, Section 55 (1).
2. Bahamas Powers and Privileges Act, Ch 8, Section 4; Barbados Parliament (Privileges, Powers and Immunities) Act, Ch 9, Section 4; Grenada Legislature (Privileges, Immunities and Powers), Ch 168, Section 4.
3. See also *Reavey and Another v. Century Newspapers Ltd* (2001) NI 187.
4. (1973) QB 710, at 741.
5. Usually, if members of Parliament try to refer to a matter that is before the courts, the Speaker will stop them.
6. Erskine May, *Parliamentary Practice,* 25th ed., chapter 15, paras 15.2, 15.11. Available online at the parliament.uk website.
7. www.ttparliament.org.
8. House of Commons parliamentary debates, 24 January 1957.
9. Tony Banks, Newham North West, 19 July 1983, House of Commons Debate, vol. 46 cc268–341.
10. See chapter 5 on defences.
11. Prime Minister Patrick Manning dissolved Parliament on 8 April 2010.

CHAPTER 10

1. *North Division of the County of Louth* (1911) 6 O'M & H 103, at 163.
2. (1998) 26 EHRR 1, at para 42.
3. Ch 1:03.

4. Also Belize Representation of the People Act, Section 37; Cayman Elections Laws, Section 100 (1) (d); Dominica House of Assembly (Elections Act), Section 62(3); Grenada Representation of the People Act, Section 95; Jamaica Representation of the People Act, Section 97; St Lucia Election Act, Section 83 (3); St Vincent and the Grenadines Representation of the People Act, Section 74; Trinidad and Tobago Representation of the People Act, Section 74.

5. (2014) EWHC 662 (QB).

6. *R v. Woolas* (2012) QB 1, at 40.

7. (1911) 6 O'M & H 103.

8. 11 TLR 537.

9. 5 O'M & H 53.

10. (1959) 2 WIR 36.

11. Ch 342.

12. *Watkins v. Woolas* (2010) EWHC 2702 QB.

13. Sedition is conduct or speech inviting others to overturn the authority of the state or monarch.

14. It was formed in Montpelier, France, in 1985 by four journalists but now has international dimension. It monitors freedom of the press, violations against journalists and assists persecuted journalists.

15. Copyright permission was obtained to include excerpts in this publication. See also Lennox Grant and Wesley Gibbings, eds., *An Election Handbook for Caribbean Journalists* (Association of Caribbean Media Works, 2009). www.acmediaworkers.com.

CHAPTER 11

1. Italian inventor who in 1909 won the Nobel Prize for physics for his contribution to the development of wireless telegraphy.

2. Article 10 of the European Convention on Human Rights from which relevant sections of the regional constitutions are drawn expresses the right to freedom of expression but adds the following: "This Article shall not prevent states from requiring the licensing of broadcasting, television and cinema enterprises."

3. Section 22 (1e) of the Telecommunications Authority of Trinidad and Tobago Act provides that the concessionaire must adhere to the Broadcasting Code promulgated pursuant to the act. A draft code was published in 2014 and commented upon by media associations and press freedom groups.

4. *Observer Publications v. Matthew and Attorney General of Antigua* (2001) UKPC 11.

5. The Sanatan Dharma Maha Sabha, led by Sat Maharaj. He died on 16 November 2019.

6. *Central Broadcasting Services Ltd and Another v. the Attorney General of Trinidad and Tobago* (2018) UKPC 6.

7. (2000) Ch 274 (B).

8. Regulation 5 (h).

9. Grenada Telecommunications Act 31 of 2000, Section 68; St Vincent and the Grenadines Telecommunications Act 1 of 2000; St Lucia Telecommunications Act 27 of 2000, Section 69; St Kitts and Nevis Telecommunications Act 2 of 2000.

10. Regulation 3, Constitution (General Elections) Allocation of Broadcasting Time 1990.

11. *Surujrattan Rambachan v. Trinidad and Tobago Television and the Attorney General*, HC 4789 of 1982.

12. Justice Lennox Deyalsingh, at 64.

13. Section 12 (1) Barbados Broadcasting Regulations.

14. Section 13 (1).

15. Section D30, Concession for the Operation of a Public Telecommunications Network and/or Provision of Public Telecommunications and/or Broadcasting Services.

16. Broadcasting Amendment Act 10 of 2017. Section 2(b).

17. It first came into being in 1997, partly in response to the vilified "Green Paper", in which government sought to introduce a code of ethics for journalists, mandating that they promote "national unity" and economic and social progress.

CHAPTER 12

1. *Redmond-Bate v. DPP* (1997) 7 BHRC 375.

2. The quote originates with Finley Peter Dunne (1867–1936), who was an American humourist who wrote sketches starring a fictional Irishman named Mr Dooley. It has been famously borrowed and adapted by writers, politicians and speakers.

3. S. Coronel, "Corruption and the Watchdog Role of the News Media", in P. Norris, *Public Sentinel: News Media and Governance Reform* (Washington, DC: World Bank, 2010).

4. Ibid.

5. He held the post from 2008 to 2013.

6. www.cps.gov.uk.

7. *Francome and Another v. Mirror Group* (1984) 1 WLR 892 at 898.

8. Jamaica Cybercrime Act 2015; Belize Interception of Communications Act 2010; St Lucia Interception of Communications Act 2005; Trinidad and Tobago Interception of Communications Act, Ch 15:08. See also Antigua and Barbuda

Prevention of Terrorism Act 2005, Section 24 and Computer Misuse Act 2006; St Vincent and the Grenadines Electronic Transactions Act 2007, Section 69.

9. Examples: Barbados Telecommunications Act 2001, Section 82; British Virgin Islands Telecommunications Act 2010; Cayman Information and Communications Technology Authority Law 2011, Section 75. Guyana Telecommunications Act, Ch 47:02, Section 35; St Lucia Telecommunications Act 27 of 2000, Section 61.

10. Antigua and Barbuda Electronic Crimes Act 2013; Barbados Computer Misuse Act 2004; Cayman Computer Misuse Act 2015; Grenada Electronic Crimes Act 2013; Jamaica Cybercrimes Act 2015; Trinidad and Tobago Cybercrime Act 2017.

11. Section 2 (1), interpretation section.

12. Section 2 (1), interpretation section.

13. Hansard, 19 November 2010; 26 November 2010; 29 to 30 November 2010, 1 December 2010. www.ttparliament.org.

14. *D v. L* (2003) EWCA Civ 1169.

15. ABC reporter Sam Donaldson produced a programme on Medicare fraud and reporters posed as patients in clinics where they were told they needed cataract surgery when their eyes were fine. The clinic sued unsuccessfully for trespass, defamation and fraud. *Desnick v. American Broadcasting Co, Inc.* (7th Circuit 2000) 233 F.3d 514.

16. Third-party intervention: para 5 of written submissions by MLDI in *Haldimann and Others v. Switzerland*, Application 21820/09 to the European Court of Human Rights, in case where journalists were prosecuted for covert recording (contrary to Swiss law) in an insurance industry investigation.

17. P. Kihss, "Debate on Exposes Held Up a Pulitzer", *New York Times,* 18 April 1979, at 4.

18. *X Ltd v. Morgan Grampian Publishers* (1991) 1 AC 1.

19. *Bermuda Fire and Marine Insurance and Others v. Asbestos Claims Management Corporation and Others,* Civ 7 of 1995.

20. Under Section 16, Administration of Justice (Contempt of Court) 1979.

21. Mr Campbell said that he saw his role then as protecting the integrity of the judiciary. Personal communication: 20 September 2016. The writer was G.C.H. Thomas, author of the West Indian classic *Ruler in Hiroona.* The article appeared on 1 May 1987. On 15 May 1987, the *Vincentian* editor Nora Peacock published "An Explanation", which was an apology of sorts.

22. *Hope v. Brash* (1897) 2 QB 188.

23. (1983) QCA 043.

24. Section 69 (7) Eastern Caribbean Civil Procedure Rules; Section 69.02 (5) Guyana Civil Procedure Rules 2016.

25. A low-tech foul-up: The *New York Times* in 2004 merely blacked out some text when it published a PDF document handed over by source Edward Snowden. It revealed the name of a national security agent as well as the target of an operation in Iraq.

26. (1981) 1 AER 417.

27. "See Why I Did It", by the Steel Mole, *Sunday Times* (London), 2 November 1980, at 15.

28. *Goodwin v. UK* (1996) *The Times,* March 28.

29. OAS Inter-American Convention Against Corruption (1996) Article III, Section 8; UN Convention Against Corruption (2003) Article 33.

30. The whistle-blower legislation provides no guidance on this limitation.

31. HC Debate, 25 June 1920, cc896–7.

32. *The Times*, 3 February 1971, at 4, and 4 February 1971, at 2 and 15; *Sunday Telegraph*, 7 February 1971, at 12.

33. The legality of the order (compelling the *Guardian* to surrender the documents and thus reveal their source) was upheld in a decision of the House of Lords (*Secretary of State for Defence v. Guardian Newspapers Ltd* (1985) AC 339) by a majority of three against two.

34. (1977) 16 JLR 84.

35. In the United Kingdom, the catch-all Section 2 of the Official Secrets Act 1911 was trashed and replaced by the Official Secrets Act 1989.

36. This is different from criminal trespass, which is entering someone's premises with an unlawful purpose, such as to steal.

37. *Entick v. Carrington* (1558–1774) AER 41, at 45.

38. *Ferguson v. Welch* (1987) 3 AER 777; *Robson and Another v. Hallett* (1967) 2 AER 407.

39. *Lord Bernstein of Leigh v. Skyviews and General Ltd* (1977) 2 AER 902.

40. 100 F.3d 457 (6th Circuit 1996).

41. (1916) 2 KB. 880.

42. *State of Connecticut v. Edward Peruta*, 14 May 1991.

43. *Crevelle v. Cpl Copeland 8122*, CA Mag 83/2003.

44. See for example Code of Practice for Jamaican Journalists, para 3.

45. Section 15 (1).

46. (1995) 4 All ER 473, at 476.

47. (2001) EWCA Civ 1233.

48. Examples: Section 30A, Trinidad and Tobago Offences Against the Person Act (amendment) No. 11 of 2005; Section 3, Bermuda Stalking Act 1997; Section 118 St Lucia Criminal Code.

49. Ben Dowell and James Robinson, "Amy Winehouse Wins Court Ban on Paparazzi at Her Home", *Guardian*, 1 May 2009.

50. (2006) EWHC 41 (QB).

51. Para 13.

52. (2006) UKHL 34. This was a labour law case in which a gay man claimed he was bullied and harassed by his manager.

53. Example: Trinidad and Tobago POCA, Section 51.

54. See also Belize Financial Intelligence Act, Ch 138:02, Section 12; Jamaica Financial Investigations Division Act, No. 9 of 2010, Section 29; St Vincent and the Grenadines Financial Intelligence Unit Act 2001, Section 8; Trinidad and Tobago Financial Intelligence Unit Act, No. 11 of 2009, Section 22.

55. St Vincent and the Grenadines had similar provision in 1996 that was later repealed.

56. Bahamas Justice Protection Act 2008, Ch 64A; Jamaica Justice Protection Act 23 of 2001, Section 20; Trinidad and Tobago Justice Protection Act 78 of 2000, Section 21.

57. *Edmonton Journal v. R* (2013) ABPC 356, at para 30.

58. (1995) 2 LRC 808.

59. The principle is reinforced through the Inter-American Press Association's Declaration of Chapultepec, 1994.

CHAPTER 13

1. *Paracelsus,* 1835.

2. Section 8.

3. Section 10.

4. Section 15 (1).

5. The documents contained the personal financial information of many well-known public officials and wealthy investors. Some disclosures, such as tax avoidance in poor countries by the wealthy, raised moral and ethical issues although the transactions were legal. But some transactions also revealed money laundering through shell companies.

6. Breach of confidence may not be strictly classified as a tort but is rather an equitable doctrine. See *Vidal Hall and Others v. Google Inc.* (2014) EWHC 13 QB, at paras 52 and 71. Equity is a body of rules developed to mitigate or soften the severity of the common law. It brought about a system where, based on the overall fairness of the circumstances, judges could provide remedies beyond monetary compensation, such as injunctions.

7. (1848) 2 De G. & Sm 652.

8. *Argyll v. Argyll* (1967) Ch 302.

9. *Douglas v. Hello!* (2003) 3 AER 96.

10. (1990) 1 AC 109 HL, at 281.

11. *Francis George Polidore v. Crusader Publishing Co.,* Civil No. 380 of 1990.

12. *Folding Attic Chairs v. Loft Chairs* (2009) EWHC 1221 (Patents).

13. *Facenda Chicken v. Fowler* (1987) Ch. 117 CA.

14. (1968) 1 QB 396.

15. Page 405.

16. (1969) RPC 41, at 47–48.

17. UKPC (2017) 40. This concerned software development. The board decided that there was no breach of confidence because the information that was disclosed was of no particular value.

18. Page 48.

19. Mason J in *Commonwealth of Australia v. Fairfax and Sons* (1980) 147 CLR 39, at 45–51.

20. *Encylopaedia of Forms and Precedents,* vol. 32, 138.3.

21. Page 260.

22. (1990) 3 WLR 774.

23. UKSC (2013) 3.

24. (1990) AC 109, at 281–82.

25. (1994) EMLR 134.

26. *Creation Records Ltd v. News Group Newspapers* (1997) EMLR 444.

27. "In the public interest" is a malleable and complex concept relevant to privacy, confidentiality and defamation claims. It allows for publication of material that contributes to public debate. But the courts have stated that what is "interesting to the public" on the basis of its being scandalous or newsworthy is not necessarily in the public interest.

28. *Gartside v. Outram* (1857) 26 LJ Ch (NS) 113. Employers sought to prevent a former clerk from disclosing any of their dealings. The clerk said they conducted their business fraudulently and filed interrogatories that the employers declined to answer. There was no privilege to protect them from answering. Where an employer commits fraud in the course of business, the ordinary rule forbidding anyone employed in a confidential capacity from disclosing information obtained in such capacity does not apply. The public obligation supersedes the private.

29. *Lion Laboratories Ltd v. Evans and Others* (1984) 2 AER 417.

30. Page 422.

31. *Hubbard and Anor v. Vosper and Anor* (1972) 2 QB 84.

32. (2003) QB 195 CA, at 204.

33. (1994) Fam 192, at 203–4.

34. *Commissioner of Police and Attorney General v. Bermuda Broadcasting Co. Ltd and Others* (2007) SC Bda 38 Civ.

35. Para 33.

36. (2002) EWHC 137 QB.

37. *A v. B (a company)* 2002 12 BHRC 466; EWCA Civ 337, at 48.

38. See also *Ho v. Lendl Simmons* CV 2014-01949 (Trinidad and Tobago), in which the ex-lover of the cricketer obtained an injunction preventing him from further publishing confidential nude images. The defendant had sent the images to friends of the claimant.

39. (2008) EWCA Civ 446.

40. (2004) UKHL 22.

41. Para 51.

42. *Ho v. Lendl Simmons* CV 2014-01949 (Trinidad and Tobago, at 10).

43. *Australian Broadcasting Corp v. Lenah Game Meats Pty Ltd* (2001) HCA 63.

44. In *Applause Store Productions Ltd v. Raphael* (2008) EWHC 1781 (QB) membership details of the British National Party were leaked on a blog site. Members thereafter received malicious communications and property attacks. The blogger was fined under the Data Protection Act 1998.

45. *Z v. Finland* (1997), application 22009/93, EHRR 371.

46. 2003 AER (D) 255 (Jan).

47. 7 June 2001, unreported.

48. (2001) EWHC 32 (QB).

49. *Re S (A Child) (Identification: restriction on publications* (2004) UKHL 46, at 34.

50. *Richard v. BBC* (2018) EWHC 1837.

51. Page 57.

52. "Statement on BBC's Decision Not to Appeal the Ruling in the Sir Cliff Richard Case", 15 August 2018.

53. Tom Wells and Mike Sullivan, "Free Speech Falls Off a Cliff", *Sun*, 18 July 2018. www.thesun.co.uk/news.

54. Such as multimillionaire William Goad who was convicted for life in 2004 of sexual abuse and died in 2012. Ten of his victims came forward after reading of his arrest. Rolf Harris, television personality and family entertainer, was convicted of indecent assault in 2014. His arrest in March 2013 was not made public until several weeks after and prompted some victims to come forward.

55. The UK Leveson Inquiry into the Culture, Practices and Ethics of the Press in 2012 (vol. 2, para 2.39) recommended that it should be made abundantly clear to the police that "save in exceptional and clearly identified circumstances (for example, where there may be an immediate risk to the public), the names or

identifying details of those who are arrested or suspected of a crime should not be released to the press nor the public".

56. Bahamas Data Protection (Privacy of Personal Information) Act 2003; Trinidad and Tobago Data Protection Act 13 of 2013.

57. Due 30 September 2019.

58. Bahamas Data Protection Act 2007, Section 2: "'Data' means information in a form in which it can be processed. 'Processing' means obtaining, recording or holding the information or data or carrying out any operation or set of operation on the information or data, including organization, adaptation or alteration of the data; retrieval, consultation or use of the information or data; transmission of the data; dissemination or otherwise making available; or alignment, combination, blocking, erasure or destruction of the information or data."

59. The Cayman Islands Data Protection Law 2017 was modelled on the UK legislation and contains the journalism exemption.

60. *Douglas v. Hello!* (2003) 3 AER 96.

61. Data Protection (Amendment) Act 2003.

62. M. Guevara, et al., "Leaked Records Reveal Offshore Holdings of China's Elite", *International Consortium of Investigative Journalists,* 21 January 2014. www.icij.org.

63. Section 7.

64. T. Mioli, "St Vincent and the Grenadines Passes Cybercrime Bill that Allows Prison Sentences for Online Defamation", 2016. www.knightcenter.utexas.edu/blog.

65. The section states that a person commits an offence if that person uses a computer to send to another person any data (whether in the form of a message or otherwise) (a) that is obscene, constitutes a threat or is menacing in nature and (b) intends to cause or is reckless as to whether the sending of the data causes annoyance, inconvenience, distress or anxiety to that person or any person. See also St Kitts and Nevis Electronic Crimes Act 2009, Section 14.

66. Section 6 of the Grenada Electronic Crimes Act 2013 was in similar terms and was repealed after public criticism.

67. She responded by posting the attorney's letter on Facebook and adding the following words: *"Institute onnu bo** bl**d cl**t proceedings, oonu and Canute can f**k off, oonu sick stomach. Fi a law firm onnu nuh have no r**s sense. Move oonu p***ycl**t from yah soh."*

68. Full text available at www.dpp.gov.jm.

69. Section 14.

70. Omar Watson in 2017, three years after the charge, posted an apology online. The other case concerned the posting of intimate photographs; the defendants were sentenced to community service.

71. Reporters Without Borders published a letter to the prime minister and minister of information, expressing concern that certain clauses would have a detrimental effect on the "free flow of news and information and to public debate". The International Press Institute also expressed concern.

72. Section 18.

73. During his stewardship, the paper published leaked material provided by civil servant Sara Tisdall, who was jailed for breaching the Official Secrets Act.

74. Helen Lewis, "When Is It Ethical to Publish Stolen Data?", Nieman Reports, 1 June 2015. www.niemanreports.org.

CHAPTER 14

1. "On Publicity" from *The Works of Jeremy Bentham*, vol. 2, part 2 (1839). Bentham (1748–1832) was an English philosopher, jurist and social reformer.

2. Examples: Antigua and Barbuda Constitution, Section 12; the Bahamas Constitution, Section 23 (1); Barbados Constitution, Section 20; Belize Constitution, Section 12 (1); Dominica Constitution, Section 10 (1); Grenada Constitution, Section 10 (1); Guyana Constitution Article 146 (1); Jamaica Constitution, Section 22; St Kitts and Nevis Constitution, Section 12 (1); St Lucia Constitution, Section 12; Trinidad and Tobago Constitution, Sections 4(i) and (k).

3. It stemmed from Parliament's interest in obtaining information in the possession of the king.

4. Antigua and Barbuda Freedom of Information Act 2004; Bahamas Freedom of Information Act 2017; Belize Freedom of Information Act 2000 (revised); Bermuda Public Access to Information Act 2010; Cayman Freedom of Information Law 2015 (revised); Guyana Access to Information Act 2011; Jamaica Access to Information Act 2007; St Vincent and the Grenadines Freedom of Information Act 2003; Trinidad and Tobago Freedom of Information Act 1999.

5. The interpretation section of the act defines the term, providing a list.

6. St Lucia says twenty working days.

7. Section 7 (2) of the Jamaica Access to Information Act 2007 says application can be by telephone or other electronic means. Similarly, Section 16 (b) Guyana Access to Information Act 2011 says any electronic means may be used to make request to Commissioner of Information.

8. Examples: Antigua Freedom of Information Act, Section 17 (2); Belize Freedom of Information Act, Section 12 (4); Guyana Access to Information Act 2011, Section 17; Jamaica Access to Information Act 2007, Section 7 (3); St Vincent Freedom of Information Act 2007, Section 14; Trinidad and Tobago Freedom of Information Act 1999, Section 14 (2).

9. Antigua and Barbuda Freedom of Information Act 2004, Section 19 (1); Belize Freedom of Information Act 1994, Section 35 (1); Guyana Access to Information Act 2011, Section 26 (1); St Vincent and the Grenadines Freedom of Information Act 2003, Section 39; Trinidad and Tobago Freedom of Information Act, Ch 22:02, Sections 38A and 39.

10. Access to Information Act 2004, Sections 30 and 31.

11. Cayman Freedom of Information Law 2015 (revised), Sections 33, 42 and 47.

12. Civ App 170 of 2008.

13. Para 28.

14. Section 35.

15. L. Smith, "Freedom of Information: A Bridge too Far", *Bahama Pundit,* 17 June 2014. www.bahamapundit.com.

16. Ombudsman Seventeenth Annual Report 2018; Sixteenth Annual Report 2017. Does this mean public authorities are making more documents available more readily?

17. The information commissioner had been terminated the year earlier, and sued the state for unpaid gratuity. "Ransom Sacked as Information Commissioner since March", *Stabroek News,* 11 December 2018.

18. The judge was arrested but never charged and won a million-dollar assessment from the government; the police commissioner was fired; a senior police officer was suspended and also won a substantial settlement from the government; Martin Bridger, the chief Tempura investigator, himself became the subject of counter-allegations, and that police inquiry ran for three years. Lyndon Martin, a part-time journalist at *Cayman News Net,* who had made the allegations against Seales, was tried and acquitted of attempting to pervert the course of justice by making false allegations against a deputy police commissioner.

19. Evans admitted this in an Offshore Alert 2014 Miami conference session entitled "Inside the Cayman Islands: The Operation Tempura Affair".

20. Decision 2-01109 Royal Cayman Islands Police Service, 12 February 2010. Information Commissioner Jennifer Dilbert.

21. www.gov.uk.

CHAPTER 15

1. Recent conventions include the 1994 World Trade Organization Agreement on Trade-Related Aspects of Intellectual Property Rights (the TRIPS Agreement) and the 1996 World Intellectual Property Organization (WIPO) Copyright Treaty. The TRIPS agreement places copyright in a world trade context.

2. Article 2(1). www.wipo.int.

3. There are 175 member states as of December 2017. www.wipo.int.

4. Author means the natural person who created the work.

5. Section 13A. "Where, pursuant to an agreement between employer and employee, the copyright in a work created by the employee has vested in the employer, the copyright expires at the end of the period of ninety-five years from the end of the calendar year in which the work was created." See also *Paymaster v. Grace Kennedy* (2017) UKPC 40.

6. (2007) 1 LRC 343.

7. Page 346.

8. Copyright Act 21 of 2003, Section 8.

9. Copyright Amendment Act 2015, Section 5. The Berne Convention requires a fifty-year duration but member states are free to provide longer periods.

10. *General Tire and Rubber v. Firestone Tyre and Rubber* (1976) RPC 197, 214.

11. Section 41 (3).

12. *Dick v. Yates* (1881) 18, Ch D 76.

13. The definition section that appears at the beginning of every state's Copyright Act illustrates what works are protected. Example: Jamaica Copyright Act, Section 2, provides "graphic work includes (a) any painting, drawing, diagram, map, chart, or plan; and (b) any engraving, etching, lithograph, woodcut or similar work".

14. (1978) RPC 485.

15. Also, Antigua and Barbuda Copyright Act, Section 32 (3); Barbados Copyright Act 1998, Ch 300, Section 32 (3); Bahamas Copyright Act 2004, Section 41 (4); Belize Copyright Act 2000, Section 36 (2); Dominica Copyright Act, Section 37 (3); Grenada Copyright Act, Section 40 (2); Guyana Copyright Act 1956, Section 17 (2); St Kitts and Nevis Copyright Act, Section 32(3); St Vincent and the Grenadines Copyright Act 21 of 2003, Section 29 (2); Trinidad and Tobago Copyright Act 2008, Section 38 (2).

16. *The Lady Anne Tennant v. Associated Newspapers Group Ltd* (1979) FSR 298.

17. *Nottinghamshire NHS Trust v. News Group Newspapers* (2002) EWHC 409. The damages were £10,000 (£9,550 attributable to additional damages).

18. *Television Jamaica Ltd v. CVM Television Ltd* (2017) JMSC Comm 1.

19. The Court of Appeal noted that the IAAF live stream was intended for the ordinary citizen, not for commercial exploitation.

20. (1998) EMLR 47.

21. Antigua and Barbuda Copyright Act 2003, Section 54; Bahamas Copyright Act 2004, Sections 54, 60; Barbados Copyright Act 1998 (revised), Sections 51–52; Belize Copyright Act 2000, Sections 56–57, 61; Dominica Copyright Act 2003, Section 65; Guyana Copyright Act 1956, Sections 6, 9; St Lucia Copyright Act

1995, Section 127; St Vincent and the Grenadines Copyright Act 2003, Sections 50–52; 55–57; Trinidad and Tobago Copyright Act, Sections 10–11, 25.

22. (2000) 3 WLR 215 CA.

23. The UK Society of Authors and Publishers Association has published guidelines and considers fair use to apply to a single extract of up to four hundred words or a series of extracts of which none exceeds three hundred words to a total of eight hundred words; in a poem, up to forty lines as long as the extract does not exceed more than one quarter of the poem.

24. (1972) 2 QB 84.

25. *BBC v. BSB* (1991) 3 WLR 174.

26. (1999) 1 WLR 605.

27. (1994) EMLR 1.

28. *Ashdown v. Telegraph Group* (2001) EWCA Civ 1142.

29. The "Laddie" factors, put forward by Laddie, Prescott and Vitoria, *The Modern Law of Copyright and Designs,* 3rd ed., para 20.16.

30. Grenada Copyright Act 21 of 2011, Section 6 (1) c. Trinidad and Tobago Copyright Act 2008, Section 6 (1) c.

31. This is a core provision of the Berne Convention, Article 6bis.

32. *Lord Byron v. Johnson* (1816) 2 Mer. 29.

33. Antigua and Barbuda Copyright Act 2003, Sections 14, 15; Bahamas Copyright Act 2004, Sections 11–13; Barbados Copyright Act, Sections 14, 15; Belize Copyright Act 2000 (revised), Ch 252, Sections 14–17; Dominica Copyright Act 2003, Section 15; Jamaica Copyright Act, Sections 14, 15; St Kitts and Nevis (2002), Sections 14–16; St Lucia Copyright Act 1995, Sections 15–17; Trinidad and Tobago Copyright Act, Section 18 (1).

34. (2012) EWPCC 29.

35. (1999) FSR 168 HHJ.

36. *Moore v. News of the World* (1972) 1 QB 441 CA.

37. (1980) 1 WLR 1558.

38. Examples: Bahamas Copyright Act 2004, Section 14; Barbados Copyright Act, Ch 300, Section 18; Belize Copyright Act, Ch: 252, Section 18; Dominica Copyright Act 2003, Section 16; Jamaica Copyright Act, Section 17; St Kitts and Nevis Copyright Act 2002, Section 17; St Lucia Copyright 10 of 1995, Section 18; St Vincent and the Grenadines Copyright Act 21 of 2003, Section 16. Grenada, Guyana and Trinidad and Tobago do not include this provision in their statutes. In absence of such provisions, someone who does not own the copyright in photographs would have to rely on contractual arrangements or perhaps the tort of breach of

confidence or misuse of private information to prevent or object to unjustified exposure.

39. Commissioning means there must be an obligation by one party to pay money or money's worth and an obligation to produce the work by the other party. *Trimmingham v. Associated Newspapers Ltd* (2012) EWHC 1296 QB.

40. However, there will be an implied contract not to sell or exhibit copies for commercial purposes. Such sale would be a breach of confidence. *Pollard v. Photographic Co.* (1888) 37 WR 266.

41. 1966 F. No. 2647.

42. *Forbes v. Kemsley Newspapers Ltd* (1951) 66 RPC 183.

43. Formed in 2000, Caribbean Media Corporation is a Barbados-based content provider for regional media houses. Associated Press is a US-based news agency founded in 1846.

44. *McClatchey v. the Associated Press* (2005). Case number: 3:2005cv00145. US District Court for the Western District of Pennsylvania.

45. (1900) AC 539.

46. (2003) 2 All ER 881.

47. This was the first case in the United Kingdom in which a passing-off action succeeded in a false endorsement case.

48. *Fenty v. Arcadia Group Brands Ltd* (2015) EWCA Civ 3.

49. She gained prominence after her frontline war reporting on the Kargil Conflict between India and Pakistan in 1999.

50. *Barhka Dutt v. Easy Ticket, Kapavarapu, Vas,* Case No. D2009-1247.

51. *Fenty* (supra).

52. (1994) 3 JLR 97.

53. *Clark v. Freeman* (1850) 11 Beav 1120; *Dockrell v. Dougall* (1899) 80 LT 556.

CHAPTER 16

1. *Faaiq Mohammed v. Jack Warner* CV 2013-04726, Trinidad and Tobago.

2. Lord Kerr in *Calix v. AG* (2013) UKPC 15 said that even an eccentric living in squalid conditions has a reputation of worth and a name that deserves protection.

3. *Jamaica Observer and Paget de Freitas v. Gladstone Wright* (2014) JMCA Civ 18. The claimant was awarded J$6.5 million plus interest.

4. Para 4.

5. Where defamation proceedings are tried by a jury, a jury usually determines the amount. In Jamaica (Section 17, Defamation Act 2013), it is the judge, not the jury.

6. Justice Kokaram in *Faaiq Mohammed v. Jack Warner,* CV 2013-04726, Trinidad and Tobago, at para 30. See also *Barrick Gold Corp v. Lopehandia* (2004) 71 OR (3d) 416 and *Crampton v. Nugawela* (1996) NSWC 651.

7. *Conrad Aleong v. Trinidad Express Newspapers* CA Civ. 122 of 2009. Exemplary damages of TT$200,000 were also awarded because of the reporter's recklessness, the banner headlines and sensational writing style that the court viewed as intended to boost sales in a "revenue-earning opportunity".

8. *Rowley v. Annisette* HC 4909 of 2010. Mr Rowley became prime minister in 2015. See also *TnT News Centre Ltd v. John Rahael* CA Civ. 166 of 2006; *Robin Montano v. Harry Harrinarine* HC 3039 of 2008; *Basdeo Panday v. Ken Gordon* (2005) UKPC 36.

9. (2003) UKPC 55.

10. US$21,703.

11. US$72,345.

12. *Glen Lall and National Media Co. v. Walter Ramsahoye,* CCJ/GYC 2015/006.

13. *Jones v. Pollard* (1996) EWCA Civ 1186.

14. They settled in 2013 for an undisclosed amount.

15. See chapter 3 on difference between libel and slander. Slander per se is not actionable without proof of damage, except in certain circumstances.

16. (1942) 2 QB 669. This became the inspiration for another novel by Uris, *QB VII,* which became a television series starring Anthony Hopkins as the doctor and Ben Gazzara as the writer.

17. *Atlantis World Group of Companies v. Gruppo Editoriale L'Espresso SPA* (2008) EWHC 1323 (QB); *Jameel v. Wall Street Journal Europe SPRL* (2006) UKHL 44.

18. The juxtaposition of his Islamic faith with the baseless smear of corruption was described by the court as a sinister aspect of the defamation.

19. *Faaiq Mohammed v. Jack Warner,* CV 2013-04726, Trinidad and Tobago.

20. *A v. Bottrill* (2003) 3 WLR 1406.

21. Civ App 22 of 2003.

22. A judicial officer, whose role includes assessing damages in civil proceedings.

23. Para 17.

APPENDIX

1. The ACM was established in 2001 in Barbados and is a network of Caribbean journalists, media workers and media associations. Among its objectives are to promote professional and ethical standards; promote freedom of information and independence of journalism; protect and advance the interests of journalists and media workers at national and regional levels; and promote greater understanding of media issues through research, seminars and conferences.

SELECTED BIBLIOGRAPHY

Antoine, Rose-Marie Bell. *Commonwealth Caribbean Law and Legal Systems*. London: Routledge-Cavendish, 2006.

Bently, L., D. Sherman, D. Gangjee, and P. Johnson. *Intellectual Property Law*. 5th ed. Oxford: Oxford University Press, 2014.

Kodilinye, Gilbert. *Commonwealth Caribbean Tort Law*. 5th ed. London: Routledge, 2015.

Mullis, Alastair, and Cameron Doley, eds. *Carter-Ruck on Libel and Privacy*. 6th ed. New York: LexisNexis, 2010.

Phillips, Sir Fred. *Commonwealth Caribbean Constitutional Law*. London: Cavendish, 2002.

Robertson, Geoffrey, QC, and Andrew Nicol, QC. *Media Law*. 4th ed. London: Sweet and Maxwell, 2002.

Robinson, Tracy, Arif Bulkan and Adrian Saunders. *Fundamentals of Caribbean Constitutional Law*. London: Sweet and Maxwell, 2015.

Seetahal, Dana. *Commonwealth Caribbean Criminal Practice and Procedure*. 5th ed. London: Routledge, 2019.

INDEX

CPSIA information can be obtained
at www.ICGtesting.com
Printed in the USA
LVHW031733130320
649999LV00001B/55